MCSE Test Suc
Internet Information
Server 4

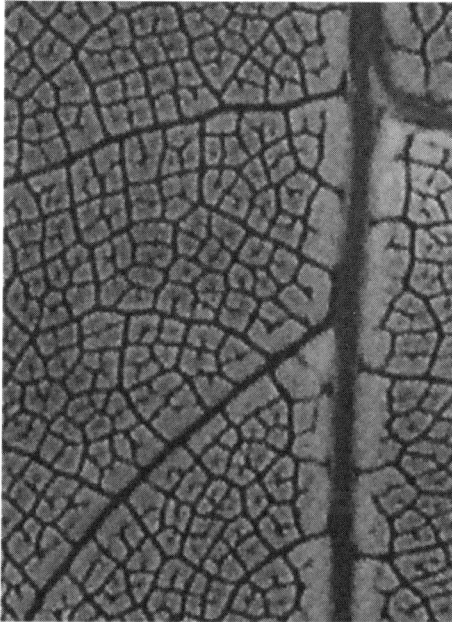

Lisa Donald

CW01424613

San Francisco • Paris • Düsseldorf • Soest

NETWORK PRESS ®
SYBEX

Associate Publisher: Guy Hart-Davis
Contracts and Licensing Manager: Kristine Plachy
Acquisitions & Developmental Editor: Bonnie Bills
Editor: Andy Carroll
Project Editor: Lisa Duran
Technical Editors: Matthew Fiedler, Don Fuller
Book Designer: Bill Gibson
Electronic Publishing Specialist: Bill Gibson
Production Coordinator: Jefferson McClure
Indexer: Matthew Spence
Cover Designer: Archer Design
Cover Illustrator/Photographer: FPG International

Screen reproductions produced with Collage Complete.

Collage Complete is a trademark of Inner Media Inc.

SYBEX, Network Press, and the Network Press logo are registered trademarks of SYBEX Inc.

Test Success is a trademark of SYBEX Inc.

TRADEMARKS: SYBEX has attempted throughout this book to distinguish proprietary trademarks from descriptive terms by following the capitalization style used by the manufacturer.

Microsoft, the Microsoft Internet Explorer logo, Windows, Windows NT, and the Windows logo are either registered trademarks or trademarks of Microsoft Corporation in the United States and/or other countries.

The author and publisher have made their best efforts to prepare this book, and the content is based upon final release software whenever possible. Portions of the manuscript may be based upon pre-release versions supplied by software manufacturer(s). The author and the publisher make no representation or warranties of any kind with regard to the completeness or accuracy of the contents herein and accept no liability of any kind including but not limited to performance, merchantability, fitness for any particular purpose, or any losses or damages of any kind caused or alleged to be caused directly or indirectly from this book.

Photographs and illustrations used in this book have been downloaded from publicly accessible file archives and are used in this book for news reportage purposes only to demonstrate the variety of graphics resources available via electronic access. Text and images available over the Internet may be subject to copyright and other rights owned by third parties. Online availability of text and images does not imply that they may be reused without the permission of rights holders, although the Copyright Act does permit certain unauthorized reuse as fair use under 17 U.S.C. Section 107.

SYBEX is an independent entity from Microsoft Corporation, and not affiliated with Microsoft Corporation in any manner. This publication may be used in assisting students to prepare for a Microsoft Certified Professional Exam. Neither Microsoft Corporation, its designated review company, nor SYBEX warrants that use of this publication will ensure passing the relevant exam. Microsoft is either a registered trademark or trademark of Microsoft Corporation in the United States and/or other countries.

Copyright ©1998 SYBEX Inc., 1151 Marina Village Parkway, Alameda, CA 94501. World rights reserved. No part of this publication may be stored in a retrieval system, transmitted, or reproduced in any way, including but not limited to photocopy, photograph, magnetic or other record, without the prior agreement and written permission of the publisher.

Library of Congress Card Number: 98-86621
ISBN: 0-7821-2334-1

Manufactured in the United States of America

10 9 8 7 6 5 4 3 2

November 1, 1997

Dear SYBEX Customer:

Microsoft is pleased to inform you that SYBEX is a participant in the Microsoft® Independent Courseware Vendor (ICV) program. Microsoft ICVs design, develop, and market self-paced courseware, books, and other products that support Microsoft software and the Microsoft Certified Professional (MCP) program.

To be accepted into the Microsoft ICV program, an ICV must meet set criteria. In addition, Microsoft reviews and approves each ICV training product before permission is granted to use the Microsoft Certified Professional Approved Study Guide logo on that product. This logo assures the consumer that the product has passed the following Microsoft standards:

- The course contains accurate product information.
- The course includes labs and activities during which the student can apply knowledge and skills learned from the course.
- The course teaches skills that help prepare the student to take corresponding MCP exams.

Microsoft ICVs continually develop and release new MCP Approved Study Guides. To prepare for a particular Microsoft certification exam, a student may choose one or more single, self-paced training courses or a series of training courses.

You will be pleased with the quality and effectiveness of the MCP Approved Study Guides available from SYBEX.

Sincerely,

Holly Heath
ICV Account Manager
Microsoft Training & Certification

MICROSOFT INDEPENDENT COURSEWARE VENDOR PROGRAM

For the Rickster. The hard work is done, now it's time to play. This is also for all of those who want to be MCSEs. If you are ready for your elective exam, you are almost there!

MCSE Test Success:
Internet Information Server 4

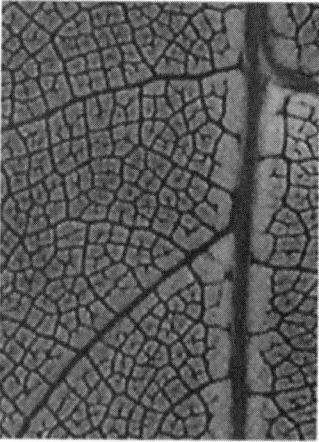

Acknowledgments

This book has really been a team effort. Thanks to Bonnie Bills of Sybex who developed the Test Success series. She has been very supportive of the entire project and has been especially patient in seeing this book done.

Lisa Duran was the project editor and did a fabulous job of keeping this book on track. She was wonderful to work with and was able to keep me sane through everything.

Andy Carroll was the editor, and Matt Fiedler was the technical editor. These guys have been real troopers through all the different iterations of the many units that were submitted, reviewed, and re-reviewed. Both did a great job editing and made the book clearer and easier to read. Andy, thank you for your patience! Matt, especially, did a good job of keeping us honest on some of the technical details. In addition, this book went through a second technical edit from Don Fuller. Thanks, Don, for taking a final "peek" and making sure we sent out the best book possible.

Thanks to Ron Reimann, who was able to come in and pinch-hit when the dealine was crashing in on my head. The work seen in Units 4 and 5 is his contribution. I also want to thank Peter Henneberry of Hewlett-Packard for his early contribution to the development of this book. His work provided the basis for Units 3 and 6 and was highly appreciated.

In addition, Jefferson McClure was the production coordinator and Bill Gibson was the desktop publisher. Everyone did a great job. Thank you.

Healthy Planet
Books for Free
You've rescued me from going to waste
healthyplanet.org
healthy_planet   healthyplanet

Contents at a Glance

Table of Contents

Introduction

One of the greatest challenges facing corporate America today is finding people who are qualified to manage corporate computer networks. Many companies have Microsoft networks, which run Windows 95, Windows NT, and other Microsoft BackOffice products (such as Microsoft SQL Server and Systems Management Server).

Microsoft developed its Microsoft certification program to certify those people who have the skills to work with Microsoft products and networks. The most highly coveted certification is the MCSE, or Microsoft Certified Systems Engineer.

Why become an MCSE? The main benefits are that you will have much greater earning potential and that an MCSE carries high industry recognition. Certification can be your key to a new job or a higher salary—or both.

So what's stopping you? If it's because you don't know what to expect from the tests or you are worried that you might not pass, then this book is for you.

Your Key to Passing Exam 70-087

This book provides you with the key to passing Exam 70-087, Implementing and Supporting Microsoft Internet Information Server 4.0. Inside, you'll find *all* the information relevant to this exam, including hundreds of practice questions, all designed to make sure that when you take the real exam, you are ready for even the most particular questions.

Understand the Exam Objectives

In order to help you prepare for certification exams, Microsoft provides a list of exam objectives for each test. This book is structured according to the objectives for Exam 70-087, designed to test your ability to implement, administer, and troubleshoot information systems that incorporate Microsoft Internet Information Server version 4.0.

At-a-glance review sections and more than 240 study questions bolster your knowledge of the information relevant to each objective and the exam itself. You learn exactly what you need to know without wasting time on background material or detailed explanations.

This book prepares you for the exam in the shortest amount of time possible—although to be ready for the real world, you need to study the subject in greater depth and get a good deal of hands-on practice.

Get Ready for the Real Thing

More than 150 sample test questions prepare you for the test-taking experience. These are multiple-choice questions that resemble actual exam questions—some are even more difficult than what you'll find on the exam. If you can pass the Sample Tests at the end of each unit and the Final Review at the end of the book, you'll know you're ready.

A New Kind of Exam

Implementing and Supporting Microsoft Internet Information Server 4.0 uses a combination of multiple choice and new simulative questions. The simulative questions use a simulation version of Microsoft Management Console to test your ability to perform common administrative tasks. This is Microsoft's way of testing that candidates know how to use a product in the real world, and not just on paper.

Out of the exam's approximately 55 questions, 8 to 10 will be simulative. So to be well-prepared for the exam, in addition to studying, you'll need to install and play with the software specified in the test objectives.

Is This Book for You?

This book is intended for those who already have some experience with Microsoft Internet Information Server and the products and services that enhance IIS. It is especially well suited for:

- Students using courseware or taking a course to prepare for the exam and who need to supplement their study material with test-based practice questions.

- Network engineers who have worked with the product, but want to make sure there are no gaps in their knowledge.

- Anyone who has studied for the exams—by using self-study guides, by participating in computer-based training or classes, or by getting on-the-job experience—and wants to make sure that they're adequately prepared.

Understanding Microsoft Certification

Microsoft offers several levels of certification for anyone who has or is pursuing a career as a network professional working with Microsoft products:

- Microsoft Certified Professional (MCP)

- Microsoft Certified Systems Engineer (MCSE)

- Microsoft Certified Professional + Internet

- Microsoft Certified Systems Engineer + Internet

- Microsoft Certified Trainer (MCT)

The one you choose depends on your area of expertise and your career goals.

Microsoft Certified Professional (MCP)   This certification is for individuals with expertise in one specific area. MCP certification is often a stepping stone to MCSE certification and allows you some benefits of Microsoft certification after just one exam.

By passing any certification exam that is current as of October 1, 1998—except for Networking Essentials—you become an MCP.

Microsoft Certified Systems Engineer (MCSE)   For network professionals, the MCSE certification requires commitment. You need to complete all of the steps required for certification. Passing the exams shows that you meet the high standards that Microsoft has set for MCSEs.

The following list applies to the NT 4.0 track. Microsoft still supports a track for 3.51, but 4.0 certification is more desirable because it is the current operating system.

To become an MCSE, you must pass a series of six exams:

1. Networking Essentials (waived for Novell CNEs)

2. Implementing and Supporting Microsoft Windows NT Workstation 4.0 (*or* Implementing and Supporting Windows 95 *or* Implementing and Supporting Windows 98)

3. Implementing and Supporting Microsoft Windows NT Server 4.0

4. Implementing and Supporting Microsoft Windows NT Server 4.0 in the Enterprise

5. Elective

6. Elective

Some of the electives include:

- Internetworking with Microsoft TCP/IP on Microsoft Windows NT 4.0

- Implementing and Supporting Microsoft Internet Information Server 4.0

- Implementing and Supporting Microsoft Exchange Server 5.5

- Implementing and Supporting Microsoft SNA Server 4.0

- Implementing and Supporting Microsoft Systems Management Server 1.2

- Implementing a Database Design on Microsoft SQL Server 6.5

- System Administration for Microsoft SQL Server 6.5

- Implementing and Supporting Microsoft Proxy Server 2

- Implementing and Supporting Microsoft Internet Explorer 4.0 by Using the Microsoft Internet Explorer Administration Kit

Microsoft Certified Systems Engineer (MCSE) + Internet   One of the newest certification designations is MCSE + Internet. This certification allows you to show that you have completed additional exams that qualify you as an Internet specialist.

For MCSE + Internet certification, you must pass a series of seven required exams:

1. Networking Essentials (waived for Novell CNEs)

2. Internetworking with Microsoft TCP/IP on Windows NT 4.0

3. Implementing and Supporting Microsoft Windows NT Workstation 4.0 (*or* Implementing and Supporting Windows 95 *or* Implementing and Supporting Windows 98)

4. Implementing and Supporting Microsoft Windows NT Server 4.0

5. Implementing and Supporting Microsoft Windows NT Server 4.0 in the Enterprise

6. Implementing and Supporting Microsoft Internet Information Server 4.0

7. Implementing and Supporting Microsoft Internet Explorer 4.0 by Using the Internet Explorer Administration Kit

You must also pass two elective exams. You can choose from:

- System Administration for Microsoft SQL Server 6.5

- Implementing a Database Design on Microsoft SQL Server 6.5

- Implementing and Supporting Web Sites Using Microsoft Site Server 3.0

- Implementing and Supporting Microsoft Exchange Server 5.5 (can also use version 5.0 exam)

- Implementing and Supporting Microsoft Proxy Server 2.0 (can also use version 1.0 exam)

- Implementing and Supporting Microsoft SNA Server 4.0

Microsoft Certified Trainer (MCT)   As an MCT, you can deliver Microsoft certified courseware through official Microsoft channels.

The MCT certification is more costly, because in addition to passing the exams, it requires that you sit through the official Microsoft courses. You also need to submit an application that must be approved by Microsoft. The number of exams you are required to pass depends on the number of courses you want to teach.

For the most up-to-date certification information, visit Microsoft's Web site at www.microsoft.com/Train_Cert.

Preparing for the MCSE Exams

To prepare for the MCSE certification exams, you should try to work with the product as much as possible. In addition, there are a variety of resources from which you can learn about the products and exams:

- You can take instructor-led courses.

- Online training is an alternative to instructor-led courses. This is a useful option for people who cannot find any courses in their area or who do not have the time to attend classes.

- If you prefer to use a book to help you prepare for the MCSE tests, you can choose from a wide variety of publications. These range from complete study guides (such as the books in the Network Press MCSE Study Guide series, which cover the core MCSE exams and most electives) to test-preparedness books similar to this one.

After you have completed your courses, training, or study guides, you'll find the MCSE Test Success books an excellent resource for making sure that you are prepared for the tests. With each of these books, you will discover if you've got the exam covered or if you still need to fill in some holes.

For more MCSE information, point your browser to the Sybex Web site, where you'll find information about the MCP program, job links, and descriptions of other quality titles in the Network Press line of MCSE-related books. Go to www.sybex.com and click on the MCSE logo.

Scheduling and Taking an Exam

Once you think you are ready to take an exam, call Prometric Testing Centers at (800) 755-EXAM (755-3926). They'll tell you where to find the closest testing center. Before you call, get out your credit card because each exam costs $100. (If you've used this book to prepare yourself thoroughly, chances are you'll only have to shell out that $100 once!)

You can schedule the exam for a time that is convenient for you. The exams are downloaded from Prometric to the testing center, then you show up at your scheduled time and take the exam on a computer.

Once you complete the exam, you will know right away whether you have passed or not. At the end of the exam, you will receive a score report. It will list the six areas that you were tested on and how you performed. If you pass the exam, you don't need to do anything else—Prometric uploads the test results to Microsoft. If you don't pass, it's another $100 to schedule the exam again. But at least you will know from the score report where you did poorly, so you can study that particular information more carefully.

Test-Taking Hints

If you know what to expect, your chances of passing the exam will be much greater. The following are some tips that can help you achieve success.

Get There Early and Be Prepared   This is your last chance to review. Bring your Test Success book and review any areas you feel unsure of. If you need a quick drink of water or a visit to the restroom, take the time to do so before the exam. Once your exam starts, it will not be paused for these needs.

When you arrive for your exam, you will be asked to present two forms of ID. You will also be asked to sign a piece of paper verifying that you understand the testing rules (for example, the rule that says that you will not cheat on the exam).

Before you start the exam, you will have an opportunity to take a practice exam. It is not related to Windows NT and is simply offered so that you will have a feel for the exam-taking process.

What You Can and Can't Take in with You   These are closed-book exams. The only thing that you can take in is scratch paper provided by the testing center. Use this paper as much as possible to diagram the questions. Many times diagramming questions will help make the answer clear. You will have to give this paper back to the test administrator at the end of the exam.

Many testing centers are very strict about what you can take into the testing room. Some centers will not even allow you to bring in items like a zipped up purse. If you feel tempted to take in any outside material, beware that many testing centers use monitoring devices such as video and audio equipment (so don't swear, even if you are alone in the room!).

Prometric Testing Centers take the test-taking process and the test validation very seriously.

Test Approach   As you take the test, if you know the answer to a question, fill it in and move on. If you're not sure of the answer, mark your best guess, then "mark" the question.

At the end of the exam, you can review the questions. Depending on the amount of time remaining, you can then view all of the questions again, or you can view only the questions that you were unsure of. I always like to double-check all of my answers, just in case I misread any of the questions on the first pass. (Sometimes half of the battle is to try to figure out exactly what the question is asking you.) Also, sometimes I find that a related question provides a clue for a question that I was unsure of.

Be sure to answer all questions. Unanswered questions are scored as incorrect and will count against you. Also, make sure that you keep an eye on the remaining time so that you can pace yourself accordingly.

If you do not pass the exam, note everything that you can remember while the exam is still fresh on your mind. This will help you prepare for your next try. Although the next exam will not be exactly the same, the questions will be similar, and you don't want to make the same mistakes.

After You Become Certified

Once you become an MCSE, Microsoft kicks in some goodies, including:

- A one-year subscription to Microsoft Technet, a valuable CD collection that contains Microsoft support information.

- A one-year subscription to the Microsoft Beta Evaluation program, which is a great way to get your hands on new software. Be the first kid on the block to play with new and upcoming software.

- Access to a secured area of the Microsoft Web site that provides technical support and product information. This certification benefit is also available for MCP certification.

- Permission to use the Microsoft Certified Professional logos (each certification has its own logo), which look great on letterhead and business cards.

- An MCP certificate (you will get a certificate for each level of certification you reach), suitable for framing or sending copies to Mom.

- A one-year subscription to *Microsoft Certified Professional Magazine*, which provides information on professional and career development.

How to Use This Book

This book is designed to help you prepare for the MCSE exam. It reviews each objective and relevant test-taking information, and offers you a chance to test your knowledge through study questions and sample tests.

The first seven units in this book correspond to the Microsoft objective groupings: Planning, Installation and Configuration, Configuring and Managing Resource Access, Integration and Interoperability, Running Applications, Monitoring and Optimization, and Troubleshooting. The eighth unit is a final review, which contains test questions pertaining to all the previous units.

For each unit:

1. Review the exam objectives list at the beginning of the unit. (You may want to check the Microsoft Train_Cert Web site to make sure the objectives haven't changed since the book was published.)

2. Read through or scan the reference material that follows the objectives list. Broken down according to the objectives, this section helps you brush up on the information you need to know for the exam.

3. Review your knowledge in the Study Questions section. These are straightforward questions designed to test your knowledge of the topic. Answers to Study Questions are listed in the Appendix, at the back of the book.

4. Once you feel sure of your knowledge of the subject area, take the Sample Test. The Sample Test's content and style matches the real exam. Set yourself a time limit based on the number of questions: a general rule of thumb is that you should be able to answer 20 questions in 30 minutes. When you've finished, check your answers with the Appendix, at the back of the book. If you answer at least 85 percent of the questions correctly within the time limit (the first time you take the Sample Test), you're in good shape. To really prepare, you should note the questions you miss and be able to score 95 to 100 percent correctly on subsequent tries.

5. After you successfully complete Units 1-7, you're ready for the Final Review in Unit 8. Allow yourself 90 minutes to complete the test of 60 questions. If you answer 85 percent of the questions correctly on the first try, you're well prepared. If not, go back and review your knowledge of the areas you struggled with, and take the test again.

6. Right before you take the real test, scan the reference material at the beginning of each unit to refresh your memory.

At this point, you are well on your way to becoming certified!
Good Luck!

UNIT

1

Planning

Test Objectives: Planning

- **Choose a security strategy for various situations. Security considerations include:**

  - Controlling anonymous access

  - Controlling access to known users and groups

  - Controlling access by host or network

  - Configuring SSL to provide encryption and authentication schemes

  - Identifying the appropriate balance between security requirements and performance requirements

- **Choose an implementation strategy for an Internet site or an intranet site for stand-alone servers, single-domain environments, and multiple-domain environments. Tasks include:**

  - Resolving host header name issues by using a HOSTS file, or DNS, or both

  - Choosing the appropriate operating system on which to install IIS

- **Choose the appropriate technology to resolve specified problems. Technology options include:**

  - WWW service

  - FTP service

  - Microsoft Transaction Server

  - Microsoft SMTP Service

  - Microsoft NNTP Service

  - Microsoft Index Server

  - Microsoft Certificate Server

NOTE Exam objectives are subject to change at any time without prior notice and at Microsoft's sole discretion. Please visit Microsoft's Training & Certification Web site (www.microsoft.com/Train_Cert) for the most current exam objectives listing.

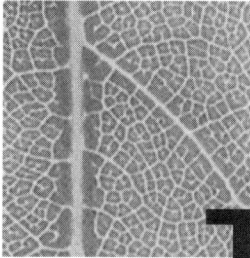

his unit introduces the options that are part of the Windows NT 4.0 Option Pack. You will learn what the Option Pack components are and be able to choose options that meet your specific technology requirements. You will also learn about planning issues that should be addressed before any software is installed.

Microsoft Internet Services

Microsoft provides support for Internet and intranet servers through the Windows NT 4.0 Option Pack. The Option Pack consists of the following components:

- Internet Information Server 4.0
- Microsoft Management Console 1.0
- Microsoft Transaction Server 2.0
- Microsoft Index Server 2.0
- Microsoft Certificate Server 1.0
- Microsoft Site Server Express 2.0

This section gives an overview of the NT Option Pack components so that you will be able to select components to meet specific technology needs.

Internet Information Server 4.0

Internet Information Server (IIS) 4.0 is the latest Web server software to ship from Microsoft. It has been designed so that it is very integrated with the NT operating system software and the Microsoft BackOffice products.

In addition to Microsoft compatibility, IIS provides strong support for existing Internet standards. Some of the key Internet services that are supported are:

- WWW service
- FTP service
- SMTP service
- NNTP service

These services are described in the following subsections.

WWW Service

WWW (World Wide Web) is the main service provided through IIS, and it is used to support HTTP (Hypertext Transfer Protocol) requests. Through HTTP you are able to publish content to the Internet.

You publish Web content through HTML (Hypertext Markup Language) documents. HTML documents can include text and links to audio, video, graphics, and animation content. A user then connects to your Web site through a Web browser, like Microsoft Internet Explorer or Netscape Communicator.

FTP Service

The File Transfer Protocol (FTP) service is another very important service offered through IIS. Through the FTP service you can transfer files between two computers over the Internet or over any other TCP/IP network.

To use FTP, you must have an FTP server and an FTP client. By configuring the FTP service within IIS, you become an FTP server, and most current Web browsers can act as FTP clients. FTP uses the services of TCP and is considered the most efficient protocol for secure file transfer.

SMTP Service

Where would we be without e-mail? It is one of the most commonly used Internet services. SMTP (Simple Mail Transfer Protocol) is the service that allows e-mail to be routed over the Internet. The IIS SMTP service is fully compatible with existing SMTP standards, and it supports standard e-mail client software.

NNTP Service

The NNTP (Network News Transfer Protocol) service is used to host newsgroup-type discussions. Through NNTP you can read information posted by other users, post information regarding a particular topic, or participate in conversation threads. The Microsoft implementation of the NNTP service follows industry standards and is compatible with other vendors' NNTP server and client software.

Microsoft Management Console 1.0

Microsoft Management Console is a new management interface that simplifies network administration. Microsoft Management Console is made up of a common primary interface that is used to support add-on snap-in modules. Each product within the Windows NT Option Pack is managed through an associated snap-in module.

The benefit of using Microsoft Management Console is that you can customize your administrative console to include only the modules that you need.

Future releases of NT and BackOffice applications will replace existing administrative tools with snap-in modules. Third-party companies are also developing snap-in modules for their specific software and hardware.

Microsoft Transaction Server 2.0

Microsoft Transaction Server is designed to be used by application developers. With Microsoft Transaction Server, developers are able to create scaleable applications.

The main feature of Microsoft Transaction Server is the ability to define a complex series of actions as a single transaction. In the event that one action within a transaction fails, all of the actions within the transaction fail.

Microsoft Index Server 2.0

Microsoft Index Server is used to index the contents of your IIS Server, and thus allows you to search the contents of the server.

With Index Server you can:

- Index files on the local computer, or on remote computers (through the creation of virtual directories)

- Index a variety of file types (.TXT, .HTM, .DOC, .XLS, .PPT—pretty much all of the Microsoft Office applications)

- Index and query documents in many different languages

- Index NNTP messages

> **NOTE** The disk space required to store an index generated through Index Server could be 30–40 percent of the size of the documents that will be indexed. The data that will be indexed is called the corpus.

Microsoft Certificate Server 1.0

The main function of Certificate Server is issuing and managing digital certificates. Digital certificates are used to verify that users are who they claim to be, beyond any doubt.

Digital certificates combine a private key and a public key. The private key is used by a user to sign a message. The user's public key is then used to verify that the private key is valid.

The Certificate Server is considered a Certificate Authority (CA) and is able to generate and store digital certificates.

Microsoft Site Server Express 2.0

Site Server Express is used to manage your Web server. The main components of Site Server Express are:

- Content Analyzer

- Usage Import

- Report Writer

- Posting Acceptor

The following subsections describe these components.

Content Analyzer

The main component of Content Analyzer (CA) is the WebMap. WebMap is used to graphically represent your entire Web site. In addition, it contains information about your Web site's objects and links, including the objects and link labels, the size, and the last date modified.

Content Analyzer can also generate Site Summary reports. Site Summary reports can be used to generate information about the number of levels and links, and the total size of objects within the Web site.

Usage Import

Through IIS you are able to generate log files that track information related to specific IIS services. These logs store raw data and are not very useful without a means of interpreting and managing the data files.

The Usage Import option allows you to take the raw data files and compile them into a format that can then be viewed through Report Writer.

Report Writer

After log files have been compiled through Usage Import, the Report Writer utility allows you to view log activity through a variety of predefined reports.

The Report Writer utility can also customize reports generated from the IIS log files. Through Report Writer you can see detailed information regarding access of your Web server.

When reports are generated, you can save the report as a document, in either HTML, Word, or Excel format.

Posting Acceptor

The Posting Acceptor component of Site Server Express allows users to add content to your Web server through an HTTP connection.

Implementation of Internet Services

When planning how your Internet services will be implemented, you should consider the following:

- Whether you will host an Internet or intranet site
- How your server and domain are currently configured
- The operating system that IIS will be installed on
- Host header name resolution issues

These items are covered in the following subsections.

Internet and Intranet Sites

You can create a Web server that will be used as an internal Web server or an external Web server. If you are using a Web server for internal use only, it is considered an intranet server. If you will publish your site on the World Wide Web through the Internet, you are considered an Internet server. Internet servers usually have more security considerations than intranet servers do.

Server and Domain Implementation

When you install an IIS server, you can configure services to support directories either on the local computer or on remote computers by using virtual directories. Virtual directories use UNC path names to connect to remote directories.

This allows you to take advantage of existing domain infrastructure. In addition to mapping virtual directories to domain resources, you can also map virtual directories to resources in other domains. This is most commonly accomplished by using a trust relationship and verifying that the resource has permissions assigned so those Web users can access the resource.

Selecting an Operating System

IIS can be installed on an NT Server, NT Workstation, or Windows 95 computer. For full IIS functionality, you should install IIS on an NT Server. If you install IIS on an NT Workstation or a Windows 95 computer, you are actually installing Peer Web Services (PWS). This book will assume that you are installing IIS on an NT Server for full functionality.

NT Workstation

There are several limitations of installing IIS on an NT Workstation or a Windows 95 computer:

- You cannot host multiple Web sites.
- You cannot connect to an ODBC database, so ODBC logging is not available.
- You cannot impose security by limiting what IP addresses can access your Web server.
- There are no process-isolation capabilities.

Windows 95

Windows 95 offers even fewer IIS features than NT Workstation does. In addition to the previous list, you are also limited in that you:

- Have no features of NT security available
- Cannot install or use the features of Index Server

Host Header Name Resolution

It is possible to host multiple Web servers on a single computer running IIS. Each Web server is considered a virtual server.

In this case, it is possible to have multiple host names that all point to the same IP address. To help resolve the name resolution, you must complete the two following steps:

- Implement a DNS (Domain Name System) server, or use a HOSTS file to resolve host names to IP addresses.
- Configure each virtual server so that you specify a Host Header Name in the property-sheet configuration dialog box.

IIS Security Strategies

Before you connect your Web server to the Internet, you should first plan and implement a security strategy that will meet the requirements of your Web site.

Some of the main considerations are:

- Does your site require anonymous access?
- How is the current NT user security defined?
- Do you want to limit access to your Web site to specific host addresses or network addresses?
- Do you require SSL for encryption and authentication?
- What is an appropriate balance between security and performance for your Web site?

These questions are explored in the following subsections.

Access Control for Anonymous Access

In order to access IIS, you must be able to log on as a valid NT user account. If you choose to allow anonymous access, you are actually using a user account called IUSR_*computername*. This user account is created when you install IIS, and it can be viewed and managed through User Manager for Domains.

This account is limited in that it only has guest access permissions (the account is added to the local group Guests). It is also limited to logging on locally. This allows users to access your Web server without having to provide a unique NT user name and password.

Access Control for Users and Groups

One way you can control Web server access is to eliminate anonymous access. In this case, you force users to be authenticated as valid NT users.

When users log on to your IIS server through an NT user account, you can specify that one of the following authentication methods be used:

- Anonymous
- Basic
- Windows NT Challenge/Response
- Client Certificate Mapping

These authentication methods are covered in the following subsections.

Anonymous

In order to access NT, you must have a valid NT account name and password. If you want to allow anonymous access, this is accomplished through the IUSR_*computername* account that is created when IIS is installed.

Allowing anonymous access provides the least amount of security, but provides the easiest mechanism for allowing site access without creating a unique user account for each user that will access your Web site.

Basic

With basic authentication, you require that users use valid NT account names and passwords to access your Web site.

Basic authentication is used for:

- Supporting clients who do not use a Microsoft Web browser

- Supporting clients who will access your IIS server through a firewall using a proxy server

Windows NT Challenge/Response

If all of your Web clients use Microsoft Internet Explorer 3.0 or later, you can use the Windows NT Challenge/Response authentication option.

This option provides the highest level of authentication since it uses a cryptographic exchange of passwords, as opposed to actually transmitting the password over the Internet.

Client Certificate Mapping

Client certificate mapping allows a client to authenticate to a Web server by using the features of Secure Socket Layer (SSL). This forces the user to present a valid digital certificate before they can be authenticated.

You can issue and manage digital certificates through:

- Trusted third-party organizations (such as Verisign)

- Microsoft Certificate Server

Access Control through Host and Network

It is possible to allow or deny access to specific IIS services based on IP addresses and host names. When you define IP address restrictions, they can be set to grant or deny access.

If you grant access by default, you specify that access is allowed for all users, except those with the specific IP addresses or domain names that are explicitly defined.

If you deny access by default, you specify that access is denied for all users, except those with the specific IP addresses or domain names that are explicitly defined.

You can also limit access by specifying an IP network address and subnet mask. For more information on IP subnet masking, see *MCSE Test Success: TCP/IP for NT Server 4.*

Using SSL for Encryption and Authentication

One way to ensure that you have a secure communication channel when communicating via the Internet is to take advantage of SSL (Secure Sockets Layer).

SSL provides the following advantages:

- There is a secure path created between the client and the server so that data cannot be diverted to a third computer.

- Because data is encrypted, even if it is diverted the diverting computer would not be able to read the data.

- The encryption ensures that the data is delivered intact and that it has not been tampered with in any way.

SSL works through a combination of public and private keys. This works in the following manner: Kevin wants to order a Roadrunner Demolition Kit from the Acme Corporation. He wants to pay by credit card, but does not want to send the credit card number over the Internet in an unsecured manner. He would then follow these steps:

1. He would get a copy of Acme's public key. This would come from Acme's Web site, a third-party organization, or even through an e-mail message.

2. Kevin's order and credit card number would be encrypted using the public key.

3. Kevin would send the data to the Acme Corporation.

4. The only way that Kevin's data could be decrypted is by using the Acme private key. Acme would decrypt the message and send Kevin his Roadrunner Demolition Kit.

Balancing Security and Performance

Using SSL has its drawbacks. Communication is much slower when all data must be encrypted and decrypted. When managing SSL, you should be careful in selecting which directories will require SSL services; you might only use it for folders that have private or sensitive data. All other data could be stored in SSL-disabled directories, which would allow much more efficient (faster) access.

STUDY QUESTIONS

Microsoft Internet Services

1. List the four key services that are supported through IIS 4.0.

_____

_____

_____

_____

2. The _____ is the new management interface that ships with the Windows NT Option Pack and that allows you to simplify administration through the use of snap-in utilities.

3. Which Windows NT Option Pack utility allows you to create and manage digital certificates?

_____

4. The _____ product is used by developers to create scaleable applications. One main benefit of using this product is that you can manage a single transaction composed of multiple actions. If any action within the transaction fails, you can rollback to a known checkpoint.

5. The _____ service is supported through IIS and allows e-mail to be routed through the Internet.

6. True or False. By using Microsoft Index Server you can index Word, Excel, PowerPoint, text documents, and NNTP messages.

7. Index Server can require as much as _____ percent of the size of the corpus in order to create the index.

8. Which IIS service would you use if you wanted to host newsgroup-type discussions?

_____

9. Which Windows NT Option Pack utility would you use to view your Web site in a graphical manner?

_____

10. Which Windows NT Option Pack utility would you use to generate predefined reports based on the log files created by IIS services?

_____

Implementation of Internet Services

11. True or False. You can install IIS and Index Server on a computer running Windows 95.

12. True or False. You can connect to an ODBC database on a Windows NT workstation that is running IIS.

13. List the three platforms that IIS can be installed on.

_____

_____

_____

14. If you install IIS onto a Windows NT Workstation or a Windows 95 computer, you are actually using _____.

15. If you host multiple Web servers on a single IIS computer, you must resolve host names through the two following steps:

_____

_____

IIS Security Strategies

16. If you allow anonymous access, users will validate through the _____ NT user account.

17. True or False. Users can authenticate to your Web site using the Windows NT Challenge/Response method as long as they use an industry-standard Web browser.

STUDY QUESTIONS

18. List the four access methods that can be used to authenticate to an IIS server.

_____

_____

_____

_____

19. Which authentication method would you use if you wanted to ensure secure communication through the use of digital certificates?

_____

20. True or False. You can limit access to specific IIS services by granting or denying access to specific IP network addresses and subnet masks.

21. True or False. You can limit access to specific IIS services by granting or denying access to specific NT user names.

22. True or False. You can limit access to specific IIS services by granting or denying access to specific IP domains.

23. When sending data using SSL services, the sender sends data using a _____(public or private) key. The receiver then decodes the data using a _____(public or private) key.

SAMPLE TEST

1-1   You are managing a Web site that is used by your company's accounting department. All of the data that is stored on your IIS Server is very sensitive, and you need a mechanism that will provide a high level of security. You decide to use digital certificates. What utility will you use?

   A. Microsoft SSL Manager 2.0

   B. Microsoft Certificate Server 1.0

   C. Microsoft Certificate Authority 1.0

   D. Microsoft SSL Authority 2.0

1-2   You originally installed IIS on a Windows 95 computer in order to host a Web site that was accessed by a single internal corporate department. The data now needs to be accessed by your entire organization. You also need to install and use the features of Index Server. What two options will best support the new requirements?

   A. You can still use the current configuration and just install Index Server.

   B. You should install IIS on a computer running NT Workstation.

   C. You should install IIS on a computer running NT Server.

   D. You should create a large FAT partition that will be used to store the index generated by Index Server.

   E. You should create a large NTFS partition that will be used to store the index generated by Index Server.

```
S A M P L E   T E S T
```

1-3 You are the new Webmaster for an existing Web server. The first thing you want to do is create a graphical representation of the Web server so that you can view the size and content of the Web site. What utility will you use?

A. Microsoft Transaction Server

B. Microsoft Index Server

C. Microsoft IIS Management Console

D. Microsoft Site Server Express

1-4 When you access an IIS Web server using anonymous access, what mechanism allows you to access the server?

A. You access the server through the NT GUEST user account.

B. You access the server through the IISUSER user account.

C. You access the server through the IUSR_*computername* user account.

D. You access the server through the ANONYMOUS user account.

1-5 You are an ISP that hosts several Web sites on a single IIS server. You have a single IP address and each client uses their own registered domain name. What two things must you configure to support this setup?

A. You must install the WINS service to resolve host names or implement LMHOST files for name resolution.

B. You must install and configure a DNS server to resolve host names or implement a HOSTS file for name resolution.

C. Each virtual server must be configured so that a Host Header Name is specified in the virtual server's property-sheet configuration.

D. You must check the Allow Virtual Servers option within the Virtual Server property tab when configuring the WWW service. This allows you to fill out a dialog sheet and map domain names to each specific virtual server.

1-6 You are a manufacturer of computers and other network products. You use an IIS server to provide support for your products. The IIS Server includes many documents related to known technical problems and you want users to be able to find answers to their support questions easily. Which product should you use to create an index of your Web site so that it can be easily searched for specific keywords or phrases?

    A. Microsoft Transaction Server

    B. Microsoft Index Server

    C. Microsoft Site Server Express

    D. Microsoft Search Service Express

1-7 You are a manufacturer of computers and other network products. You use an IIS Server to provide support for your products. You need to be able to provide updated drivers that users can download from your Web site. What product or service should you install?

    A. HTTP

    B. FTP

    C. Microsoft Site Server Express

    D. Microsoft File Publisher Express

1-8 Your company provides financial services for users that subscribe to your service. You want to set up a Web site that can be accessed only by validated subscribers. Which of the following options can be used to implement access security?

    A. You can specify that only certain users can access specific IIS services.

    B. You can specify that only certain IP domain names can access specific IIS services.

    C. You can specify that only certain IP addresses can access specific IIS services.

    D. You can disable anonymous access and force users to authenticate to your Web server by using a valid NT account name and password.

1-9   Your company is a manufacturer of computers and other network products. You host a Web server through IIS. You want to provide a mechanism so that users of your product can read or post articles, or participate in conversation threads that relate to the support of your products. What service or product should you install?

    A. WWW service

    B. NNTP service

    C. Microsoft Site Server Express

    D. Microsoft Network News Server

1-10   You are a retail company that publishes a Web site containing a customer catalog, a comments forum, and online ordering capability. You want to provide a high level of security for your customers, with the best possible access time to your site. How should you configure the site?

    A. Require SSL services when accessing any of your Web content

    B. Require SSL services when accessing online ordering, but place all other Web content in SSL-disabled folders

    C. Require that users use Windows NT Challenge/Response authentication when placing orders

    D. Require that users use Basic encryption when placing orders

1-11 You are the Webmaster for your company's internal Web server. Many of your employees are in remote locations and access the Web server via the Internet. Some of your users use Netscape Communicator and some use Microsoft Internet Explorer. You want to make sure that the only people who can access your server are valid NT users. You also want the highest level of log-on authentication. Which authentication option do you implement?

A. Anonymous

B. Basic

C. Windows NT Challenge/Response

D. C2/E2 Challenge/Response

UNIT

2

Installation and Configuration

Test Objectives: Installation and Configuration

- **Install IIS. Tasks include:**

  - Configuring a Microsoft Windows NT Server 4.0 computer for the installation of IIS

  - Identifying differences to a Windows NT Server 4.0 computer made by the installation of IIS

- **Configure IIS to support the FTP service. Tasks include:**

  - Setting bandwidth and user connections

  - Setting user logon requirements and authentication requirements

  - Modifying port settings

  - Setting directory listing style

  - Configuring virtual directories and servers

- **Configure IIS to support the WWW service. Tasks include:**

  - Setting bandwidth and user connections

  - Setting user logon requirements and authentication requirements

  - Modifying port settings

  - Setting default pages

  - Setting HTTP 1.1 host header names to host multiple Web sites

  - Enabling HTTP Keep-Alives

- **Configure and save consoles by using Microsoft Management Console.**

- **Choose the appropriate administration method.**

- **Install and configure Certificate Server.**

- **Install and configure Microsoft SMTP Service.**

- **Install and configure Microsoft NNTP Service.**

- **Customize the installation of Microsoft Site Server Express Content Analyzer.**

- **Customize the installation of Microsoft Site Server Express Usage Import and Report Writer.**

NOTE Exam objectives are subject to change at any time without prior notice and at Microsoft's sole discretion. Please visit Microsoft's Training & Certification Web site (www.microsoft.com/Train_Cert) for the most current exam objectives listing.

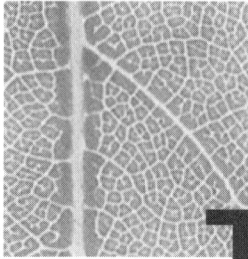

This section focuses on IIS installation and configuration. You will learn how to support the FTP and WWW services. In addition, you will learn about Microsoft Management Console and the different utilities that can be used to manage IIS. Finally, an overview of the installation and configuration of Certificate Server and the SMTP service will be provided.

IIS Installation

This section will outline what steps should be taken to prepare your NT server for IIS installation, how to perform the IIS installation, and what changes are made to your NT Server when IIS is installed.

Preparing Your NT Server for IIS Installation

Before IIS is installed, you need to prepare your NT server. The three considerations are:

- Minimum system requirements
- Transport protocol configuration
- NTFS partition

These options are covered in the following subsections.

Minimum System Requirements

Before you install IIS on your NT Server, you should first confirm that your system meets the minimum requirements to install IIS. The minimum requirements are listed in Table 2.1.

TABLE 2.1	Hardware	Minimum Requirement	Recommended Minimum
IIS Installation Requirements	Processor	486DX/50	Pentium/90
	Memory	16MB	64MB
	Free Disk Space	50MB	200MB

While this list provides minimum requirements, you would use more upgraded equipment to support a production IIS server.

You should also note that IIS can be installed on an NT Workstation or a Windows 95 computer. However, in order to be fully functional, IIS should be installed on an NT Server.

Transport Protocol Configuration

Any time you attach a computer to the Internet, you must use the TCP/IP protocol. In order to be fully functional, your NT Server should already be configured to use the TCP/IP protocol and have a static IP address assigned.

NTFS Partition

Because IIS is able to take advantage of inherent NT security, you should have at least one NTFS partition. This allows you to take advantage of NTFS security when publishing folders and files through IIS.

In order to support the SMTP service, NTFS is required.

IIS Installation Options

IIS is installed as a component of Microsoft Windows NT 4.0 Option Pack. This pack contains software and services that can be used in conjunction with IIS to support a Web server.

When installing the Microsoft Windows NT 4.0 Option Pack, you can choose from Minimum, Typical, or Custom installation options. The components offered through the Microsoft Windows NT 4.0 Option Pack are listed in Table 2.2.

T A B L E 2.2: Windows NT 4.0 Option Pack Components

Component	Description	Installed With: Minimum (M), Typical (T), Custom (C)
Microsoft Management Console (MMC)	New administrative utility that allows you to manage your network through a single utility. Administrative tools are snap-in components. By installing different components, different snap-ins are made available.	M, T, C
Internet Information Server (IIS)	The software that allows you to host a Web server using the TCP/IP protocol.	M, T, C
Internet Service Manager snap-in	Used to manage the services provided by IIS. The main administrative utility is Internet Service Manager.	M, T, C
Microsoft Transaction Server (MTS)	Used with applications that support multiple processes per transaction. By using the services of MTS, you can avoid corruption caused by transaction failures.	M, T, C
Microsoft Transaction Server snap-in	Used to manage the services provided by MTS. This includes help information and Transaction Server Explorer.	M, T, C
Index Server	Index Server is used to create an index file of key words within your site. Index files can contain information from text files, as well as files created by most Microsoft applications. Users can then search for specific text.	M, T, C
Index Server snap-in	Used to manage the services provided through Index Server. The specific utility used to manage Index Server is Index Server Manager.	M, T, C

T A B L E 2.2:   Windows NT 4.0 Option Pack Components *(continued)*

Component	Description	Installed With: Minimum (M), Typical (T), Custom (C)
Active Server Pages	Used to create Active Server pages that can then be accessed by independent Web browsers. Also used to support server-side scripting.	M, T, C
Microsoft Data Access Components	Used to support database connectivity.	M, T, C
Posting Acceptor	Provides the ability to allow users to upload data to a Web server.	M, T, C
FrontPage Extensions	This component allows you to use FrontPage to manage and maintain your Web server.	M, T, C
Help	Context-sensitive help for the MMC components.	M, T, C
File Transfer Protocol (FTP) Service	Service that allows IIS to act as an FTP server. The FTP server provides a mechanism for file transfer with FTP clients.	T, C
Microsoft Script Debugger	Tool that can be used to debug client and server scripts as well as Web document scripts.	T, C
Java Virtual Machine	Used to support Java applications on the Web server.	T, C
Internet Service Manager (HTML version)	This version of Internet Service Manager is used to manage IIS from a Web browser.	T, C
Online Documentation	More detailed documentation than you get with the online help.	T, C

T A B L E 2.2:   Windows NT 4.0 Option Pack Components *(continued)*

Component	Description	Installed With: Minimum (M), Typical (T), Custom (C)
Site Server Express	Allows you to graphically view and manage your Web site. Can also be used for verifying that all links are functioning. In addition, it provides statistics on access and usage of your Web site.	C
Site Server Express snap-in	Used to manage and support Site Server Express.	C
Simple Mail Transfer Protocol (SMTP) Service	Supports the transfer of mail documents over the Internet via the TCP/IP protocol.	C
Network News Transfer Protocol (NNTP) Service	Supports the hosting of electronic discussion groups.	C
Certificate Server	Used to create and manage digital certificates for both clients and servers.	C
Windows Scripting Host	Allows you to manage your Web server from a command prompt using Cscript or Wscript.	C

Changes Made to NT Server 4 by IIS

After IIS is installed, you will notice several changes. They include:

- The addition of the Microsoft Management Console
- Services are added to your computer
- A metabase is added
- A new user has been created
- There are additional counters within Performance Monitor

These items are covered in more detail in the following subsections.

Microsoft Management Console

MMC is used to manage your network through a single utility. Administrative tools are snap-in components. By installing different components, different snap-ins are made available.

After installing IIS, you will notice a new program group called Windows NT 4.0 Option Pack. This group includes the MMC interface. Within this group you will see all of the snap-ins that have been installed.

Figure 2.1 shows the graphical nature of MMC. In this case, the Internet Service Manager snap-in is loaded.

FIGURE 2.1

Microsoft Management Console window

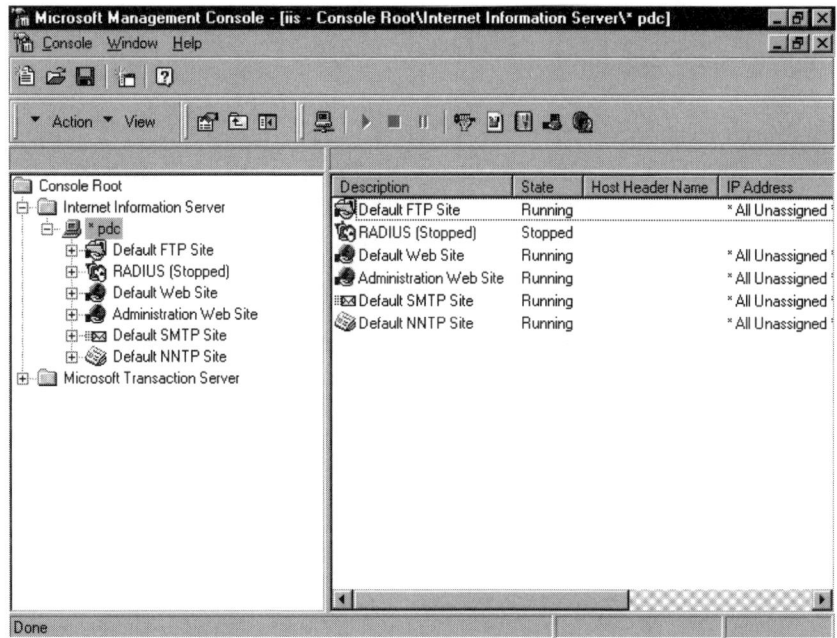

Services Installed

After IIS is installed, you will notice that there are new services. These are used to support IIS and can be viewed through Control Panel ➤ Services or Server Manager. The new services include:

- Content Index
- FTP Publishing service

- IIS Admin service
- Microsoft NNTP service
- Microsoft SMTP service
- MSDTC (Microsoft Distributed Transaction Coordinator)
- World Wide Web Publishing service

Metabase

The metabase is used to store configuration settings used by IIS. Normally NT configuration settings are stored within the registry. IIS settings are stored in the metabase as opposed to the registry because the metabase uses disk space more efficiently.

New User Creation

After IIS is installed, you will notice a new user within User Manager for Domains. The IIS installation creates a user named IUSR_*computername*. This user can provide anonymous access to your Web server if you choose to allow it.

New Performance Monitor Counters

Performance Monitor is used to track the resources used by specific objects. Once IIS is installed, it extends the schema of Performance Monitor to include the following objects that relate to IIS.

- Active Server Pages
- Content Index
- Content Index filter
- FTP service
- HTTP Content Index
- Internet Information Services global
- NNTP commands
- NNTP Server
- SMTP Server
- Web service

In the next section you will learn how to configure the FTP service.

Managing FTP

The FTP service is used to transfer files between an FTP server and an FTP client. In this section you will learn how to create an FTP site and how to configure the FTP service.

Creation of an FTP Site

To create an FTP site, you would take the following steps:

1. From Start ➣ Programs ➣ Windows NT 4.0 Option Pack ➣ Microsoft Internet Information Server ➣ Internet Service Manager, click on the Internet Information Server folder to expand it. Highlight the computer that will host the FTP server, and from Action, select New FTP Site as shown in Figure 2.2.

FIGURE 2.2

Creating a new
FTP site

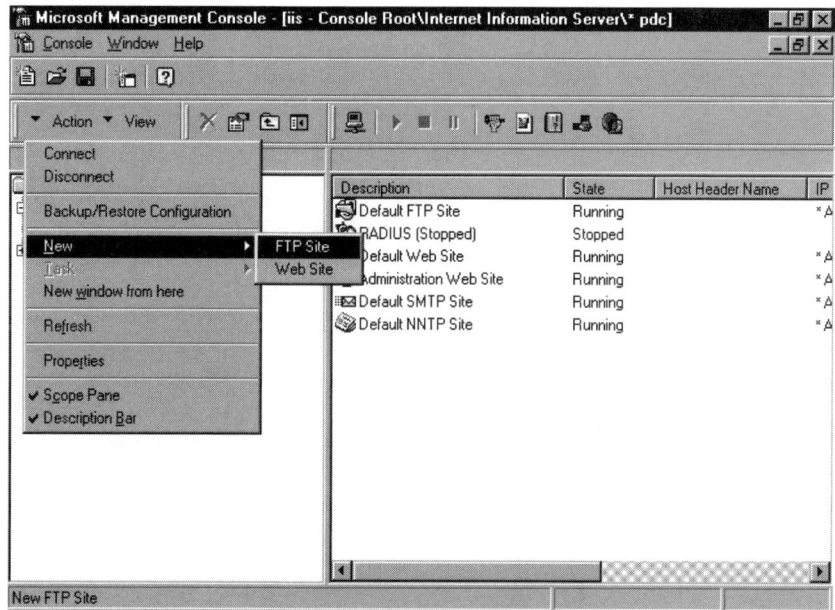

2. The FTP Site Wizard will appear. Type in the name of your FTP site. Click Next.

3. The next dialog box will prompt you for the IP address of the FTP site and the TCP port the FTP site will use. Make the appropriate selection and click Next.

4. In the next dialog box, select the root folder location for your FTP site and click Next.

5. The next dialog box will prompt you to choose what access permissions you want to apply for your home directory. You can select Read and/or Write access. Click Finish.

6. You will need to manually Start the FTP site after creation.

You should definitely install and play with IIS through the MMC before taking this exam. Many of the questions are simulative in nature. For example, you might be asked to create a new FTP site and configure it with parameters provided. You've been warned!

You will learn how to configure the FTP service in the following sections.

Configuration of FTP Service

This section will cover configuration of the FTP service. The main topics are the FTP configuration options and specific FTP properties.

FTP Configuration Options

When you configure FTP, you must first consider what level you want to configure. You can configure:

- FTP inherited defaults
- Specific FTP sites

These options are covered in the following subsections.

FTP Inherited Defaults (Master Properties)

You can configure master properties for all FTP sites created on a specific computer running IIS. This allows you to centrally manage all FTP properties.

If you have FTP servers that were configured before you set the master properties, you have the option of replacing existing configurations with the new master properties.

New FTP servers will automatically inherit the master properties that you have configured.

To configure the FTP master properties:

1. Click on the computer that hosts the IIS Server within Internet Service Manager. Then use your secondary mouse button to access the Properties option. You will see the dialog box shown in Figure 2.3.

2. Select the FTP Service and click the Edit button.

FIGURE 2.3

Computer Properties for Internet Information Server dialog box

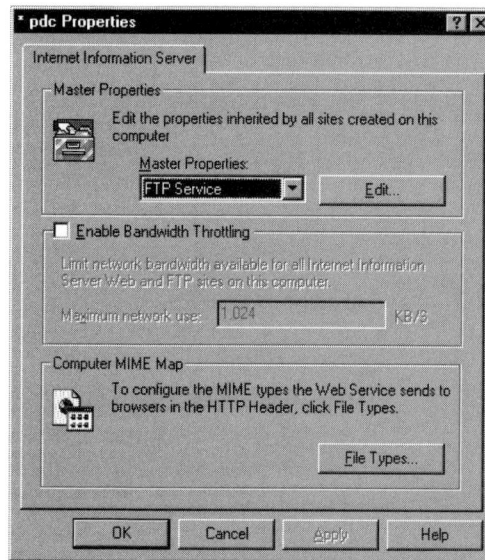

The options you can configure are covered in the following "Configuring FTP Properties" subsection.

Configuration of Specific FTP Sites

You can also configure specific FTP sites. If you configure both master properties and specific FTP sites, the specific configuration will override the master property. This allows you to have complete control over how FTP is configured.

To configure a specific FTP site, click on the site within Internet Service Manager and click the site with the secondary mouse button to access Properties.

Now as promised, the FTP property configurations.

Configuring FTP Properties

Once you have decided whether you will configure the FTP master properties or a specific FTP site, access the FTP properties.

This section will outline each tab used to configure the FTP properties. They include:

- FTP Site properties

- Security Accounts

- Messages

- Home Directory

- Directory Security

FTP Site Properties

In Figure 2.4 you can see the FTP site properties. The various Site properties are defined in Table 2.3.

F I G U R E   2.4
FTP Site tab of the
FTP Site Properties
dialog box

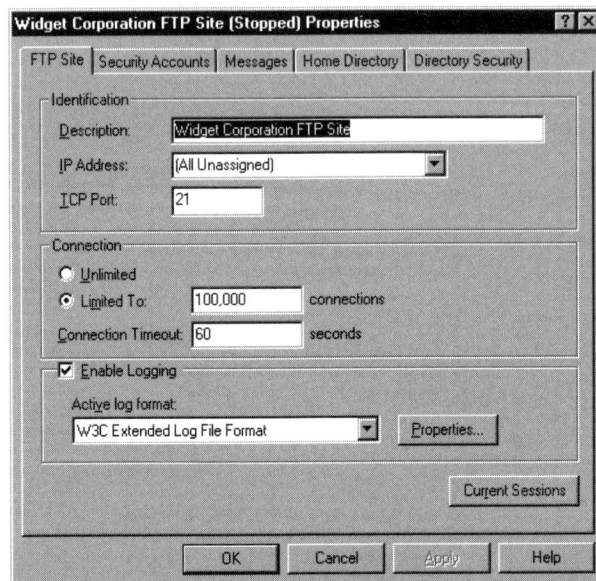

T A B L E 2.3: FTP Site Properties Defined

Category	Item	Description	Default Value
Identification	Description	The tag that identifies the FTP site.	Whatever you specified when you created the FTP site (through the FTP Site Wizard).
Identification	IP Address	The IP address you want to associate with this FTP site. The IP address must already be configured for the NT computer through Control Panel ➢ Network.	All Unassigned
Identification	TCP Port	Specifies the TCP port the FTP service will use. If you change the default port, clients must know to request the port number you define, or their connection will be refused. Some FTP sites change the default port as part of their security strategy.	Port 21
Connection	Unlimited	Specifies that you will allow an unlimited number of connections to your FTP server.	Not Selected
Connection	Limited To	Specifies a finite number of users that can simultaneously connect to your FTP server.	100,000 connections
Connection	Connection Timeout	This number specifies the number of seconds that a connection can remain inactive before it is automatically disconnected.	60 seconds
Enable Logging	Active log format	You can enable or disable logging capabilities. If you enable logging, you can specify the time period that each log will use, the location of the log file, and the file format the log file will use.	Set to use W3C Extended Log File Format

Security Accounts

In Figure 2.5 you see the FTP Security Accounts properties. The main Security Accounts configuration options are whether or not you will allow anonymous connections and which users are granted operator privileges.

FIGURE 2.5

Security Accounts tab
of the FTP Site Proper-
ties dialog box

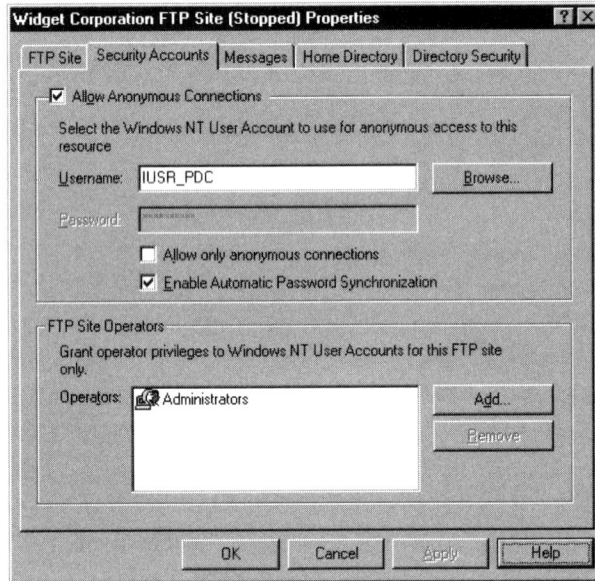

You can specify whether or not you will allow anonymous access to your FTP site. By default, anonymous access is allowed. The user account that provides anonymous access is IUSR_*computername*. It is possible to specify a different user account be used for anonymous access.

You can also select whether or not you will allow only anonymous connections and if you want to Enable Automatic Password Synchronization.

Allow only anonymous connections is used to prevent users from accessing your FTP site using an NT user name and password. This prevents someone from having more permissions than the Anonymous account has been assigned. This option is not selected by default.

Enable Automatic Password Synchronization is used to automatically manage the synchronization of the password used by the FTP account and the NT account. This option is selected by default.

By default, only members of the Administrators group can administer an FTP site. You can specify that other users or groups have the permissions necessary to manage an FTP site by adding them to the FTP Site Operators.

Messages

You can see the FTP Messages dialog box in Figure 2.6. This dialog box allows you to specify:

- A Welcome message

- An Exit message

- A message that appears if the Maximum Connections have been exceeded

FIGURE 2.6

Messages tab of the
FTP Site Properties
dialog box

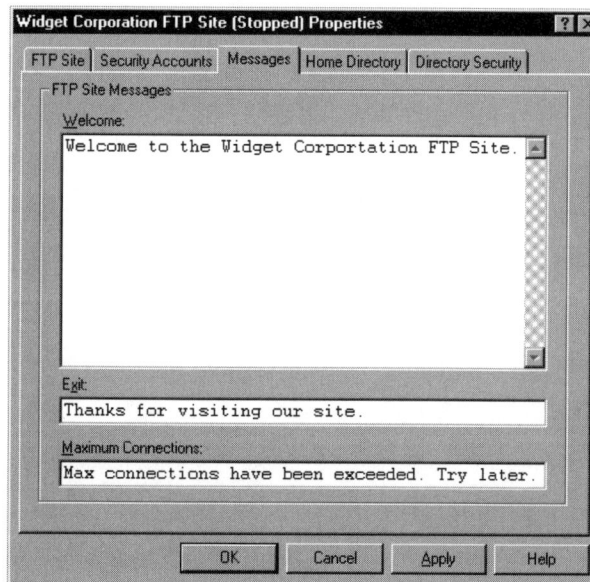

Home Directory

This is one of the most important configuration tabs for your FTP site. The dialog box shown in Figure 2.7 allows you to configure:

- Whether FTP content is local or remote

- The FTP Site Directory and Permissions

- The Directory Listing Style that will be used

These options are covered in Table 2.4.

F I G U R E   2.7

Home Directory tab of
the FTP Site Properties
dialog box

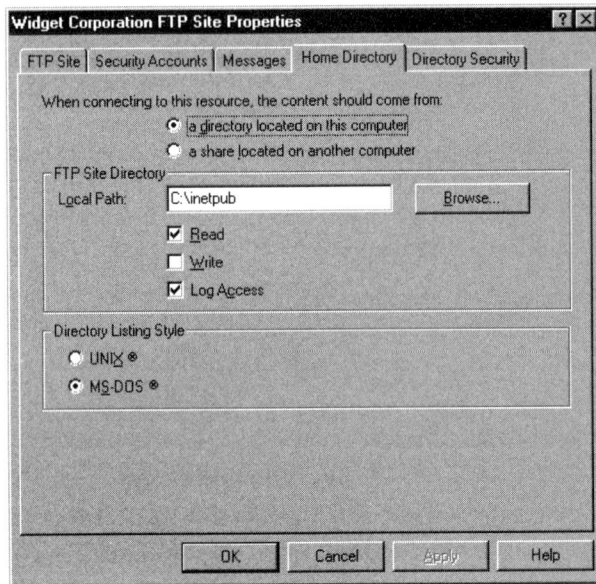

T A B L E   2.4: FTP Home Directory Properties Defined

Category	Item	Description	Default Value
Content Location	a directory located on this computer	Specifies that you are using a local directory.	If you look at the default FTP site, then the default directory is \INETPUB\FTPROOT (on the drive that you specified during the IIS installation). Otherwise, this would depend on where you pointed the FTP Site Wizard when the site was created.
Content Location	a share located on another computer	This option allows you to specify that the FTP home directory is located on another computer. The directory must be shared and the FTP users must have access permission to the directory. This is called a virtual directory.	This is not selected unless you pointed the FTP Site Wizard to a network share for the FTP home directory when the site was created.

T A B L E 2.4: FTP Home Directory Properties Defined *(continued)*

Category	Item	Description	Default Value
FTP Site Directory	Local Path	This allows you to specify the path for your FTP home directory. It can be a local path or a network share.	If you look at the default FTP site, then the default directory is \INETPUB\FTPROOT (on the drive that you specified during the IIS installation). Otherwise this would depend on where you pointed the FTP Site Wizard when the site was created.
FTP Site Directory	Permissions	You can specify what access users have to the FTP home directory. Permissions include Read, Write, and/or Log Access permission. If NTFS permissions and share permissions are applied, users will be bound by the most restrictive access.	Read and Log Access
Directory Listing Style	UNIX or MS-DOS	Specifies whether users will see the listing in UNIX or MS-DOS format. For maximum compatibility, it is recommended that you use UNIX-style listing.	MS-DOS

Directory Security

Directory Security allows you to specify access to your FTP site based on TCP/IP access restrictions. You can grant or deny access to all computers with exceptions based on:

- An IP address
- An IP network address and subnet mask
- A domain name (this requires DNS reverse lookup capabilities)

You can see the Directory Security dialog box in Figure 2.8.

FIGURE 2.8

Directory Security tab of the FTP Site Properties dialog box

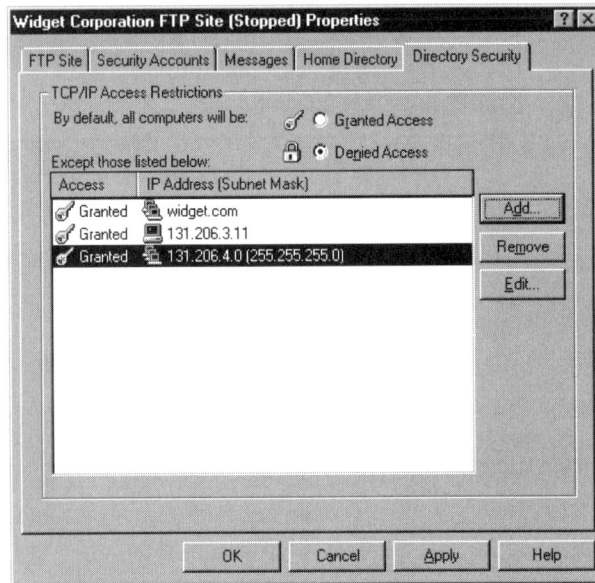

Virtual Directories and Virtual Servers

With FTP and WWW you can create virtual directories and virtual servers. These are covered in the following subsections.

Virtual Directories

A virtual directory is a directory that does not physically exist on the computer that is hosting the FTP site or that is not a part of the home directory for the FTP site. You point to the virtual directory using a UNC name or a physical path to the directory that contains the data you wish to publish. The virtual directory appears to the FTP client as if it is physically part of the FTP site.

Virtual Servers

Virtual servers exist when a single computer running IIS hosts more than one FTP or Web server. For example, you might be an ISP that has been contracted to host five separate FTP sites. Instead of using five different computers, you could use a single computer with multiple virtual servers.

> **NOTE**
>
> More detailed configuration information on virtual servers is provided in Unit 3.

Managing WWW

WWW (the World Wide Web) uses HTTP (Hypertext Transfer Protocol) to allow Web servers and Web clients to communicate. In this section, you will learn how to create a Web site and how to configure the WWW service.

Creation of a New Web Site

To create a new Web site, you would take the following steps:

1. From Start ➢ Programs ➢ Windows NT 4.0 Option Pack ➢ Microsoft Internet Information Server ➢ Internet Service Manager, click on the Internet Information Server folder to expand it. Highlight the computer that will host the Web site, right-click to see Action, then select New Web Site.

2. The New Web Wizard will appear. Type in the name of your Web site. Click Next.

3. The next dialog box will prompt you for the IP address of the Web site and the TCP port the Web site will use. Make the appropriate selection and click Next.

4. In the next dialog box, select the root folder location for your Web site and whether or not you will allow anonymous access to your Web site. Click Next.

5. The next dialog box will prompt you to choose what access permissions you want to apply for your home directory. After you select from the following list, click Finish.

- Allow Read Access (default)
- Allow Script Access (default)

- Allow Execute Access (includes Script Access)
- Allow Write Access
- Allow Directory Browsing

6. You will need to manually Start the WWW site after creation.

The next section provides more detailed information on the configuration of the WWW site.

Configuration of the WWW Site

This section will outline what is involved in configuring the following WWW properties:

- Web site
- Operators
- Performance
- ISAPI filters
- Home directory
- Documents
- Directory security
- HTTP headers
- Custom errors
- Configuring virtual servers to use host headers

Web Site

Web site properties are shown in Figure 2.9. The properties are similar to the FTP site properties that were covered in Table 2.3.

Operators

You can configure which users and groups are able to manage the Web site through the Operators dialog box shown in Figure 2.10.

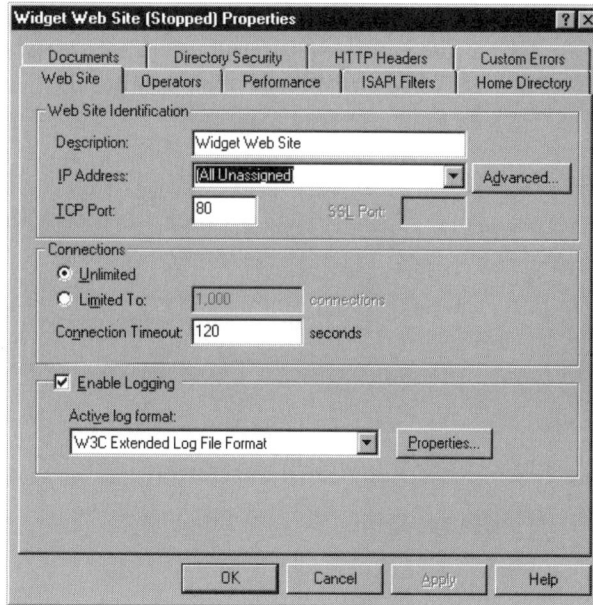

F I G U R E   2.10

Operators tab of the
WWW Properties
dialog box

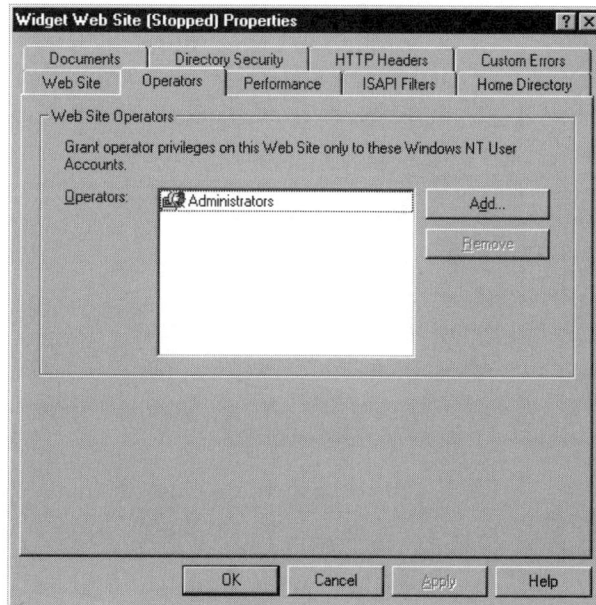

By granting operator privileges, you can delegate Web site management without giving administrative permissions to the NT Server or IIS Server. This might be used to allow an ISP to host multiple virtual servers and allow customers to manage their specific sites.

Operators can:

- Manage the properties of the Web site
- Specify security properties of the Web site

Operators cannot:

- Change port numbers
- Configure the Anonymous user or the Anonymous user password
- Set bandwidth throttling
- Add virtual directories
- Configure ISAPI filters
- Stop, pause, or restart a site
- Change the identification of a Web site

Performance

The Performance tab of your Web Site Properties dialog box allows you to configure the properties that affect the Web site's use of memory and bandwidth. The main areas of configuration can be seen in Figure 2.11 and are:

- Performance Tuning
- Bandwidth Throttling
- HTTP Keep-Alives

Performance Tuning

Performance tuning allows you to tune your Web site based on the number of hits your Web site is expected to receive each day. The tuning options allow you to specify:

- Fewer than 10,000 hits (default)
- Fewer than 100,000 hits
- More than 100,000 hits

FIGURE 2.11

Performance tab of the
WWW Properties
dialog box

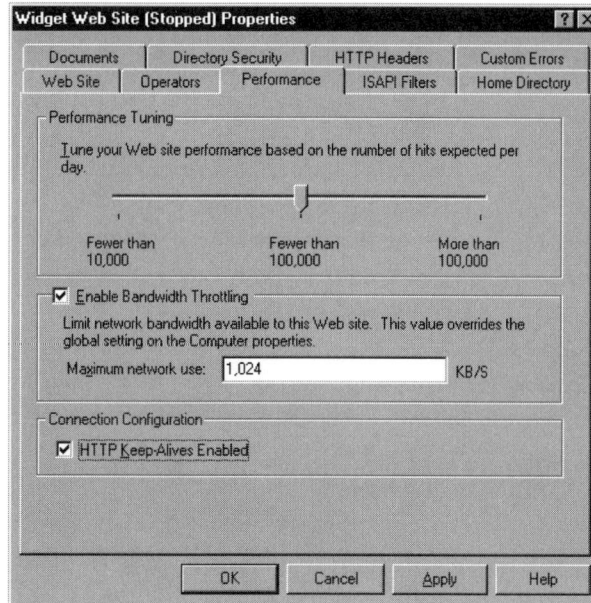

FIGURE 2.11

Performance tab of the WWW Properties dialog box

Bandwidth Throttling

Bandwidth is defined as the total capacity of your transmission media. This can be expressed as bps (bits per second) or as Hz (frequency). IIS allows you to specify how much bandwidth is used in terms of KB/S.

By default, your Web server could use your maximum bandwidth capability. If the server is used for multiple purposes (for example, it also hosts your e-mail application), you might want to limit the total bandwidth that is used by your Web server. This is called bandwidth throttling.

If you use multiple virtual servers, then bandwidth throttling is one way of managing the amount of bandwidth each server can use. This prevents a single Web site from monopolizing bandwidth.

HTTP Keep-Alives

By default, HTTP keep-alives are enabled. This means that when a client connects to your server, they will maintain an open connection to your server. This allows the client to make new requests without reestablishing a new connection with each request.

ISAPI Filters

Within the ISAPI Filters property dialog box you can set ISAPI (Internet Server Application Programming Interface) filters. ISAPI filters direct Web browser requests for specific URLs to specific ISAPI applications, which are then run.

ISAPI filters are commonly used to manage customized logging and authentication. ISAPI filters work by monitoring HTTP requests and responding to specific events that are defined through the filter. The filter is loaded from the Web site's memory. You can define which filters you will use within the dialog screen shown in Figure 2.12.

FIGURE 2.12

ISAPI Filters tab of the
WWW Properties
dialog box

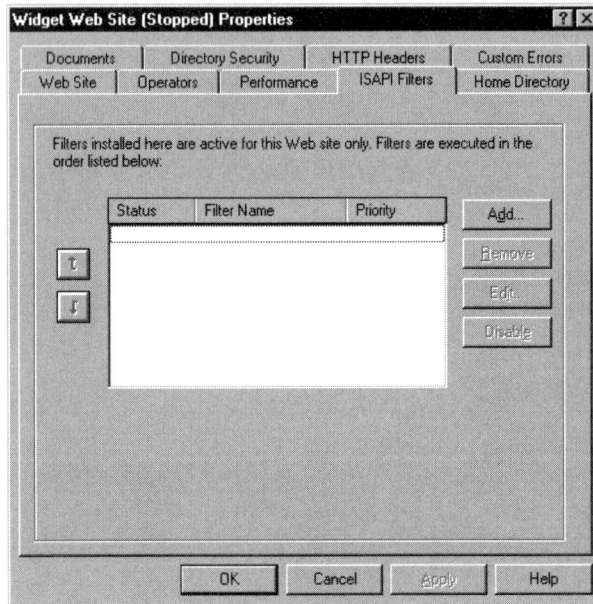

Home Directory

This option is used to specify and manage the home directory that is used to provide Web content. The default Web site will use a home directory called \INETPUB\WWWROOT on the drive that IIS is installed on.

As seen in Figure 2.13, the Home Directory properties tab allows you to configure:

- Content location

- Access permissions and content control

- Application settings

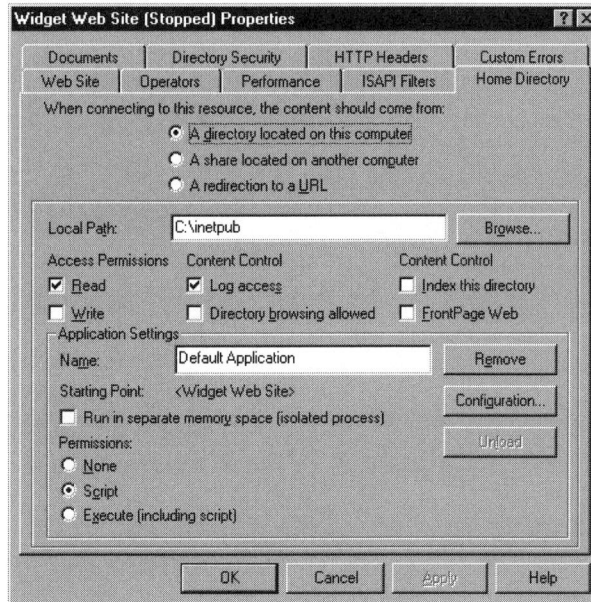

Content Location

Content location specifies where the home directory is located. This can be:

- A directory located on this computer (a local resource)

- A share located on another computer (within the local network using a UNC name)

- A redirection to a URL (a redirection to a resource using a Uniform Resource Locator)

Access Permissions and Content Control

If your content is local or from a network share, you can specify the access permissions and content control that will be applied. The access permissions and content control are defined in Table 2.5.

T A B L E 2.5: Access Permissions and Content Control Defined

Category	Option	Description	Default Selection
Access Permissions	Read	This allows users to read or download files located in your home folder. This is used if your home folder contains HTML files. If your home folder contains CGI applications or ISAPI applications, you should uncheck this option so that users cannot download your application files.	Set
Access Permissions	Write	Write allows users to modify or add to your Web content. This access should be granted with extreme caution.	Not set
Content Control	Log access	This option allows you to log any access to your Web site. In order to log access, the Enable Logging box must be checked within the Web Site Properties dialog box.	Set
Content Control	Directory browsing allowed	This option is not commonly used because it exposes your directory structure to users who access your Web site without specifying a specific HTML file.	Not set
Content Control	Index this directory	This option is used if you are using Microsoft Index Server and you want to include your home folder in the Index Servers index.	Not set
Content Control	FrontPage Web	This option is used to specify that you want to create a FrontPage Web document that will be used by the Web site.	Not set

If NTFS permissions and access permissions are defined, the more restrictive permission will be the effective permission.

Application Settings

Application, in this context, is defined as the starting point of a specific folder (and its subfolders and files) that has been defined as an application. For example, if you specify that your home directory is an application, every local directory and virtual directory that is contained in your site is able to participate in the application. You can specify whether applications will run in separate memory spaces and what permissions will be applied.

If you specify that the application will run in a separate memory space (isolated process), then the application will run in a memory space that is separate from everything else, including the Web site service. This is used for fault tolerance. In the event of failure, the Web site will not be affected. However, this configuration uses more memory resources.

The Permissions option specifies how applications can be accessed within this folder.

- None: no applications or scripts can be executed from this folder.

- Script: allows you to run script engines, even if no execute permissions have been set. This permission should be used for folders that contain ASP scripts or IDC scripts.

- Execute (including script): specifies that you can run script engines and NT binary files that include .EXE and .DLL extensions.

Documents

The Documents Property tab allows you to specify the default document a user will see if they access your Web site without specifying a particular document. You normally set your default document to be your Web site's home page.

You can specify multiple default documents. This way, if a document is unavailable, the Web server will access the next default document that has been defined.

You are also able to specify document footers. A document footer is an HTML document that will appear at the bottom of each Web page that is sent to Web clients.

The Documents properties dialog box is shown in Figure 2.14.

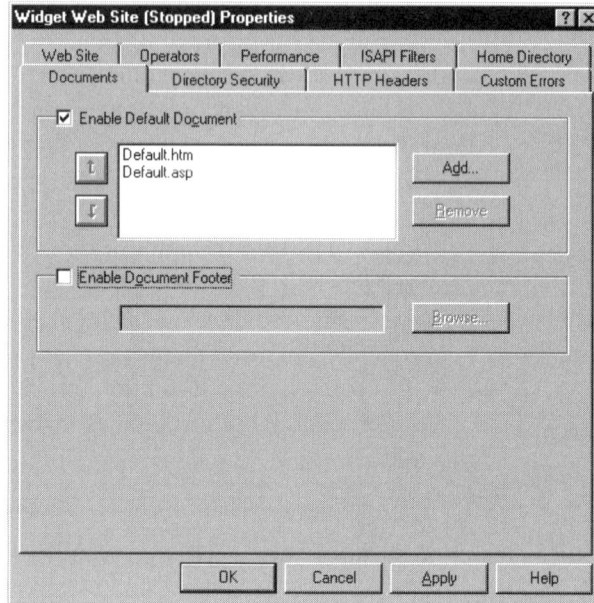

Directory Security

As seen in Figure 2.15, the Directory Security properties dialog box of your Web site allows you to configure:

- Anonymous Access and Authentication Control

- Secure Communications

- IP Address and Domain Name Restrictions

Anonymous Access and Authentication Control

This area of directory security allows you to control who can access your Web site and the authentication method users will use when they do access it. You can select from the authentication methods listed in Table 2.6.

F I G U R E   2.15

Directory Security tab
of the WWW Proper-
ties dialog box

T A B L E   2.6: Authentication Methods Used with Web Site Access

Authentication Method	Description
Allow Anonymous Access	If your Web site is available for public use, you will most likely allow anonymous access. If you allow anonymous access, by default the system uses the IUSR_*computername* user account. You should limit the access the Anonymous user account has by applying NTFS permissions to your Web content.
Basic Authentication	If anonymous access is disabled or the Anonymous account tries to access data that the account has no permission to, the system will prompt the user for a valid NT account. One way that users can be authenticated is through Basic authentication. The advantage of Basic authentication is that it is supported by most Web browsers. The disadvantage is that passwords are transmitted in an unencrypted format.

TABLE 2.6: Authentication Methods Used with Web Site Access *(continued)*

Authentication Method	Description
Windows NT Challenge/ Response	If anonymous access is disabled or the Anonymous account tries to access data that the account has no permission to, the system will prompt the user for a valid NT account. The most secure method for transmitting the user password is to use the Windows NT Challenge/Response authentication method. This method uses a cryptographic exchange of passwords. The disadvantage is that the only Web browser that supports this encryption is Internet Explorer 3.0 or later.

Secure Communications

You can increase the security of your Web site by using secure communications. Within the Secure Communications section, you can create and manage Key requests and Key certificates.

This allows you to then specify that you require a secure channel (using certificates) when accessing the Web site. If you require a secure channel, then clients will be required to present valid key certificates in order to access your Web site. (See Figure 2.16)

FIGURE 2.16

Secure Communications properties dialog box

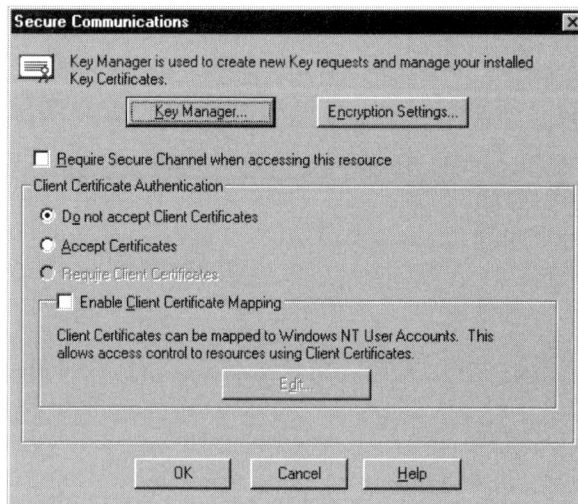

> **NOTE** Digital certificates can be created and managed through Microsoft Certificate Server.

IP Address and Domain Name Restrictions

Directory Security allows you to specify access to your Web site based on TCP/IP access restrictions. You can grant or deny access to all computers with exceptions based on:

- An IP address
- An IP network address and subnet mask
- A domain name (this requires DNS reverse lookup capabilities)

HTTP Headers

You can specify the values that are returned to Web browsers in the HTML headers of Web pages.

The HTTP Headers property dialog box is shown in Figure 2.17.

FIGURE 2.17

HTTP Headers tab of the WWW Properties dialog box

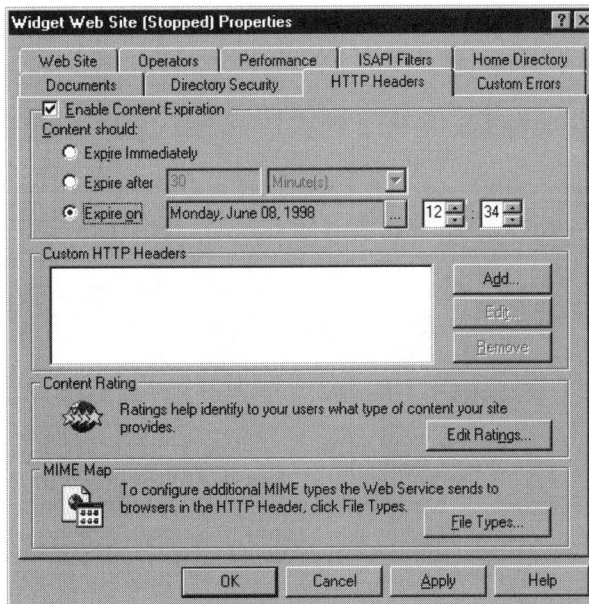

Through this dialog box, you can specify:

- Content Expiration
- Custom HTTP Headers
- Content Rating
- MIME Map

Content Expiration

If your Web site displays information that is time-sensitive, you can specify that you want to use content expiration. You can set content to expire immediately, after a specified number of minutes, or on a specific date.

This helps the Web browser determine if it should use a cached copy of a requested page or whether it should request an updated copy of the page from the Web site.

Custom HTTP Headers

This option is used to specify that you want to use custom HTTP headers.

Content Rating

Because some Web sites are known to contain information that is objectionable to some users, IIS supports the ability to specify content ratings.

Content ratings allow you to specify appropriate restrictions if a site contains violence, sex, nudity, or adult language. Most Web browsers can then be configured to block objectionable material based on how the content rating has been defined.

MIME Map

MIME stands for Multipurpose Internet Mail Extensions. By specifying MIME maps, you can configure Web browsers so that they can view files that have been configured with different formats extensions.

Custom Errors

If a Web browser encounters an error, it will get an error message. There are predefined error messages, and you also have the option of customizing the error message displayed.

To create custom error messages, you create an .HTM file, which can then be mapped to a specific HTTP error. This is configured through the Custom Errors property sheet of the Web site, as shown in Figure 2.18.

FIGURE 2.18

Custom Errors tab of
the WWW Properties
dialog box

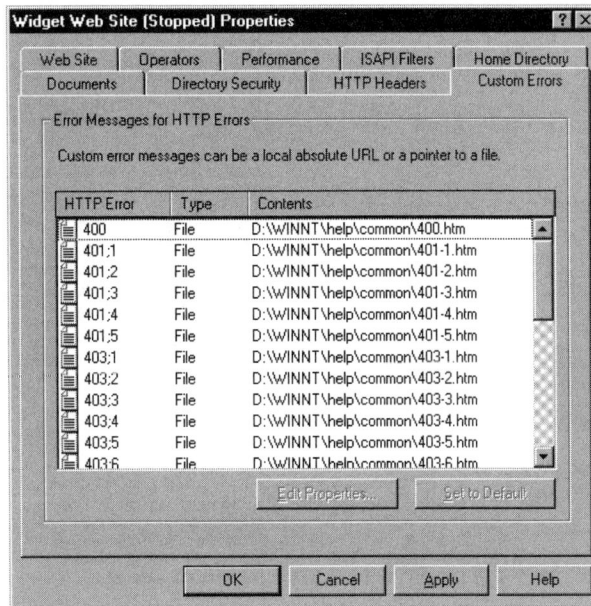

FIGURE 2.18

Custom Errors tab of the WWW Properties dialog box

Configuring Virtual Servers to Use Host Headers

If you have multiple virtual servers that are configured with the same IP address, you have to have some mechanism for specifying how a Web client will access the correct site. In this case, you basically have multiple host names that point to a single IP address. This is managed through two steps:

- You must provide name-resolution through a DNS Server or a HOSTS file

- You must configure host headers for each virtual server

To configure a host header, take the following steps:

1. Within Internet Service Manager, click on the virtual Web site you wish to configure. Access the properties of the Web site, and from the Web Site tab, click the advanced button.

2. Within the dialog box you will see Multiple Identities for this Web site. Click the Add button.

3. You will see a dialog box similar to Figure 2.19. From this dialog box you can configure the host header information.

F I G U R E 2.19

Advanced Web
Site Identification
dialog box

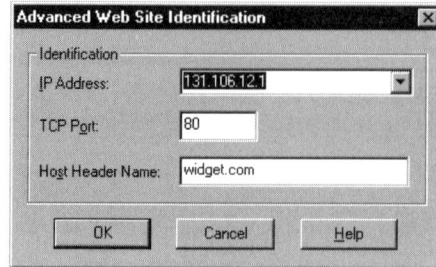

Configure and Save Consoles with MMC

As mentioned earlier, MMC provides a consistent interface that can be used to administer your NT network. MMC gains functionality through added management components called snap-ins that are installed with each Windows NT 4.0 Option Pack component.

Microsoft has announced that in the future all management tasks for NT Server and BackOffice applications will be accomplished through MMC. One advantage of MMC is that you can customize the MMC console any way you like. You can save the customized consoles and share them with other administrators.

To create a customized console, you access MMC and arrange the console to suit your preferences. Once this is done, you would select Console ➤ Save As and specify the file name you want to use to save the customized console. The saved console should have an .MSC extension. This file can then be accessed at a later time or possibly e-mailed to another administrator.

Administration Methods of IIS

You can manage IIS through:

- The Internet Service Manager (ISM) snap-in
- Internet Service Manager (HTML version)
- Windows Scripting Host

The Internet Service Manager Snap-In

The Internet Service Manager snap-in is accessed through MMC. Take the following steps to access Internet Service Manager through MMC. Select Start ➤ Programs ➤ Windows NT 4.0 Option Pack ➤ Microsoft Internet Information Server ➤ Internet Service Manager.

This will call up the graphical interface for administering IIS that has been used for all of the previous tasks and figures within this unit.

Internet Service Manager (HTML Version)

It is also possible to administer IIS through an HTML version of Internet Service Manager. The HTML version of Internet Service Manager allows you to manage many of the same tasks that the snap-in version of ISM allows. In Figure 2.20 you see the default home page that is loaded with Internet Service Manager (HTML).

> If you want to use the HTML version of ISM for remote management, you should use SSL services for security purposes.

FIGURE 2.20

Internet Service Manager (HTML version) home page

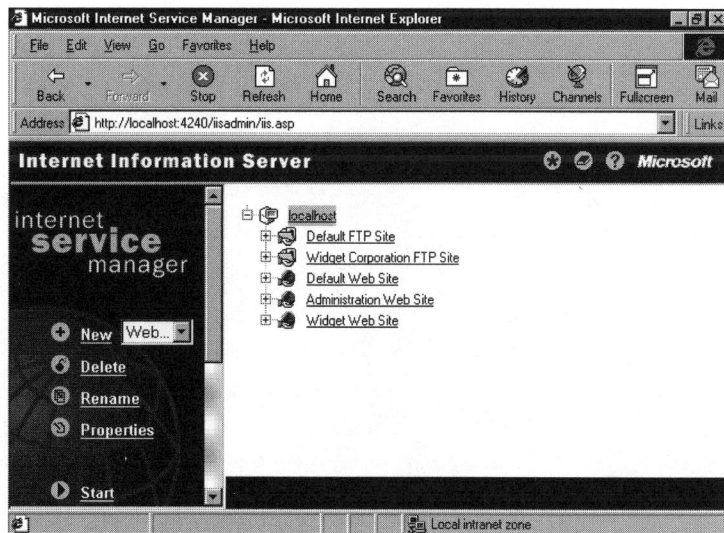

To access the Internet Service Manager (HTML version) select Start ➤ Programs ➤ Windows NT 4.0 Option Pack ➤ Microsoft Internet Information Server ➤ Internet Service Manager (HTML).

> **NOTE** Certificate mapping support is not supported through the HTML version of ISM.

Windows Scripting Host

Windows Scripting Host (WSH) is used to execute scripts from the command line using Wscript (scripting for the Windows desktop) or Cscript (scripting from a console prompt). This allows you to automate non-interactive administrative tasks through the use of scripts.

Installing and Configuring Certificate Server

Certificate Server is used to provide services for creating and managing digital certificates for both clients and servers. Digital certificates are used to provide high levels of security by using public-key cryptography.

In order to install Certificate Server, you must choose the custom installation option of Microsoft Windows NT 4.0 Option Pack Setup.

Once you select the option to install Certificate Server, you will see the dialog box shown in Figure 2.21.

FIGURE 2.21
Microsoft Certificate Server Setup location dialog box

Through this dialog box, you configure:

- The location of your data storage
- The location of your database
- The location of your log
- Whether or not you will perform advanced configuration

The dialog box shown in Figure 2.22 is used to specify identifying information for your Certificate Server.

F I G U R E 2.22

Microsoft Certificate Server Setup identification dialog box

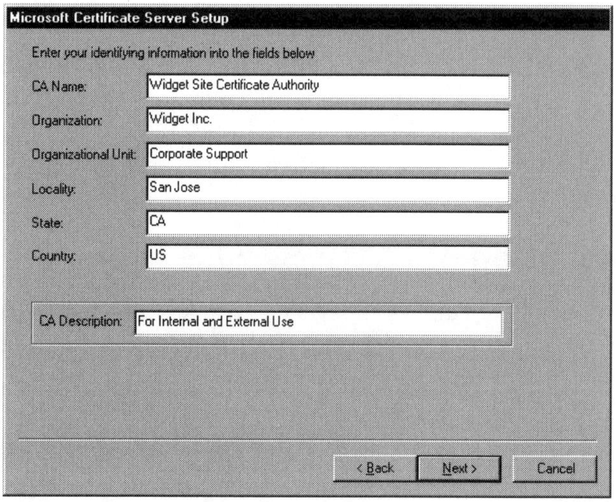

The identification information includes:

- CA Name: the name used by your Certificate Authority, for example, Widget Site Certificate Authority
- Organization: your company name, for example, Widget Inc.
- Organizational Unit: your organizational unit, usually a division or department, for example, Corporate Support
- Locality: your city, for example, San Jose
- State: your state, for example, CA

- Country: your country, for example, US

- CA Description: any descriptive information you want to provide

Once you enter this information, the installation of Certificate Server is complete.

Installing and Configuring SMTP Service

The SMTP Service is offered through the custom installation option of Microsoft Windows NT 4.0 Option Pack Setup. SMTP stands for Simple Mail Transfer Protocol. The SMTP Service is designed to provide support for managing and supporting high levels of traffic generated through SMTP applications (such as e-mail).

This section will outline how to install and configure the SMTP Service.

Installation of SMTP Service

You install SMTP as a subcomponent of Internet Information Server by selecting a check box as shown in Figure 2.23.

FIGURE 2.23

Subcomponents of Internet Information Server dialog box

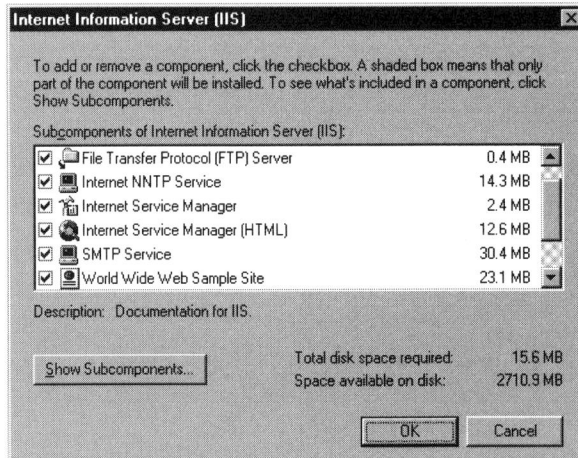

Configuration of the SMTP Service

Once the SMTP Service has been installed, you can manage the service through Internet Service Manager. You can configure the following SMTP properties:

- SMTP site
- Operators
- Messages
- Delivery
- Directory security

These options are covered in the following subsections.

SMTP Site

The SMTP Site properties dialog box is shown in Figure 2.24. The configuration options are defined in Table 2.7.

F I G U R E 2.24

SMTP Site tab of the
SMTP Properties
dialog box

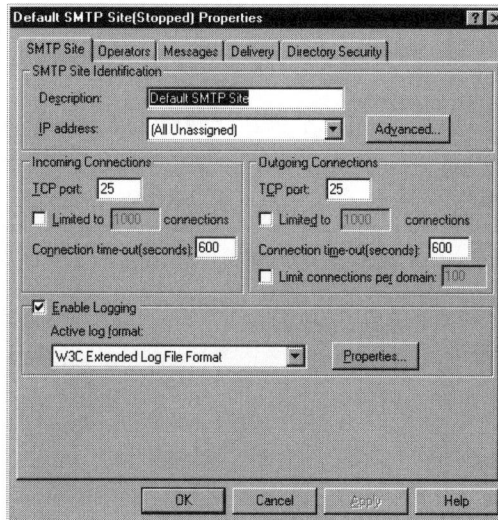

T A B L E 2.7: SMTP Site Properties Defined

Category	Property	Description	Default Value
SMTP Site Identification	Description	This is the name of your SMTP site.	Default SMTP site
SMTP Site Identification	IP address	This is the IP address used to process SMTP connection requests.	All unassigned
Incoming Connections and Outgoing Connections	TCP port	This is the TCP port that is used to process SMTP connection requests.	Port 25
Incoming Connections and Outgoing Connections	Limited to	This is used to limit concurrent incoming and outgoing connections. If you check the check box to limit connections, the default values are activated and can be changed.	By default, not enabled. If you check the limitation boxes, incoming and outgoing connections are limited to 1,000 by default.
Incoming Connections and Outgoing Connections	Connection time-out (seconds)	This specifies that if an incoming or outgoing connection is inactive for the specified number of seconds, the connection will be closed.	600 seconds
Outgoing Connections	Limit connections per domain	This value is used to limit the maximum number of connections the SMTP site will accept from a single remote domain.	100
Enable Logging	Enable Logging	This is used to log SMTP activity.	Enabled

T A B L E 2.7: SMTP Site Properties Defined *(continued)*

Category	Property	Description	Default Value
Enable Logging	Active log format	If you choose to enable logging, you can choose from Microsoft IIS Log Format, NCSA Common Log File Format, ODBC Logging, or W3C Extended Log File Format.	W3C Extended Log File Format

Operators

The Operators property tab allows you to specify which users and groups should have operator rights to the SMTP Service. By default, the Administrators group is added to the Operators group.

Messages

The Messages property dialog box is shown in Figure 2.25. The configuration options are defined in Table 2.8.

F I G U R E 2.25

Messages tab of the
SMTP Properties
dialog box

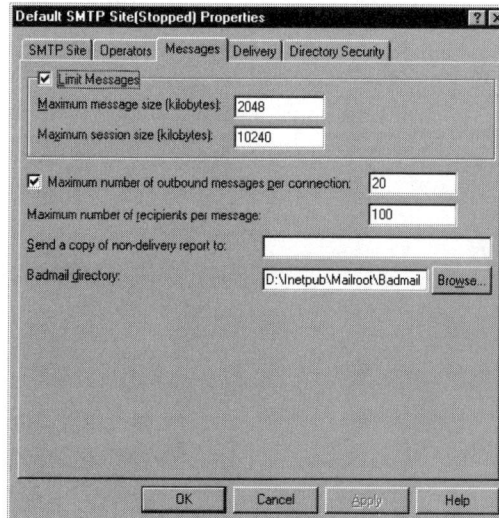

T A B L E 2.8: SMTP Message Properties Defined

Property	Description	Default Value
Limit Messages	Maximum message size and Maximum session size allows you to limit the size of messages that the server will accept. Maximum message size is the maximum message size that will be accepted. It is a value set in kilobytes (KB). Maximum session size specifies that if a message exceeds the session's size value, the connection will be closed automatically.	By default, Maximum message size is 2048KB and Maximum session size is 10240KB.
Maximum number of outbound messages per connection	This specifies the number of outbound messages that are supported per connection. If this number is exceeded, a new connection is established. By using multiple connections, as opposed to a single streaming connection, you will have better performance.	20
Maximum number of recipients per message	This specifies the maximum number of recipients that a message can be sent to. By default, this number is set to 100. If more than 100 recipients are specified, additional connections are created. For example, if the message is sent to 150 recipients, the first 100 recipients would use one connection, then another connection would be used for the remaining 50 recipients.	100
Send a copy of non-delivery report to	This is used to specify the e-mail address of the user who should receive copies of the non-delivery report. The non-delivery report includes information about mail that is not able to be delivered.	Not specified
Badmail directory	This allows you to specify the folder that the non-delivery report should be sent to.	the root drive: \INETPUB\ MAILROOT\ BADMAIL

Delivery

The Delivery tab of the SMTP Properties dialog box allows you to configure the SMTP delivery and routing properties. This dialog box is shown in Figure 2.26, and the options are defined in Table 2.9.

F I G U R E 2.26

Delivery tab of the
SMTP Properties
dialog box

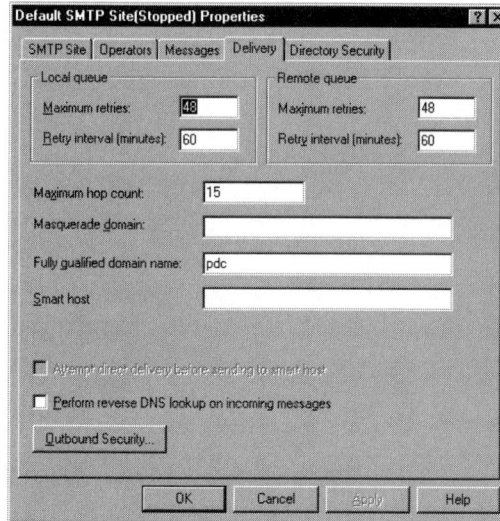

T A B L E 2.9: SMTP Delivery Properties Defined

Property	Description	Default Value
Maximum retries	When you send a message through SMTP, you deal with a sender (remote) and a receiver (local) queue. If the message cannot be delivered, the system will attempt to resend the message. This value can be set for the remote and local queues to specify how many retries should be attempted before the message is considered undeliverable and a non-delivery report is sent.	48 tries
Retry interval (minutes)	This specifies the number of minutes between retries if a message is undeliverable.	60 minutes

T A B L E 2.9:   SMTP Delivery Properties Defined *(continued)*

Property	Description	Default Value
Maximum hop count	Hop count is related to routing. Each time your message passes through a router, it has taken one hop. You can set the maximum hop count to prevent a message from looping through the network.	15 hops
Masquerade domain	This option allows you to specify an alias domain name to appear in the From line of the message instead of your local domain name.	Not defined
Fully qualified domain name	In order to process mail messages, the SMTP Service uses a record called mail exchanger (MX). The MX record relies on the fully qualified domain name (FQDN) to associate a computer with a domain name. You specify the FQDN in this field. An alternative to using this field is to specify resolution-mapping through a DNS server.	Whatever your computer NetBIOS name is, or the FQDN you have defined
Smart host	This is a routing option that controls how messages are routed. This may allow you to specify a more direct route.	Not defined
Attempt direct delivery before sending to smart host	This option specifies that SMTP should attempt a local delivery before messages are forwarded to a smart host.	Not defined
Perform reverse DNS lookup on incoming messages	This option is used to confirm the IP address that e-mail messages have originated from. This offers enhanced security, but is process-intensive and could affect performance.	Not specified
Outbound Security	This option is used to enable the SMTP site to provide authentication credentials to the server that is receiving the SMTP messages. This would be required if the receiving SMTP site was configured to require Windows NT Challenge/Response authentication.	No authentication

Directory Security

Directory security allows you to specify security restrictions for accessing your SMTP site. The options you can configure are:

- Anonymous Access and Authentication Control

- Secure Communications

- IP Address and Domain Name Restrictions

- Relay Restrictions

The dialog box is shown in Figure 2.27, and the options are defined in the following subsections.

FIGURE 2.27

Directory Security tab of the SMTP Properties dialog box

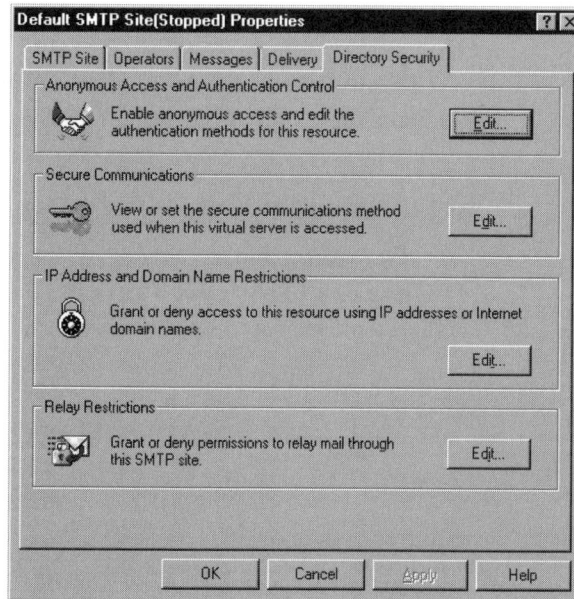

Anonymous Access and Authentication Control

Through this dialog box, you can select the following options:

- Whether or not you will allow anonymous access

- Whether clients are allowed to use Basic authentication or not, and the default domain that will provide the client authentication

- Whether clients will be required to authenticate using the Windows NT Challenge/Response authentication method or not

> **NOTE** These options are similar to the Anonymous Access and Authentication Control options that were covered in the "Configuration of the WWW Site" subsection of this unit.

Secure Communications

You can increase the security of your SMTP site by using secure communications. Within the Secure Communications option, you can create and manage Key requests and Key certificates.

This allows you to then specify that you require a secure channel when accessing the SMTP site. If you require a secure channel, then clients will be required to present valid key certificates in order to access your SMTP site.

IP Address and Domain Name Restrictions

Directory Security allows you to specify access to your SMTP site based on TCP/IP access restrictions. You can grant or deny access to all computers with exceptions based on:

- An IP address

- An IP network address and subnet mask

- A domain name (this requires DNS reverse lookup capabilities)

Relay Restrictions

You can specify which IP addresses are allowed relay access to your SMTP site through this option. By default, all IP addresses are allowed to relay as long as they meet authentication requirements.

Installing and Configuring NNTP Service

The Network News Transfer Protocol (NNTP) is used to support electronic newsgroups. Through NNTP you can:

- Create and manage news discussion groups
- Specify which users can access your discussion groups
- Require that users who access your discussion groups use a specific authentication method

Installing the NNTP Service

The NNTP Service is installed through the custom installation of Windows NT 4.0 Option Pack.

Configuration of the NNTP Service

Once the NNTP Service has been installed, you can manage it through Internet Service Manager.

The NNTP Property tabs are:

- News Site
- Security Accounts
- NNTP Settings
- Home Directory
- Directory Security
- Groups

The property settings are defined in the following subsections.

News Site

The News Site tab is used to configure the News site properties. The dialog box for this screen is shown in Figure 2.28. Through this dialog box, you can configure the properties defined in Table 2.10.

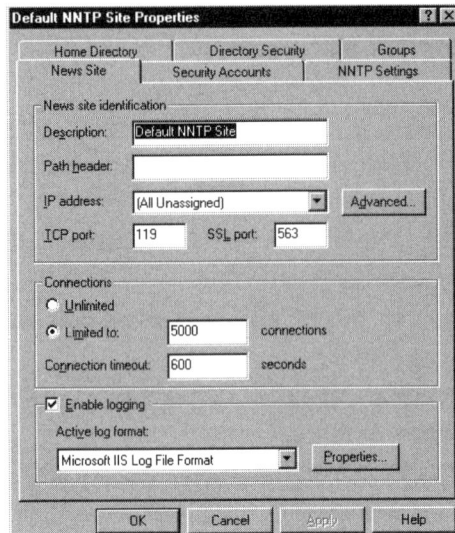

T A B L E 2.10: NNTP News Site Properties Defined

Property	Description	Default Values
Description	Specifies the name of your NNTP site	Default NNTP site
Path header	The string that will be displayed in the path line of each news posting	Not defined
IP address	The IP address that the NNTP site is hosted on	Not defined
TCP port	Specifies the TCP port that the NNTP service should use	Port 119
SSL port	Specifies the TCP port that clients should use if they connect via SSL	Port 563
Connections: Unlimited or Limited to	Specifies whether or not you will allow unlimited connections, or whether you want to limit the simultaneous connections your NNTP site will host	Limited to 5,000 connections

TABLE 2.10: NNTP News Site Properties Defined *(continued)*

Property	Description	Default Values
Connection timeout	Used to configure the number of seconds an inactive client session will be held open before it is automatically disconnected	600 seconds
Enable Logging	Used to track NNTP activity to the log file format you specify	Enabled to Microsoft IIS Log Format

Security Accounts

As shown in Figure 2.29, the Security Accounts tab is used to define:

- Whether or not you will allow anonymous access, and if so, what user account will be used for anonymous access

- Which users and groups are defined as News Site Operators

FIGURE 2.29

Security Accounts tab of the NNTP Properties dialog box

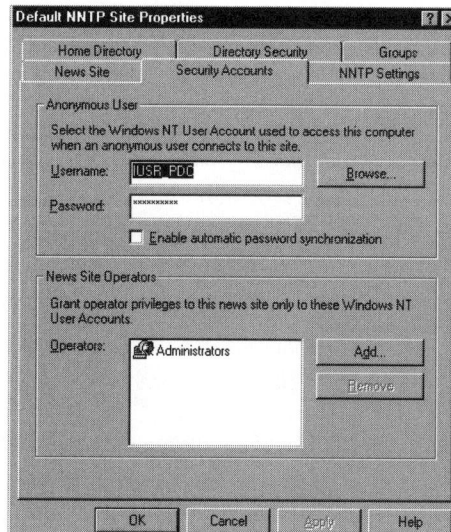

NNTP Settings

The NNTP Settings tab is used to specify client posting and moderator configuration. The NNTP Settings tab is shown in Figure 2.30, and the NNTP settings are defined in Table 2.11.

F I G U R E 2.30

NNTP Settings tab
of the Properties
dialog box

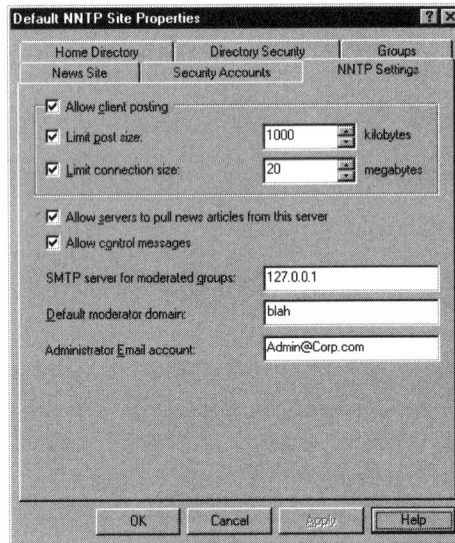

T A B L E 2.11: NNTP Settings Properties Defined

Property	Description	Default Value
Allow client posting	This option enables clients to post information to your NNTP site	Enabled
Limit post size	Specifies the maximum article size that clients can post to your NNTP site	1000KB
Limit connection size	Specifies the maximum size for all articles that clients can post to your NNTP site within a single session	20MB
Allow servers to pull news articles from this server	If set, this option allows other news servers to pull articles from your NNTP site	Enabled

T A B L E   2.11:   NNTP Settings Properties Defined *(continued)*

Property	Description	Default Value
Allow control messages	Specifies that control messages should be processed and logged	Enabled
SMTP server for moderated groups	Specifies the IP address or computer name of the SMTP server that will receive forwarded postings	Not defined
Default moderator domain	Specifies the FQDN of the domain that will host the moderated postings	Not defined
Administrator Email account	Specifies the e-mail address of the user you want to receive non-delivery reports of moderated newsgroup articles that cannot be forwarded to the appropriate moderator.	Not defined

Home Directory

The Home Directory tab of your NNTP site property configuration (shown in Figure 2.31) allows you to specify:

- The path to your NNTP home directory
- The access restrictions for your home directory
  - Allow posting
  - Restrict newsgroup visibility
- The content control configuration for your home directory
  - Log access
  - Index news content
- Whether or not you require secure communications

FIGURE 2.31

Home Directory tab of
the NNTP Properties
dialog box

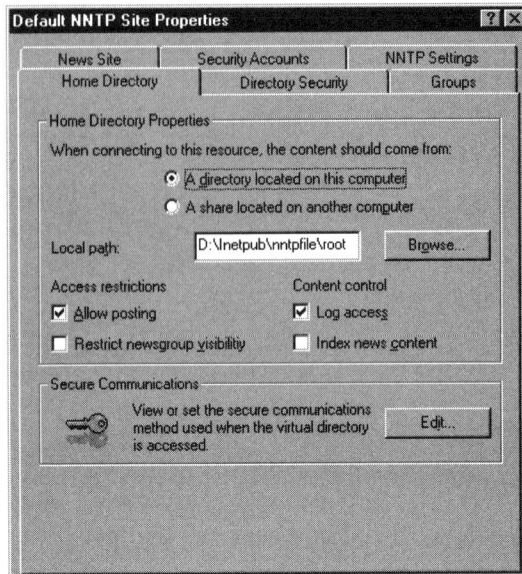

FIGURE 2.31

Home Directory tab of
the NNTP Properties
dialog box

Directory Security

Directory Security specifies:

- The password authentication method you require:

  - Allow anonymous access

  - Basic authentication

  - Windows NT Challenge/Response

  - Enable SSL client authentication

This is shown in Figure 2.32.

- IP address and domain name restrictions, which grant or deny access based on:

  - Single IP address restriction

  - IP network address restriction

  - Domain name

This is shown in Figure 2.33.

F I G U R E 2.32

NNTP Authentication
Methods dialog box

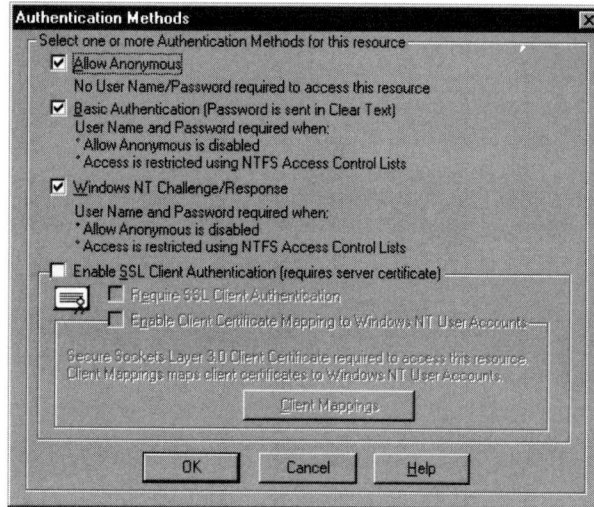

F I G U R E 2.33

NNTP IP Address and
Domain Name Restric-
tions dialog box

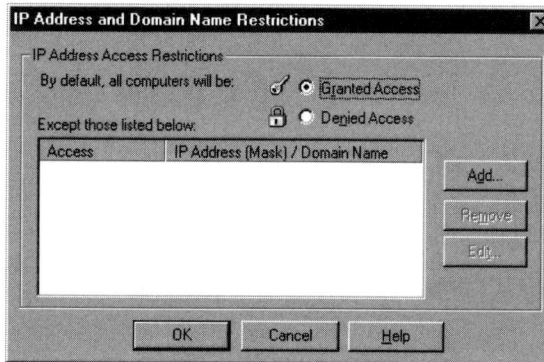

Groups

The Groups tab of NNTP site configuration allows you to add, delete, and
modify newsgroups as shown in Figure 2.34.

FIGURE 2.34

Groups tab of the
NNTP Properties
dialog box

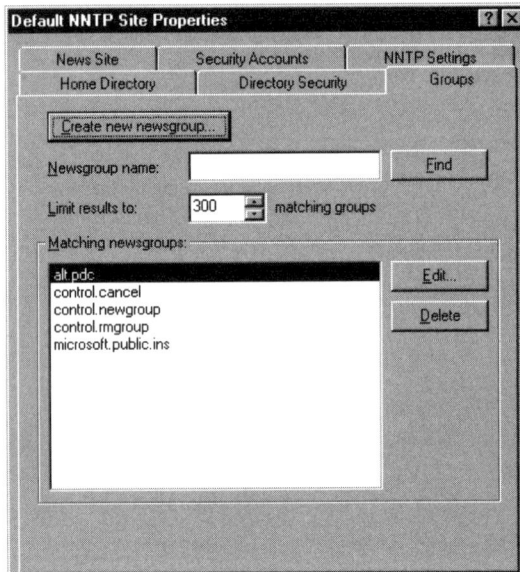

Installing and Configuring Site Server Express

You can install Site Server Express through the custom installation of the Windows NT 4.0 Option Pack.

Components of Site Server Express

Site Server Express 2.0 is mainly used to analyze and control your Web content. It is made up of the following components:

- Content Analyzer: allows you to create a graphical map of your Web site, test your links, and create HTML reports based on the content of your site

- Usage Import and Report Writer: used to import log files that have been created by IIS services and port them into one of 21 predefined reports

- Posting Acceptor: allows you to accept Web content from Web clients using HTTP

NOTE

The Site Server Express Content Analyzer, Usage Import, and Report Writer utilities are covered in more detail in Unit 6.

IIS Installation

1. The _____ transport protocol must be installed on your NT server prior to IIS installation so that IIS will be fully functional.

2. True or False. If you place your Web content on an NTFS partition, IIS will be able to take advantage of NTFS security. If IIS permissions and NTFS permissions do not match, the more restrictive permission will apply.

3. What user account is created by the IIS installation?

_____

4. The _____ is used to store IIS configuration information. It is used as opposed to the registry.

5. True or False. One of the installation requirements of IIS is that it must be installed on an NTFS partition.

6. After IIS is installed, the _____ utility is added to your computer to support IIS administration.

7.   List the seven services that are added to your computer after IIS is installed.

_____

_____

_____

_____

_____

_____

_____

8.   After IIS is installed, additional counters are added to the _____

utility to allow you to track the resources used by IIS.

9.   IIS is installed as a component of _____.

10.   True or False. One of the installation requirements of the SMTP service is that it must be installed on an NTFS partition.

11.   The three options that can be used to install Windows NT 4.0 Option Pack are:

_____

_____

_____

Managing FTP

12. True or False. You can host more than one FTP site on a single IIS server.

13. The _____ snap-in of MMC is used to create new FTP sites.

14. True or False. If you configure FTP master properties, and you also configure specific FTP site properties, the FTP master properties will be applied.

15. List the two directory listing styles supported by FTP.

_____

_____

16. True or False. The FTP site directory can exist on a local drive or a network share.

17. What is the definition of a virtual directory?

_____

18. What is the definition of a virtual server?

_____

19. List the three TCP/IP restrictions that can be applied through Directory Security to specify who can access your FTP site.

_____

_____

_____

20. List the three FTP site messages that can be defined.

_____

_____

_____

21. By default, the _____ group is able to administer FTP.

22. List the three permissions that can be applied to FTP site directories.

_____

_____

_____

23. True or False. If you change the default FTP port setting, then clients are required to specify the FTP port you define through their client software in order to access your FTP site.

Managing WWW

24. If you want to limit the amount of bandwidth that can be used by your WWW site, you should configure _____.

25. Which WWW property tab allows you to define the content rating for your WWW site?

_____

26. List the three possible locations for WWW content.

_____

_____

_____

27. Which WWW site property tab is used to specify that ISAPI applications be associated with specific file extensions?

_____

28. You have specified that your WWW site folder be assigned the Read access permission. The NTFS permission for the site folder specifies that group Everyone has Full Control. What access will users have to your site folder?

_____

29. You have specified that your WWW site folder be assigned the Read and Write access permission. The NTFS permission for the site folder specifies that group Everyone has Read access (this is the only permission assigned). What access will users have to your site folder?

_____

30. What WWW site option allows you to specify that applications should run in a separate memory space from the WWW site service.

_____

31. How do you specify whether or not the WWW home directory is part of an Index Server index?

_____

32. What happens if no default document is defined for your Web site?

_____

33. Which WWW option allows you to specify how long an interactive user's connection will remain open before it is automatically closed?

_____

34. Which WWW option allows you to specify that you want to log activity that pertains to your WWW site?

_____

35. True or False. Performance tuning of your WWW site is based on the number of simultaneous connections your WWW site will host at any given time.

36. What are HTTP keep-alives used for?

_____

37. What types of files would you assign Script application permission to?

_____

38. What types of files would you assign Execute application permission to?

_____

39. List the three authentication methods used by WWW.

_____

_____

_____

40. Why would you use the Basic authentication method?

_____

41. True or False. If you restrict access to your Web site based on domain name, you must be able to support DNS reverse lookups.

Configure and Save Consoles with MMC

42. True or False. You can create customized consoles through MMC that can be saved and shared with other administrators.

Administration Methods of IIS

43. List the three utilities that can be used to manage IIS.

_____

_____

_____

44. What service can be used to make administration of IIS through Internet Service Manager (HTML version) more secure?

_____

45. Which utility allows you to automate administration of IIS through the use of non-interactive scripts?

_____

Installing and Configuring Certificate Server

46. True or False. You can create and manage the digital certificates required by SSL through Certificate Server.

Installing and Configuring SMTP Service

47. True or False. You can define the maximum number of retries (including unlimited) that SMTP will use before a message is determined to be undeliverable.

48. Which SMTP option specifies how many routers an SMTP message can take before the message is discarded?

_____

49. Which SMTP option allows you to route outgoing messages through this option as opposed to sending messages directly to the recipient domain?

_____

Installing and Configuring NNTP Service

50. How do you configure the maximum article size that can be posted to your NNTP site?

_____

51. Which NNTP property configuration tab is used to specify that users must use SSL to connect to your NNTP site?

_____

52. True or False. You can configure the NNTP site to forward news articles to other NNTP sites.

Installing and Configuring Site Server Express

53. The _____ component of Site Server Express allows you to create a graphical map of your Web site, test your links, and create HTML reports based on the content of your site.

54. The _____ component of Site Server Express allows you to accept Web content from Web clients using HTTP.

55. The _____ component of Site Server Express is used to port log files into predefined report templates.

SAMPLE TEST

2-1   Your users have complained that some of the error messages returned from your WWW site are not very informative. You want to replace the default messages with customized messages. How do you accomplish this task?

   A. Create .TXT files with your specific error messages and specify that the .TXT files you create replace the default files through the Custom Errors property tab of the WWW site.

   B. Create .HTM files with your specific error messages and specify that the .HTM files you create replace the default files through the Custom Errors property tab of the WWW site.

   C. Create .DOC files with your specific error messages and specify that the .DOC files you create replace the default files through the Custom Errors property tab of the WWW site.

   D. Directly edit the text files that contain the error messages that you want to customize.

2-2   You host an FTP site that users are attempting to access. You are very concerned about security, so you specify that you will only allow anonymous access and use NTFS permissions to limit access for the IUSR_*computername* account. You also change the default port that the FTP service uses. In addition, you specify that the FTP site folder only be allowed Read access. A client calls and complains that when he attempts to access your FTP site, he is denied access. You test the connection and find that it works for you. What is the most likely problem?

   A. The IUSR_*computername* account has been disabled.

   B. The NTFS permissions for the FTP site folder have been configured so that the IUSR_*computername* account has No Access.

   C. The IUSR_*computername* account has not been assigned permissions for the FTP site folder.

   D. The FTP client software has not been configured to use the alternate FTP port you defined.

2-3 You are very concerned about security and want to ensure that only authorized users are able to access your Web site. All users have valid NT account names and use Internet Explorer as their Web browser. Which of the following options should you implement? Choose all that apply.

    A. Specify that users use Basic authentication to access your Web site.

    B. Specify that users use Windows NT Challenge/Response to access your Web site.

    C. Through Directory Security, specify the NT user account names that have permission to access your Web site.

    D. Through Directory Security, specify that Secure Communications be required.

2-4 Which two options must be configured if you have multiple virtual servers that use the same IP address?

    A. You must use a LMHOST file or a WINS server.

    B. You must use a HOST file or a DNS server.

    C. You must configure a host header for each virtual server.

    D. You must configure an HTTP header for each virtual server.

2-5 Which utility allows you to manage IIS by executing scripts that can be used to automate non-interactive tasks?

    A. Internet Service Manager

    B. Internet Service Manager (HTML version)

    C. Windows Scripting Host

    D. Internet Service Manager Scripting Manager

2-6 What two requirements should be met before IIS is installed on your NT Server?

  A. You should create a user called IUSR_*computername*.

  B. You should make sure that the TCP/IP protocol has been installed and properly configured.

  C. You should make sure that your server has DNS and WINS installed and properly configured.

  D. You should make sure that you have an NTFS partition.

2-7 Your company is an ISP. One of the services you offer is the ability to host your clients' Web sites. You want to use a single computer to host multiple sites. Which of the following statements best represents the configuration that will be required?

  A. You can create multiple virtual servers from a single IIS server.

  B. You need to install a separate instance of IIS for each virtual server you will host.

  C. You can create multiple virtual directories on a single IIS server. Each virtual directory can be used to support virtual Web sites.

  D. This configuration requires a separate computer for each Web site.

2-8 You have created a virtual directory that stores .DLL files. What application setting permission should be applied so that users can access these files properly?

  A. Read

  B. Execute

  C. Script

  D. Write

2-9 You have created a virtual directory that stores .ASP script files. What application setting permission should be applied so that users can access these files properly?

    A. Read

    B. Execute

    C. Script

    D. Write

2-10 Which protocol provides secure authentication through the use of public-key and symmetric encryption?

    A. SSL

    B. DES

    C. Secure Java

    D. C2 Encryption Services

2-11 You manage a Web site that contains highly sensitive corporate information. You specify that you require a secure channel when accessing the Web site through the Web site properties. What utility allows you to create and manage the digital certificates required by the secure channel option?

    A. Certificate Server

    B. Secure Communications Manager

    C. SSL Manager

    D. IIS Security Manager

2-12 Which WWW property configuration option allows clients to maintain active connections with your Web site so that they can make new requests without reestablishing new sessions?

    A. Bandwidth throttling

    B. HTTP keep-alives

    C. Cookie connector manager

    D. HTTP connection maximizer

2-13 You want to manage your Web site from your desktop. You are running NT Workstation and have installed Internet Service Manager (HTML version). What service will support more secure communication?

    A. SSL

    B. DES

    C. Secure Java

    D. C2 Encryption Services

2-14 What permission would you apply to an FTP site directory that you wanted users to be able to download files from, but not upload files to?

    A. List

    B. Read

    C. Execute

    D. Write

2-15   You need to change the port used by the WWW service on 75 IIS computers to use Port 167 for internal security purposes. What is the most efficient way to accomplish this task?

   A. Configure the ports through Internet Service Manager.

   B. Configure the ports through Internet Service Manager (HTML).

   C. Configure the ports through WSH.

   D. Delete the sites and reconfigure them from scratch through ISM.

2-16   You recently sent an e-mail to another user and accidentally typed in an incorrect e-mail address. You did not get an error message back until two days later. What should be configured to reduce the time it takes to get an error message returned? Choose two answers.

   A. Configure maximum retries for the SMTP service.

   B. Configure retry interval for the SMTP service.

   C. Configure maximum hop count for the SMTP service.

   D. Configure the BADMAIL directory for the SMTP service.

UNIT

3

Configuring and
Managing Resource Access

Test Objectives: Configuring and Managing Resource Access

■ **Create and share directories with appropriate permissions. Tasks include:**

- Setting directory-level permissions

- Setting file-level permissions

■ **Create and share local and remote virtual directories with appropriate permissions. Tasks include:**

- Creating a virtual directory and assigning an alias

- Setting directory-level permissions

- Setting file-level permissions

■ **Create and share virtual servers with appropriate permissions. Tasks include:**

- Assigning IP addresses

■ **Write scripts to manage the FTP service or the WWW service.**

■ **Manage a Web site by using Content Analyzer. Tasks include:**

- Creating, customizing, and navigating WebMaps

- Examining a Web site by using the various reports provided by Content Analyzer

- Tracking links by using a WebMap

■ **Configure Microsoft SMTP Service to host message traffic.**

■ **Configure Microsoft NNTP Service to host a newsgroup.**

■ **Configure Certificate Server to issue certificates.**

■ **Configure Index Server to index a Web site.**

- **Manage MIME types.**

- **Manage the FTP service.**

- **Manage the WWW service.**

Exam objectives are subject to change at any time without prior notice and at Microsoft's sole discretion. Please visit Microsoft's Training & Certification Web site (www.microsoft.com/Train_Cert) for the most current exam objectives listing.

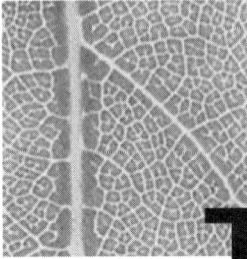

The configuration and management of resources in IIS 4.0 is significantly different from the previous versions of the software package. In addition to all of the previous applications that had resource issues (Web Service, FTP Service, Index Server, and Certificate Server), several of IIS's new applications, the SMTP and NNTP services and Site Server Express, now must be factored into the resource game plan. While there are other parts of the IIS package, the focus in this section is on the access to resources required by those services listed above.

Of course, the other major change in IIS 4.0 is the debut of the Microsoft Management Console (MMC). The MMC concept must be understood and mastered. Microsoft has specified that future versions of NT will use administration plug-in modules for NT administration, as well as to administer many of the NT products and services. The IIS 4.0 exam is the first certification exam to use a simulation section to test the candidate's skills in actually configuring various services. Mastery of the MMC application is critical to passing this exam! Be ready!

Now, on to the resource access issues...

Creating and Sharing Directories

This section will address how you can manage NTFS permissions and shared directories through NT.

NTFS

Directory access issues revolve around the selection of the storage medium format and the location of the directory with respect to the IIS server. As a rule, NTFS-formatted hard disk partitions offer greater security, because of the access-control mechanism in the NT operating system's security module, than is possible using File Allocation Table (FAT) partitions, which offer no local security. NTFS offers the following features:

- Directory Security, limited at the NT user and group level

- File Security, limited at the NT user and group level

- Directory and File Auditing for your Web server's files and directories through NTFS

By contrast, the FAT file system can only offer access control and security to directories that are remotely shared from another computer. This allows you to implement share level security. To maximize security of the IIS directories, both content and application, the NTFS file system should be used.

> Establishing the New Technology File System (NTFS) on any computer, including an IIS server, usually requires converting an existing FAT partition to NTFS through the CONVERT command line utility.

NTFS permissions are used to define the level of access that is to be granted to specific users and groups of users using Windows NT accounts. User and group accounts are created in User Manager for Domains. Once created, these accounts can be given individual (or collective) permissions to directories or files. When IIS is installed on NT Server, an additional user account, the Internet Guest account, is automatically created: IUSR_ *computername.* This account is designed to handle anonymous Web site users that access the account from outside the network, such as via the Internet.

All directories and files that reside on an NTFS partition are given the same default access on creation. They are accessible to the collective group Everyone and are given Full Control permission. The Internet Guest account, IUSR_*computername,* is automatically included within the Guest group and the Everyone group, thereby creating the potential for a huge security issue on all of the directories and files created. This is one reason to remove the group Everyone from NTFS and share permission security.

NTFS Permissions

NTFS permissions can be applied to folders and files. Commonly permissions are set at the folder level but can be applied at the file level for greater control. Permissions set at the file level override permissions set at the folder level. The NTFS permissions are as follows:

- **Full Control:** This permission is granted to the group Everyone by default. This permission allows users to modify, delete, or even change permissions or take ownership of resources.

- **Change:** With Change permission, a user can read, modify, or delete files and directories, but not change NTFS permissions.

- **Add and Read:** This permission combines the access granted through the Add and Read permissions.

- **Add:** Add permission allows you to add files and subdirectories. If Add is the only access granted, it is almost like a mail drop. You can add the file, but once it has been added, you can't read, modify, or delete anything you added.

- **Read:** Users can read, execute, and copy files and directory contents.

- **List:** List allows you to see what files and subdirectories exist. However, you cannot view or execute anything within the folder.

- **No Access:** With No Access a user cannot access any data within a file or folder. This right overrides any other permissions the user might have from other group memberships.

- **Special (Directory or File) Access:** This permission allows you to customize the access that will be granted.

NTFS permissions allow Administrators (or the owner of a file or directory) to set different permissions for various groups or individuals so that, for example, some users would be allowed to view and modify a particular file, while others would be able to copy, move, or execute the same file. Proper configuration of file and directory permissions is crucial for preventing unauthorized access.

To set NTFS permissions on either a file or a directory, the following process applies:

1. Select the file or directory in either the My Computer or Windows Explorer window.

2. Using a right-mouse click, select Properties from the pop-up menu.

3. Select the Security tab.

4. Click on the Permissions button.

5. In most cases, it will be desirable to remove the Everyone Full Control entry (see Figure 3.1).

6. Click the Add button to get the Add User and Groups dialog box.

7. Select a user or group from the Names list.

8. Select the Type of Access.

9. Click Add.

10. Repeat steps 6–9 until all permissions are assigned, then click OK.

FIGURE 3.1
NTFS Directory Permissions dialog box

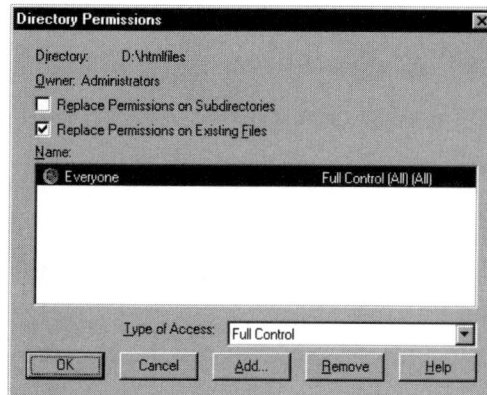

WARNING   Exercise caution when configuring a Web server's NTFS permissions. Inappropriately set permissions can deny valid Web users access to required files and directories. For example, even though a user has the right to view and execute a program, the user may not have permission to access a particular dynamic-link library (DLL) required to run that program. To guarantee users secure and uninterrupted file access, place linked files in subfolders allowing the NTFS permissions to "flow" down to all subfolders at the time of assigning the rights. If there are conflicts between NTFS and Web server permissions, the most restrictive settings will be used. In addition, if the user has No Access permission through NTFS, this explicitly denies access and will always take precedence over those permissions that grant access.

NTFS Auditing

NTFS also provides the ability to audit actions to directories and files. While this feature is very resource intensive and not usually used, it can provide an audit trail for critical files that must be protected or help detect attempted or successful accesses to an NTFS resource. Auditing must be set up on each individual file or directory that is to be covered. Once established, logged activity is reviewed using the NT Event Viewer, Security log.

Shared Folders

As previously noted, you cannot apply local security on a FAT partition, as you can with NTFS. If the FAT partition is on a remote computer (using a virtual directory), you are able to apply share permissions. Share permissions can apply to both FAT and NTFS partitions. To create a remote share on a FAT or NTFS directory:

1. Select the directory in either the My Computer or Windows Explorer window.

2. Using a right-mouse click, select Properties from the pop-up menu.

3. Select the Sharing tab (see Figure 3.2).

4. Set Sharing on by selecting Shared As.

5. Modify the Share Name if desired.

6. Select the Permissions button to get the Access Through Share Permissions dialog box.

7. At this point you may want to delete the Everyone Full Control permission. Select a user or group from the Names list that you want to grant access to.

8. Select a Type of Access.

9. Click Add.

10. Repeat steps 6–9 until all permissions are assigned, then click OK.

11. Verify the addition of the hand icon to the file or directory icon.

F I G U R E 3.2

The Sharing tab of the
Properties window

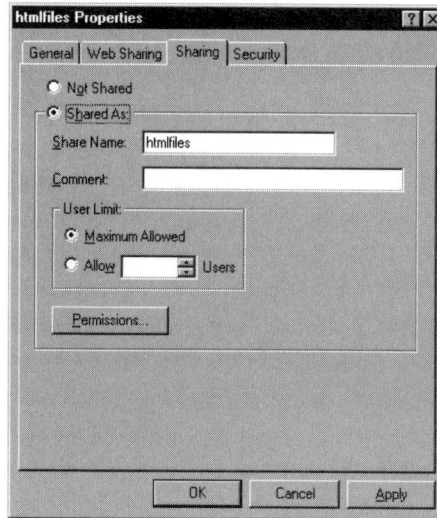

F I G U R E 3.2

The Sharing tab of the
Properties window

Share permissions can be defined as:

- Full Control
- Read
- Change
- No Access

Share permissions are similar to NTFS permissions.

If you have a folder that has share, NTFS, and IIS permissions applied, the most restrictive permission set will be the user's effective permission.

> **NOTE** In order to create a share, a user must be logged in as a member of the group Administrators or Server Operators on the computer that will contain the folder to be shared. On NT Workstation, you could be a member of the Power Users group.

Virtual Directories

A Web or FTP site may contain files that are located on different directory paths than the home or root WWW or FTP directory. The files may also be located on a different computer than the server that is running Internet Information Server. In either of these cases, a virtual directory must be created to include those files in the site. A *virtual directory* is a directory that is not contained in the home directory but appears to client browsers as though it were.

One of the main reasons that virtual directories are used and are located on other servers is to allow the load of Web sites and files to be shared across multiple NT servers. However, this sharing doesn't necessarily improve performance. In fact, if poorly planned, it can reduce Web or FTP site response time depending on how many files must be transferred across the network to support IIS.

Virtual Directory Alias

A virtual directory has an *alias*, a name that client browsers use to access that directory. Because the alias is often shorter than the UNC path name of the directory, it is more convenient for users to type. An alias can also be more secure; users do not know where the files are physically located on the server and cannot use that information to modify them. Aliases also make it easier to move directories within the site. Instead of changing the URL for the directory, the mapping between the alias and the physical location of the directory is changed.

A virtual directory can be created and mapped to any of the following:

- A directory located on the IIS server computer.

- A directory located on another computer. When prompted, type the user name and password needed to access that network shared directory.

- A URL. Browsers requesting a resource at the original URL are automatically given a new, revised destination URL.

Local and Remote Virtual Directories

A Virtual Directory that is located in a directory on the same server as the IIS service is known as a Local Virtual Directory. A virtual directory on another computer is known as a Remote Virtual Directory.

For simple Web sites, virtual directories usually are not needed. It is easier to simply place all of the content files in the site's home directory. For a complex site, or if a different URL is desired for different locations in the site, virtual directories can be added as needed.

Creation of Virtual Directories

To create a virtual directory from within the Internet Service Manager MMC plug-in:

1. Select the Web site or FTP site to which the virtual directory will be added.

2. Click the Action button, and then point to New and select Virtual Directory (see Figure 3.3).

3. Use the New Virtual Directory Wizard to complete this task.

4. Enter the name that the virtual directory will be labeled, click Next.

5. Enter the physical path of the data to be published in the virtual directory, click Next.

6. Click Finish.

7. From a Web browser, access `http://site_name/virtual_directory_name` to verify proper operation of the virtual directory.

Deletion of Virtual Directories

To delete a virtual directory:

1. In Internet Service Manager, select the virtual directory you want to delete.

2. Click the Action button, and select Delete. Deleting a virtual directory does not delete the corresponding physical directory or files.

FIGURE 3.3

Creation of a new virtual directory

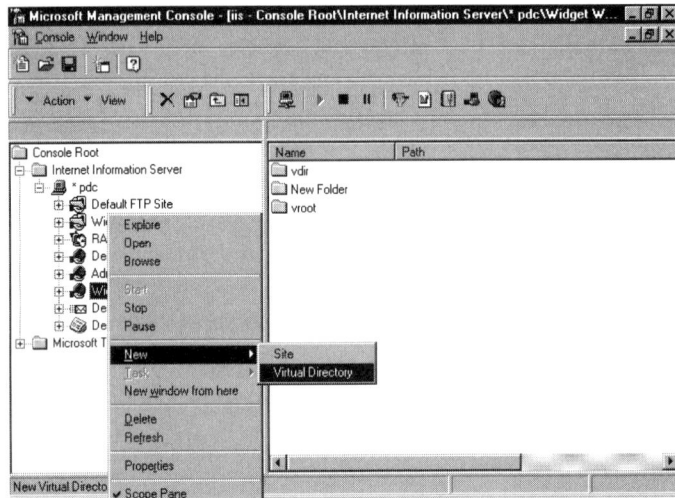

Virtual Directory Path Requirements

Depending on the location of the virtual directory, you will need to provide path information as shown in Table 3.1.

TABLE 3.1: Virtual Directory Path Requirements

Virtual Directory Type	Path Requirements
Local Directory	Use the full path to the folder; for example, root\Support\Patches. You can also click the Browse button to select a local directory rather than typing the path.
Network Share	Use a Universal Naming Convention (UNC) server and share name, for example, \\computername\sharename.
Redirected URL	Use a valid URL for the destination. To map requests to another Web site, use a fully qualified URL, for example, http://www.whitehouse.gov. To map requests to a virtual directory, use a virtual path defined by your IIS, for example, /interns. You can use redirect variables and wildcards in the destination URL to control which portions of the original URL are mapped into the destination URL.

Planning Virtual Directories

When planning the Web and FTP sites, determine the structure of the Web page and FTP file organization before creating directories.

The *home directory* is the central location for the site's published pages. By default, the root home directory is *rootdrive*:\InetPub\Wwwroot. However, you can specify any location you like for your root folder when the WWW site is created, or after creation by editing the home directory location through MMC. Likewise, for an FTP site, the default folder is *rootdrive*: \InetPub\Ftproot. As with the WWW root folder, you can also specify an alternate location for the FTP root folder. The root folder should contain a home page or index file that welcomes viewers and contains links to other pages. Once you have finished changing the default location of the files, the directories that are located on other hard disks or on computers across the network are added to the site.

Each Web or FTP site must have one home directory for each host name or alias name. (An alias name may be an IP address when using NT as a multi-homed system.) The home directory is mapped to the site's domain name or to the specific server name.

For example, if your site's Internet domain name is www.sybex.com and your home directory is *root*\Website\Sybex, then browsers use the URL http://www.sybex.com to access files in your home directory. On an intranet, if your server name is SybexIntraWebSrv, then browsers use the URL http://sybexintrawebsrv to access files in your home directory.

The Web and FTP home directories are created during the installation of IIS. A home directory is also created when a new Web or FTP site is added. The home directory can be changed by selecting the Home Directory tab as a property of the Web site.

Virtual Directory Security

After you create a virtual directory, you can define the directory's properties through Access Permissions, Content Control, and Application Settings. The window used to define the properties of a virtual directory is shown in Figure 3.4.

F I G U R E 3.4

The Directory tab of
the virtual directory
Properties window

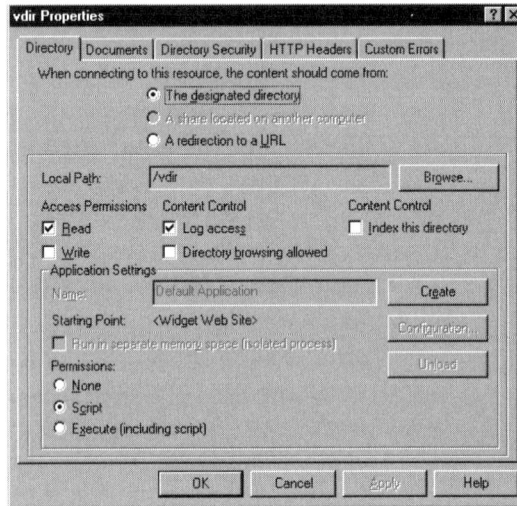

Access Permissions

The Access Permissions properties are displayed when a virtual directory is created from a local directory or a network share. This dialog box is used to set the type of access allowed to the directory. If the directory is on an NTFS partition, the NTFS settings for the directory must match the Access Permissions settings; otherwise the more limiting permissions are used. For example, if a directory is given the Write permission on the Directory property sheet through IIS configuration, but on the NTFS side a particular user group has only Read access permission, those users cannot write files to the directory because the Read permission (on the NTFS side) is more restrictive.

The permissions that can be specified through virtual directory security are defined in Table 3.2.

T A B L E 3.2: Virtual Directory Access Permissions Settings

Access Permission	Description
Read	The Read permission specifies that clients can read or download files stored in the home directory. This is the most common access granted. If the folder contains CGI applications or ISAPI DLLs, you should deny Read access, since this would allow a Web browser to download your application files. In this case, you would assign Application permissions.

T A B L E 3.2: Virtual Directory Access Permissions Settings *(continued)*

Access Permission	Description
Write	With Write permission, Web clients can modify or upload files within the folder. This is a very powerful permission and should be granted with extreme caution.

Content Control

The Content Control properties appear when working with a local directory or a network share. This property is used to control the manner in which IIS allows access, performs logging, and controls the indexing of the virtual directory. The possible virtual directory content control settings are described in Table 3.3.

T A B L E 3.3: Virtual Directory Content Control Settings

Content Control Option	Description
Log Access	This option specifies that activity on the folder is logged. This option is enabled by default, but only works if you have enabled logging for the Web site.
Directory Browsing Allowed	This option specifies that a user can see a hypertext listing of the files and subdirectories. The user would see this list if they did not specify a specific document. This option is considered a security risk and is disabled by default. You should enable this option with caution.
Index This Directory	Permits indexing of the directory by the Index Server and includes the results in a full-text index of the Web site.

Application Settings

Within the properties of virtual directories, you can define application settings. Application settings are used to define how applications, such as CGI applications or ISAPI DLL applications, are processed. The application properties are defined in Table 3.4.

T A B L E 3.4: Virtual Directory Application Settings

Name	Description
Name	Defines the name that will identify the application.
Run in Separate Memory Space (Isolated Process)	If selected, this runs the application in a separate process (out process) from IIS. This protects other applications, including the Web Server service itself, from being affected if the application crashes.
Permissions	The application permissions properties control whether applications can be run in this directory. The permissions are as follows: • **None**: Similar to the NTFS No Access permission in that it denies access so that programs or scripts can not be run from the directory. • **Script**: Script allows an application to be executed, even if the Execute permission was not defined. This option is used for folders that contain ASP or IDC scripts. • **Execute**: This permission specifies that script engines can be executed. This is commonly assigned to folders that contain `.EXE` or `.DLL` files.

Virtual Servers

When a single IIS server hosts several Web sites, it appears to be several separate servers to a user and the browser. A server that hosts multiple Web sites simultaneously is known as a *virtual server*.

For people to be able to reach a site on an intranet or the Internet, the hosting site must have a unique IP address that identifies the computer on the network. This address takes the form of the four-octet IP address, but because they are difficult to remember, text names are used by sites to provide visitors with an easy-to-remember address. The text name must be resolved by a naming system to the correct numerical address. To select the name resolution system best suited to a site situation, this section describes how different systems resolve text names to numerical addresses.

An *intranet* is a private local area network (LAN) that uses Internet technology. To receive and deliver information packets successfully, each computer on the intranet must have a unique address. Unlike the Internet, a computer can connect using methods other than or in addition to the IP address. Usually, each computer has a text name, known in Windows networks as the *NetBIOS* name. If another addressing schema, such as IP, is also used, the computer names and addresses can be assigned and linked by using any of several different systems. The system is selected based on the size of the network, scope of the intranet, how often computers are added or moved, and the software installed on Windows NT Server. Understanding these methods is important in fully understanding *virtual servers*. This subsection will cover:

- IP address assignment
- Name resolution systems
- Internet name resolution
- Host header names, addresses, and ports

IP Address Assignment

Each Web site should be configured with an IP address. The IP address must already be defined for the IIS computer through Control Panel ➤ Network ➤ Protocols ➤ TCP/IP ➤ Properties. The IP address that is assigned should be static, as opposed to an IP address that is defined through DHCP.

To configure the IP address that your Web site will use, access Internet Service Manager, click your Web site, and access the Web Site tab of the WWW Properties dialog box. On the Web Site tab, define the IP address that you will use. This is shown in Figure 3.5.

FIGURE 3.5

The Web Site tab of the WWW Properties dialog box

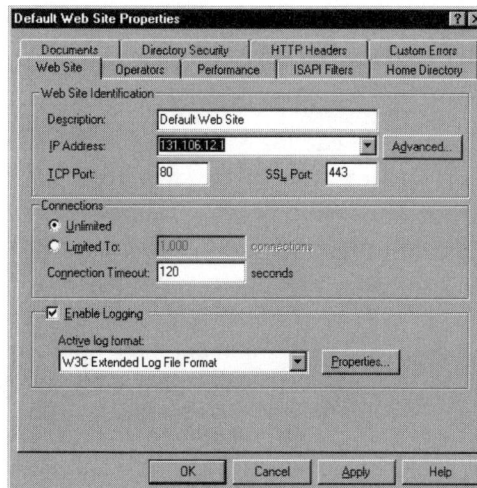

Name Resolution Systems

Windows NT networking components rely on the NetBIOS naming convention, while TCP/IP relies on the Domain Name System (DNS). Windows NT defaults the DNS host name to the NetBIOS computer name. The mapping of host computer names to IP addresses can be done in two ways:

- **Static:** A text file, called a HOSTS file (for DNS names), or an LMHOSTS file (for NetBIOS names), equates each computer name and IP address. The file is then distributed to each computer on the network. When a request for a connection to another computer is made, the file is used to resolve the name to the correct IP address. This works well for simple networks that change infrequently.

- **Dynamic:** When a client computer logs on, a WINS server registers the computer's name and IP address. When a request is made for a NetBIOS computer name, the WINS server resolves the name to the correct IP address. This automatic recognition and mapping of computer names and addresses removes the manual task of configuring and updating host files.

DNS names are typically resolved using cached information. The DNS server contains a portion of the database listing host names and addresses. If the requested name is not in the DNS server's portion of the database, it sends a query to other DNS servers to get the requested information. The DNS server that runs on Windows NT can be configured to query a WINS server for name resolution of the lower levels of the DNS hierarchical naming structure. Because WINS assigns computer names dynamically, this effectively changes DNS from a static system to a dynamic system.

Internet Name Resolution

On the Internet, the Domain Name System (DNS) is used to resolve fully qualified host names to IP addresses for sites. This section describes how Internet sites receive their names.

The Internet DNS names are currently recorded by InterNIC, an organization that manages name and address assignments on the Internet. InterNIC currently operates a distributed database that contains all the registered domain names. When a client computer requests a connection to a site using a domain name, the request is transmitted to a series of computers called the Domain Name Servers.

The Domain Name Servers are located in thousands of computers around the world. They communicate in DNS, a remarkably fast and compact language. The Domain Name Servers return the IP address that corresponds to the requested domain name, and then the client request is routed to the appropriate site.

Host Header Names, Addresses, and Ports

All this background leads to the concepts behind virtual servers and how a client gets to the multiple Web sites. Each Web site has a unique, three-part identity it uses to receive and respond to requests:

- An IP address

- A port number

- A host header name

If IIS is configured for the default of one Web site and one FTP site, it will respond to the NetBIOS or DNS name for the computer or the IP address assigned to the network card installed in the computer. Keep in mind that the default Web port is port 80, and the default FTP port is port 21. When sites use these default port numbers, client browsers do not have to append a port number to the address; otherwise, they must append the URL with a non-standard number. As an example, if the site was sybex.com, running from port 8080, a client would enter the URL http://www.sybex.com:8080, but using the standard port, they would simply type http://www.sybex.com.

Suppose the site is renamed to a different Internet suffix, such as .edu. Because changing a URL may leave a lot of users out in the cold, it may be desirable to retain the old name associated with the address of the site for a period of time. The Web site can be configured to respond to both the previous name and the new name, provided your network correctly routes both requests to your computer. This way, visitors can still reach you using the old name, while becoming familiar with the new name.

One solution is to install multiple network cards in your computer, each with its own IP address. By default, a Web site responds to all IP addresses not assigned to another Web site. Additional Web sites can be created that share a name and port number, but respond to different addresses. Each Web site can also be assigned one or more IP addresses.

The other way is to create a host header. This information links any number of IP addresses, TCP ports, and host header name combinations to a specific Web site. In the case above, `www.sybex.com:8080` could be answered by the same Web site as `www.sybex.edu`, even if they both had separate IP addresses. To configure a virtual server using host headers:

1. Start Internet Service Manager.

2. Expand the IIS Server.

3. If necessary, create the Web site that will be virtually hosted.

4. Right-click the Web site that will be the virtual server and select Properties.

5. From the Web Site tab, click the Advanced button.

6. Select the Add button in the Multiple Identities for this Web Site dialog box.

7. Enter the IP Address, TCP Port, and Host Header Name as shown in Figure 3.6.

8. Repeat for each multiple entry.

9. Click OK twice.

FIGURE 3.6

Advanced Web Site
Identification
dialog box

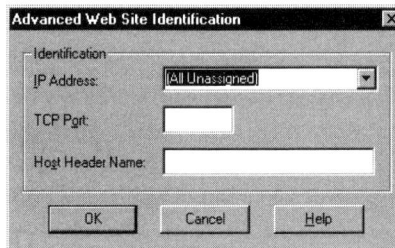

When creating additional Web sites, ensure that each Web site has a unique identity. Multiple Web sites can share any two of the three identity parts, but must be differentiated by the third. This means that two sites can share their host header name and IP address, but must use different ports. Alternatively, they could share a host header name and port, but have different IP addresses.

> **NOTE**
>
> Be aware that older browsers that are not HTTP 1.1 compliant are not able to pass the names that they are requesting in the header. Visitors using older browsers reach the default Web site for the IP address and will require additional support to reach the correct site. Newer browsers pass the name requested in their header. IIS routes these visitors to the correct Web site.

Scripts with WWW and FTP Services

IIS 4.0 permits the Windows Scripting Host (WSH) to allow script control of routine events, such as starting a service, stopping a service, copying files, or even mapping printers. You can use the console-based (Cscript) or the Windows-based (Wscript) utilities to write scripts. Both the VBScript and JScript languages are supported. Even some DOS commands and ActiveX controls are supported.

While developing scripts is beyond the scope of the exam, it is important to know that many functions of IIS can be replicated by creating and executing scripts. If a function is replicated time and time again, consider writing a script to automate it.

> **TIP**
>
> IIS provides several sample administration scripts in the software developers kit (SDK), which is an optional installation option during the IIS setup. These sample scripts are located at `http://localhost/iishelp/iis/htm/adminsamples/default.htm`.

Microsoft Content Analyzer

Content Analyzer, one of the tools in Site Server Express, provides Webmasters with visual maps of how sites are laid out, including page and link identification. It also reports on site content, including total numbers of pages, images, and links.

Content Analyzer is designed to provide graphical maps of a Web site, called WebMaps. The WebMap is, in essence, a database of all the site resources, as well as the associated properties (URLs, hyperlink texts, MIME types, etc.). The map can be customized to specific user needs.

Creating, Customizing, and Navigating WebMaps

Site WebMaps are created and controlled by several methods. The maps are viewed in one of two formats:

- **Tree view:** A hierarchical view of the files and objects that looks similar to the Windows Explorer or File Manager

- **Cyberbolic view:** A relational view of all linked Web objects that can be centered on any item in the map

Maps can be created for nearly any Web site, regardless of location. Maps can be made for sites on a local or networked file system, an internal Web server, or even public sites located on the Internet. WebMaps allow a site to be copied from a Web server to a local hard disk or to another Web server.

Content Analyzer contains settings to control the size and scope of a WebMap. These include:

- Page number limits (default 100)

- Site level limits

- URL name limits

Depending on the site and the task to be accomplished, mapping options can be set to prevent accidentally trying to copy the entire www.microsoft.com site, for example.

After a WebMap is created, it can be updated to show areas of the site that weren't explored during the first mapping of the site. Further exploration can include the entire site or only specified portions.

Additionally, WebMaps will display only selected objects if necessary— just pages, all objects, or some combination of specific object types. Different resources can be shown in each view, for example, just pages in the cyberbolic view, but pages and images in the tree view.

All in all, WebMaps provide a very powerful yet flexible way of viewing a Web site that can help the site personnel view the complex composition and interlinks of modern sites.

Creating a WebMap

Making a WebMap in Content Analyzer is a very simple process. It requires selecting the New Map command for either a URL or a file.

The location can be a path and domain name if the site is on a local or networked file system, or it can be a URL if the site is on a Web server (either an internal Web server or the public Web).

Microsoft Content Analyzer will then explore the entire site up to 100 pages, create a map, and generate reports (in HTML format) that give summary information about the target site (its structure, any broken links, and so on).

While this is the easiest way to create a map, there are a number of options that can be changed to customize the process. For example, you can set a different page limit, extend or restrict the domains and/or site paths to be mapped, and much more. When a map is created, it can start at the home page, or it can map just part of a site.

WARNING If you're using a proxy server, or if there are password-protected pages in the site you want to map, you'll want to change some of Microsoft Content Analyzer's program options before you begin mapping.

The next two procedures create a WebMap from either:

- A file system
- A URL

Map from a File System

To create a WebMap from a file system, follow these steps:

1. From the Windows NT Option Pack, start Microsoft Site Server Express 2.0, Content Analyzer.

2. Select File ➤ New ➤ Map From File. Enter the path and file name for the home page (or any other page in the site where you want to start mapping) in the Home Page Path and File Name text box.

3. In the Domain and Site Root text box, enter the domain and root directory for the site.

4. If you want to start mapping the site from a page other than the site's top home page, add the path to that page after the domain name (but don't include the page's file name).

5. If you have any CGI scripts in your site, and they're *not* in the disk directory \cgi-bin (where "\" is the root site on disk), enter or browse for their location in the CGI Bin Directory text box. If you don't enter a location, Microsoft Content Analyzer won't be able to find the scripts, and they'll show up as broken links in the map. For instance, if you've created an alias directory for your CGI scripts called /usr/bin, you'd enter that alias in the CGI Bin Directory box.

6. Click OK.

Map from a URL

To create a WebMap from a URL, follow these steps:

1. From the Windows NT Option Pack, start Microsoft Site Server Express 2.0, Content Analyzer.

2. Select File ➢ New ➢ Map from URL.

3. In the New Map from URL dialog box, enter the URL of the site's home page (or any other page in the site).

4. Click OK.

WARNING Before using Content Analyzer to map an Internet site, keep in mind that this function can generate a great deal of traffic to the Web server at the remote site.

To cancel the mapping process at any point, click Cancel, or press Esc; the map will contain as much of the site as Microsoft Content Analyzer has mapped so far.

Once you have created a WebMap, you will see a window that is similar to Figure 3.7.

FIGURE 3.7

A sample WebMap
produced by Content
Analyzer

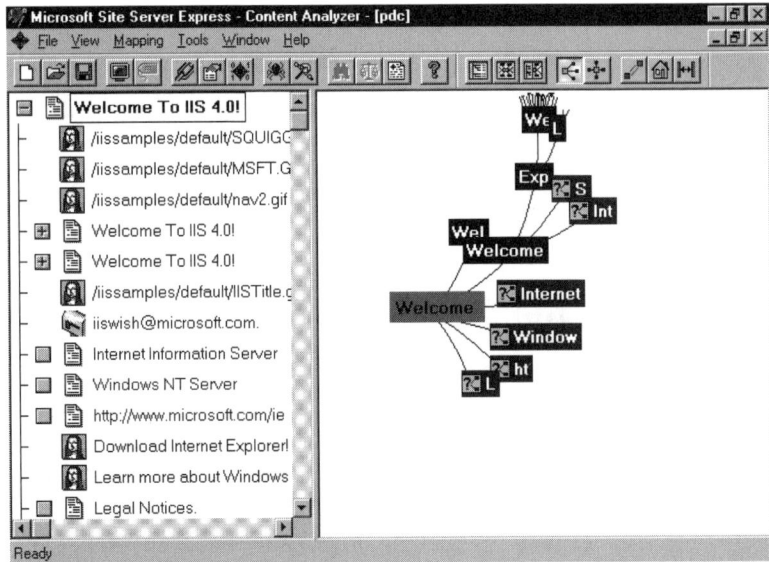

Customizing the Content Analyzer

By default, the Set Routes by URL Hierarchy check box is selected in the
New Map dialog box. This causes Microsoft Content Analyzer to build the
map according to the hierarchy of URLs in the site. If this check box is
cleared, the map will be built according to the order in which links are dis-
covered, without regard for where the links lead to in the hierarchy.

By default, the Explore Entire Site and Generate Site Reports check boxes
are selected in the New Map dialog box. Content Analyzer maps the whole
site, regardless of how many pages it contains. It also generates HTML site
reports that can be viewed in a browser when mapping is completed.

If a site is very large, consider clearing one or both of these check boxes.
If the Explore Entire Site box is cleared, the Explore dialog box appears,
allowing the creation of a smaller map by limiting the number of pages or
levels to be mapped.

To change any default mapping options, click the Options button on the
New Map from URL or New Map from File dialog box. Typically, this
might be done to change the default when mapping from a URL to copy the
site to a local file system. Depending on whether the mapping is from a URL
or the file system, some options may not be available.

Mapping options are saved with the map. To retain these options the next time a map of that site is made, use the Remap command to map the site again, without losing any settings.

To look at or change mapping options later, without exploring or creating a new map, access them with the Mapping Options command on the Mapping menu.

Exploring the Structure of a Web Site

Content Analyzer allows the user to define the scope of the map for as much or as little of a site as necessary. By default, Content Analyzer will explore the URLs for all pages and objects linked to them in the site, or limits can be set for exploring only a portion of them. Subsequent mappings can explore the remaining parts of the site or even expand the outer limits of the initial scope to include other parts and domains.

In summary, there are several ways to explore a site, or part of a site:

- When creating a new map, clear the Explore Entire Site check box and use the Explore dialog box.

- Click the question mark icon next to any unexplored page. This manually explores the target page (tree view).

- Right-click a WebMap page and select Explore Branch. This explores that branch region of the site.

- Right-click a WebMap page and select Explore Page. This explores the page (cyberbolic view).

- Choose Explore ➤ Site from the Mapping menu (or click the Explore Site button on the Main toolbar) to start the WebMap sequence for a user-defined number of pages or site levels.

- Choose Explore ➤ Branch from the Mapping menu to explore a particular region of the site.

Examining Your Web Site with Reports

Once you have generated a WebMap, you can generate Site Reports by accessing Tools ≻ Generate Site Reports from the WebMap main screen. Figure 3.8 shows a sample report.

FIGURE 3.8

Sample WebMap report

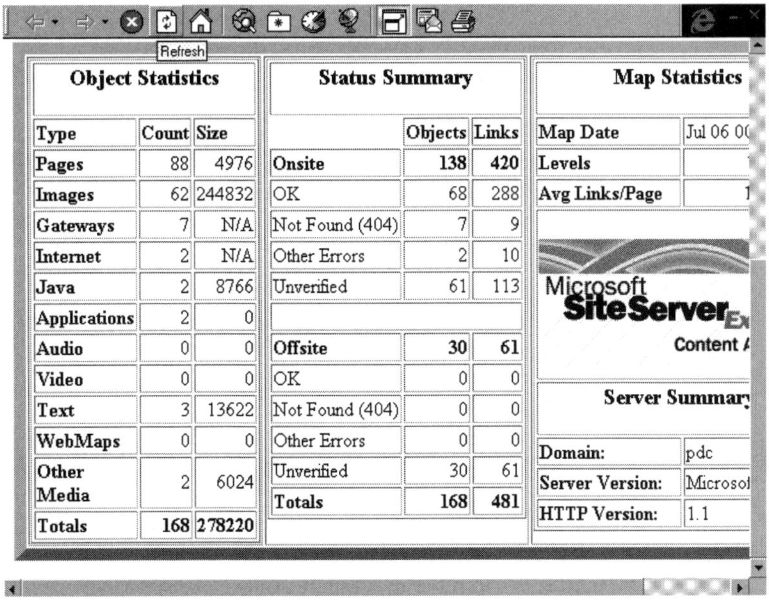

Object Statistics		
Type	Count	Size
Pages	88	4976
Images	62	244832
Gateways	7	N/A
Internet	2	N/A
Java	2	8766
Applications	2	0
Audio	0	0
Video	0	0
Text	3	13622
WebMaps	0	0
Other Media	2	6024
Totals	168	278220

Status Summary		
	Objects	Links
Onsite	138	420
OK	68	288
Not Found (404)	7	9
Other Errors	2	10
Unverified	61	113
Offsite	30	61
OK	0	0
Not Found (404)	0	0
Other Errors	0	0
Unverified	30	61
Totals	168	481

Map Statistics	
Map Date	Jul 06 00
Levels	
Avg Links/Page	1

Microsoft **SiteServer**Ex
Content /

Server Summary

Domain:	pdc
Server Version:	Microsof
HTTP Version:	1.1

Using the Site Report, you can view your site's configuration through:

- Object statistics, which specify the number of resources your site is using.

- Status summary, which specifies the number of local and remote objects. This also specifies whether links are valid or invalid.

- Map statistics, which define a time stamp for the map, the number of levels the map explored, and the average number of links each page defines.

- Server summary, which provides an overview of your Web site.

Microsoft NNTP Service

Microsoft's NNTP Service supports the Network News Transfer Protocol (NNTP), which is used for both client-to-server and server-to-server communications. The service supports popular NNTP extensions and is fully compatible with other NNTP clients and servers. It also supports numerous content formats, including:

- Multipurpose Internet Mail Extensions (MIME)
- Hypertext Markup Language (HTML)
- Graphics Interchange Format (GIF)
- Joint Photographic Experts Group (JPEG)

This support enables users to post pictures and to include Web links in articles.

Like all the other IIS 4.0 services, NNTP offers MMC-based or HTML-based administration tools, either of which enable you to perform all administration tasks.

The NNTP Service can write to the IIS access log, collecting usage statistics and tracking transactions.

How the NNTP Service Works

The NNTP Service is a client/server protocol, running as a service on Windows NT Server, and is configured to start automatically when you install IIS. The service name in the Services application in Control Panel is Microsoft NNTP Service. Microsoft NNTP Service functions as the server; Microsoft Internet Mail and News are examples of typical clients. Clients connect to Microsoft NNTP Service through a Transmission Control Protocol/Internet Protocol (TCP/IP) network. For normal connections, the default TCP port is 119; for optional encrypted SSL connections, the default TCP port is 563.

In the following subsections you will learn how to post and view articles.

Posting Articles

Newsgroup articles are sent to the NNTP Service using a news client, such as Microsoft Internet Mail and News. The client connects to an NNTP Service newsgroup and requests that an article be posted to one or more newsgroups. The NNTP Service receives the connection request and verifies the user's authorization to post to the specified newsgroups. Then, NNTP adds the article to the newsgroups and updates the newsgroup index.

Viewing Articles

Newsgroup articles on Microsoft NNTP Service are viewed using a news client, such as Microsoft Internet Mail and News. The first step in viewing newsgroup articles is getting a list of available newsgroups. The client connects to Microsoft NNTP Service and requests the list of available newsgroups. Microsoft NNTP Service receives the connection request, verifies that user access to newsgroups is authorized, and then sends the client a list of all available newsgroups.

The second step is selecting the newsgroup the user wants to view. The client requests the list of articles for the selected newsgroup. Microsoft NNTP Service verifies that user access to the specified newsgroup is authorized and then sends the client a list of all articles in that newsgroup. Then, as the user selects articles, the client requests the articles from Microsoft NNTP Service, and Microsoft NNTP Service returns the contents of the articles.

Configuring the NNTP Service

In this section, the main areas of NNTP Service are described. They include:

- The NNTP directory structure
- Creating newsgroups
- NNTP expiration policies
- Starting, stopping, and pausing the NNTP service

NNTP Directory Structures

Microsoft NNTP Service stores newsgroup articles in one or more directory hierarchies. Each newsgroup has its own directory, and each article is stored as a file in that directory.

The main directory is *rootdrive*:\Inetpub\Nntpfile\root by default, which can be changed in the Home Directory property sheet of Microsoft NNTP Service. You can create additional directory hierarchies on other disk drives or other computers by creating virtual directories.

The newsgroup directory has the same name as the newsgroup. The NNTP Service automatically creates the required directories when you create new newsgroups. For example, the newsgroup named entertainment.news is stored in the directory \Entertainment\News under the root directory by default (i.e., *rootdrive*:\Inetpub\Nntpfile\root\Entertainment\News). All newsgroup article files have an .NWS extension. Microsoft NNTP Service also creates files that list the subjects of the stored articles; these files have an .XIX extension. Microsoft NNTP Service creates one of these subject files for every 128 articles in a newsgroup.

Microsoft NNTP Service also maintains a number of internal data structure files with .HSH, .HDR, .LST, and .TXT extensions. The default location of these files is *rootdrive*:\Inetpub\Nntpfile. Do not modify or delete these files. The rebuilding of Microsoft NNTP Service restores these files if they are accidentally deleted or damaged.

> By placing the newsgroup folders on multiple disk I/O channels, you can improve performance.

Creating Newsgroups

In either Internet Service Manager or Internet Service Manager (HTML), create newsgroups with the following steps:

1. In the Internet Service Manager, select the NNTP server you wish to add the newsgroup to.

2. Right-click the mouse and choose Properties.

3. Choose the Groups tab in the NNTP Server Properties.

4. Choose Create New Newsgroup.

5. In the Newsgroup text box, type the name of the newsgroup you want to create.

6. In the Description text box, type a brief description of the newsgroup function.

7. If desired, you can specify that the newsgroup is Read-only and whether or not the newsgroup is moderated. Click OK.

NNTP Expiration Policies

The NNTP expiration policies allow you to define how long newsgroup articles are saved for and how much disk space a newsgroup can use. If you define an expiration policy, the default values are that articles over seven days old are deleted, and the maximum amount of disk space that a newsgroup can use is 500MB. If you combine the policies, then the oldest files are always deleted first.

Starting, Stopping, and Pausing the NNTP Service

When the NNTP Service is started, it accepts new connections from users. Likewise, when it is stopped, it disconnects current users and does not accept new connections. When paused, it does not accept new connections but continues to service existing connections.

Certificate Server and Certificates

Certificate requests can be created and submitted through a variety of means, such as HTML-based or file-based requests, depending on what kind of certificate is needed and who is requesting the certificate.

To demonstrate the process of generating and submitting a certificate request, the IIS Key Manager and the CertReq program will be used to request a server certificate. Key Manager can be used to generate a certificate request file by creating a new key pair.

Creating a Certificate Request File

To create a certificate request file:

1. Start Internet Server Manager.

2. Access the IIS virtual root.

3. Run IIS Key Manager from the Internet Service Manager user interface. (There is a toolbar button for Key Manager in the Microsoft Management Console, for which Internet Service Manager is a snap-in.)

4. Use Key Manager to generate a key pair and certificate request. The request file, NewKey.req, will be created in the root directory.

5. Run CertReq to submit the certificate request to Microsoft Certificate Server and obtain a certificate by entering the following:

```
certreq NewKey.req NewCert.crt
```

If Certificate Server accepts the request submitted by CertReq, the certificate file, NewCert.crt, will be created. The certificate file can then be installed into IIS using Key Manager. Once installed, the server certificate will allow any client to perform server authentication when accessing the server.

> **WARNING** You should use SSL services selectively, as they will decrease performance since requests are encrypted and decrypted.

Index Server and Web Sites

You install Index Server through the IIS setup program. During installation, a list box will show you the optional components that you can install with IIS. Once installed, the Index Server, itself, has no options that can be configured in the Internet Service Manager. You can control which virtual directories the Index Server will examine, but you must use the HTML interface to configure the Index Server parameters.

A directory named CATALOG.WCI will be created in the folder where you installed Index Server through the IIS setup program. You can change this directory during setup, if you want. The maximum index size can be up to 40 percent of the size of the original files, so if you do change the default, be sure to choose a location with enough free disk space.

Also, during setup the Index Server files are copied to your computer in the following locations:

- Sample HTML and script files will be copied into /IISSAMPLES/ IISSAMPLES.

- Administration files will be copied into /IISADMIN/IISADMIN.

- Documentation files will be copied into /IISHELP/IX.

In addition to copying sample files and the default index to your computer, Setup also does the following:

- Copies dynamic-link library files (DLLs) to the \%WINROOT%\SYSTEM32 directory

- Adds keys to the registry

- Installs performance counters

- Creates the IISADMIN folder for the administration page and administration sample pages

- Creates, by default, the IX folder under %WINROOT%\HELP for the Index Server documentation, if the documentation is installed

- Installs and starts the Content Index service

> **NOTE** For security reasons, it is recommended that Index Server data be stored on a Windows NT (NTFS) drive.

Recommended Configuration

The recommended configuration for Index Server depends upon the following factors:

- Number of documents in the corpus.

- Size of the corpus.

- Rate of search requests arriving at the server.

- Kind of queries. Complex queries will run faster on a computer with a faster CPU.

Table 3.5 lists the recommended memory configuration based on the number of documents. The size of the corpus (the collection of files to be indexed) affects the disk space needed for storing Index Server data. The disk space needed for Index Server data in all the cases is approximately 40 percent of the size of the corpus. While the average usage is less than 30 percent of the corpus, the peak usage of disk space can be 40 percent.

T A B L E 3.5: Memory Requirements for Index Server

Number of Documents	Minimum Memory	Recommended Memory
Fewer than 10,000	32MB	32MB
Fewer than 100,000	32MB	32MB
100,000–250,000	32MB	64–128MB
250,000–500,000	64MB	128–256MB
500,000 or more	128MB	256MB or more

A faster CPU and additional memory will improve the performance in the creation and updating of the index, as well as the responsiveness of queries. If the number of documents in the corpus is very large, not having enough memory will seriously affect performance. If you see that performance is slow when Index Server is running, add more memory.

For security reasons, it is recommended that Index Server data be stored on a Windows NT (NTFS) drive.

Creating an Index

After you have installed Index Server, the Content Index service is started and it begins indexing all documents in all virtual directories set by IIS. You can check to see if the Content Index service is running by looking in the Windows NT Control Panel, under Services. If the Content Index service is not running, you should start it by selecting Content Index and clicking Start.

> After the initial indexing, the Content Index service continues to index whatever you add to IIS. You can add new documents to existing virtual directories or add new virtual directories and put documents into them. The Content Index service continues to monitor and index all virtual directories on the server even when the WWW service is not running.

Index Server Processing

When a query is made to the Index Server, by default it will use the following three files: QUERY.HTM, QUERY.IDQ, and QUERY.

After you have installed Index Server, the Content Index service is started and begins indexing all documents in all virtual directories set by IIS.

To search for a word, open the Index Server Sample Query Form from the Windows NT 4.0 Option Pack. In the text box below the words "Enter your query below", type any word or phrase. For example, type Microsoft, and then click the Go button.

After a few seconds, a search-results page will appear with a list of documents that contain the word or phrase you are searching for. Click a link to see a document listed by your search. To return to the query form, click your browser's Back button.

Index Server Status and Performance

NT's Index Server provides two ways to check indexing status:

- Windows NT Performance Monitor
- Any Web browser

Windows NT Performance Monitor can verify the indexing process for you. Index Server installs nine performance counters to monitor the state of Index Server:

- # of documents filtered
- Files to be filtered
- Index size
- Merge progress
- Persistent indexes
- Running queries
- Total # of documents
- Unique keys
- Wordlists

MIME Types

MIMEs are very special things. MIME, more formally known as Multipurpose Internet Mail Extensions, is a standard that allows binary data to be published and read on the Internet. The header of a file with binary data contains the MIME type of the data; this informs client programs (Web browsers and mail packages, for instance) how to interpret and present the incoming data. For example, the header of a Web document containing a JPEG graphic contains the MIME type specific to the JPEG file format. This allows a browser to display the file with its JPEG viewer, if one is present.

To configure the MIME mapping for your IIS server, perform the following steps:

1. From Internet Service Manager, right-click the IIS server you wish to configure.

2. Select Properties.

3. Click File Types in the Compute Mime Maps Section of the Properties dialog box.

Use the MIME Map property sheet to configure Multipurpose Internet Mail Extensions (MIME) mappings. These mappings set the various File Types that the Web service returns to browsers. The registered File Types that are installed by default on Windows NT are listed in the Registered File Types dialog box. To configure MIME mappings, click the New Type button. In the File Type dialog box, enter the extension that is associated with the file in the Associated Extension box. In the Content Type (MIME) dialog box, enter the MIME type followed by the filename extension in the form *mime_type* / *filename_extension*.

To remove MIME mappings, select the file type in the Registered File Types dialog box and click the Remove button.

Setting MIME mappings in the master property sheets for your computer allows the Web sites and directories on your computer to use the same mappings. The only values displayed are those you changed—not all the MIME mapping values. If you then reapply the master properties, the master properties completely replace the modified properties for the Web site or directory; the properties are not merged.

NOTE   The objectives for this Unit also list the configuration of SMTP, WWW, and FTP. These services were covered in Unit 2.

Creating and Sharing Directories

1. In order to apply local permissions to a file or folder, you must be using a(n) _____ partition type.

2. True or False. If an IIS root folder is on an NTFS partition and the user has permissions set through IIS, then you do not need to also define NTFS permissions.

3. Andy is a member of the Sales and Everyone groups. The IIS WWW root folder specifies that the Everyone group has Read permission. The NTFS folder specifies that Everyone has Read and Sales has Change. What will Andy's permission be when accessing the IIS WWW root folder through his Web browser?

_____

4. True or False. To specify an additional level of security, you can define auditing of FAT or NTFS partitions.

5. True or False. NTFS provides directory-level security on local and remote shares, while FAT offers no local security.

6. True or False. In order to specify a remote virtual directory, you must point to an NTFS folder.

7. Which NTFS permission would you apply if you wanted users to be able to read or execute the contents of your Web folder, but not be able to make any modifications?

_____

8. In order to create a remote share on an NT server, you must be logged on as a member of the

_____ or _____

groups on the computer that will contain the remote share.

Virtual Directories

9. True or False. An NT Server running IIS can support a maximum of 256 virtual directories.

10. List the three mappings that can be used to reference a virtual directory.

_____

_____

_____

11. True or False. You can create virtual directories for FTP and WWW sites.

12. Other than the UNC path, what information must be supplied when you map a virtual directory to a remote computer within your network?

_____

13. True or False. The home directory for your Web site can be a virtual directory.

14. List and define the two access permissions that can be applied to virtual directories (excluding application permissions).

_____

_____

15. Which option would you configure if you wanted Web browsers to see a listing of all of your files in the virtual directory?

_____

16. Which configuration option within a virtual directory specifies that it be included in an Index Server index?

_____

17. List the three application permissions that can be applied to a virtual directory.

_____

_____

_____

18. Which application setting permission would you apply to a virtual directory that included NT binary files (.DLL and .EXE extensions)?

_____

19. Which application setting permission would you apply to a virtual directory that contains ASP and IDC scripts?

_____

20. True or False. When configuring a virtual directory, if you do not grant Read permission, but do grant Execute permission, users could still execute .EXE and .DLL files.

21. True or False. To specify a virtual directory on a network share, you would supply the URL to the network directory.

22. What is the default directory that is specified by IIS for the WWW root folder?

_____

Virtual Servers

23. When resolving Static TCP/IP or NetBIOS naming conventions, without using Domain Name System, the administrator may use a text file called _____ for DNS names.

24. On the Internet, the Domain Name System is used to resolve _____ to IP addresses for sites.

25. What three options uniquely identify a Web site?

_____

_____

_____

26. What is a virtual server?

_____

27. When resolving Static TCP/IP or NetBIOS naming conventions without using WINS, the administrator may use a text file called _____ .

28. True or False. In order to host multiple virtual servers, you must supply a unique IP address for each virtual server.

29. What standard must the Web client support in order to be able to recognize host header names?

_____

Scripts with WWW and FTP Services

30. What is the main purpose of Windows Scripting Host?

_____

31.   Which utility allows you to create console-based scripts?

_____

32.   Which utility allows you to create Windows-based scripts?

_____

Microsoft Content Analyzer

33.   True or False. Content Analyzer can be used to copy an entire Web site when creating a mirror site.

34.   List the two views that can be seen through WebMap.

_____

_____

35.   List the two options that can be used to create a WebMap.

_____

_____

36.   True or False. You can identify links that have become invalid through the WebMap report option.

37.   What four main items will be displayed when you create a Site Report from your WebMap?

_____

_____

_____

_____

Microsoft NNTP Service

38.   What is the main function of the NNTP service?

_____

39.   True or False. NNTP supports common NNTP extensions, such as MIME, HTML, and JPEG.

40.   What Microsoft client software would allow you to access an NNTP server?

_____

41.   True or False. You can store NNTP newsgroup articles in a virtual directory.

42.   List the two options that can be set for NNTP expiration policies.

_____

_____

Certificate Server and Certificates

43. What utility is used to submit certificates to Microsoft Certificate Server?

_____

44. True or False. You can create digital certificates through the Key Manager utility.

Index Server and Web Sites

45. You want to index a site that is 100MB (defined as the corpus). How much space should you allocate for the index?

_____

46. What two hardware upgrade options will normally improve performance on an Index Server that is performing slowly?

_____

_____

47. True or False. You can monitor the performance of Index Server through Performance Monitor.

MIME Types

48. What is the main purpose of a MIME map?

_____

SAMPLE TEST

3-1   A Scripts directory, which contains executable server-side scripts, needs to be shared between several virtual servers. This can be accomplished by doing which of the following?

   A. In the virtual server's directory properties dialog, select the Virtual Server check box and add each virtual server to the list.

   B. Choose the Make Directory Available to All Virtual Servers check box in the directory properties in the Internet Service Manager.

   C. Leave the Virtual Server check box unchecked in the directory properties in the Internet Service Manager.

   D. Create an entry for the directory containing the scripts for each virtual server root.

3-2   At what level of detail or granularity can directory browsing be activated?

   A. Per page

   B. Per directory

   C. Per virtual server

   D. Per site

3-3   You have specified that the NNTP expiration policy is that articles will expire after 10 days and that each newsgroup can only use 500MB of disk space. What is the result?

   A. Articles will only be deleted after 10 days.

   B. Articles will only be deleted after the newsgroup reaches 500MB.

   C. As long as there is disk space, articles will not be deleted until the 500MB limit is reached.

   D. If an article is over 10 days old, it will be deleted. If the 500MB is exceeded before the 10 day limit is reached, the oldest articles will be deleted first.

3-4 How much memory would be required for an Index Server to index approximately 50,000 documents?

    A. 16MB

    B. 32MB

    C. 64MB

    D. 128MB

3-5 You want to configure a virtual directory on an NT server. The NetBIOS name of the computer is NTS1 and the folder you want to share is called `C:\WebDocs`. Which of the following requirements must be met?

    A. You must specify a user name and password for a user with valid rights to share and create the virtual directory.

    B. The folder must be located on an NTFS partition.

    C. You must be able to provide a valid URL to the folder that will be shared.

    D. The remote computer must be running the WWW service.

3-6 Which three of the following locations can be used to specify a virtual directory?

    A. A directory on the local IIS computer

    B. A network directory accessing a share name

    C. A directory on a remote computer referencing the local path

    D. A redirection to a valid URL

3-7   What is the default home directory specified by IIS for the home folder?

    A. *rootdrive*:\Inetpub\www

    B. *rootdrive*:\winnt\system32\Inetpub\wwwroot

    C. *rootdrive*:\winnt\Inetpub\wwwroot

    D. *rootdrive*:\Inetpub\wwwroot

3-8   Your Internet users get an error message that says access to some Web pages is denied, but some are not. What is the likely cause of this?

    A. The IUSR_*computername* account is disabled.

    B. Web virtual directories do not have proper permissions established for the NT user account IUSR_*computername*.

    C. Web virtual directories do not have proper permissions established for all NT user accounts.

    D. Web home directories do not have proper permissions established for the NT user account IUSR_*computername*.

3-9   Which three things are used to uniquely identify a Web site?

    A. IP address

    B. TCP socket

    C. Port number

    D. Host header name

SAMPLE TEST

3-10   You have defined multiple virtual servers on your server running IIS. Some users are able to access virtual sites correctly, while other clients can only access the default site. What is the most likely problem?

    A. The users who only access the default site do not have NTFS permissions to access the virtual sites.

    B. The users who can only access the default site do not have IIS permissions to access the virtual sites.

    C. The users who can only access the default site are not specifying the port that is used by the virtual sites.

    D. The users who can only access the default site are using browsers that are not HTTP 1.1 compliant.

3-11   What is the fastest way of automating the configuration of IIS?

    A. Use MMC

    B. Use MMC HTML version

    C. Use WSH

    D. Use WHS

3-12   Which of the following configuration options are required to configure virtual Web sites on IIS? Choose all that apply.

    A. Each virtual server requires an IP address.

    B. Each virtual server requires a port number.

    C. Each virtual server requires a unique home folder.

    D. Each virtual server requires a host header entry.

3-13   Scripts for IIS can be written in the following environments and have native support:

   A. JScript

   B. VBScript

   C. DOS commands

   D. Perl

3-14   After migrating a Web site from an older UNIX server to a new NT Server running IIS, users report that the Web site can't be reached. The likely cause and best fix is:

   A. DNS resolves the domain name to the wrong IP address. Install a domain name redirection on the UNIX machine.

   B. DNS resolves the domain name to the wrong IP address. Reassign the IP address to the new NT IIS server.

   C. DNS resolves the domain name to the wrong NetBIOS name. Install a domain name redirection on the UNIX machine.

   D. DNS resolves the domain name to the wrong IP address. Power down the UNIX server and renew the IP address lease on the NT IIS Server.

3-15   Users report receiving an `HTTP 404 "File Not Found"` error. The most likely causes are (choose all that apply):

   A. The domain URL is not defined in the DNS.

   B. The domain URL is not spelled correctly.

   C. The domain does not have a default file.

   D. The domain IP address does not exist.

3-16 How does SSL affect the performance of the IIS Web Server?

    A. IIS performance is increased because SSL provides resources for services that provide encryption of data.

    B. IIS performance is decreased because SSL uses resources for services that provide encryption of data.

    C. IIS performance is increased because SSL uses resources for verifying client browser capability to support encryption of data.

    D. IIS performance is decreased because SSL uses resources for verifying client browser capability to support encryption of data.

3-17 Which utility would you use to create a graphical map of your Web site?

    A. Content Analyzer

    B. Web Mapper Express

    C. Content Mapper Express

    D. Map Analyzer

3-18 Which two options can be used to create a WebMap?

    A. A map from a virtual directory

    B. A map from a virtual server

    C. A map from a file system

    D. A map from a URL

3-19   To create a new Newsgroup, you should do which of the following:

A. Right-click the NNTP site, select Properties, select the Directories tab, click New, enter the name of the Newsgroup Name, click Next, enter the file path, click Finish.

B. Right-click the NNTP site, select New ➤ Virtual Directory, enter the name of the Newsgroup Name, click Next, enter the file path, click Finish.

C. Right-click the NNTP site, select Properties, select Groups, click Create New Newsgroup, enter the name under Newsgroup Name, click OK.

D. Right-click the NNTP site, select Properties, select Groups, click New Newsgroup, enter the name under Newsgroup Name, click Next, enter the file path, click Finish.

3-20   A Web site has been replicated on three different servers. The same domain name must be able to get to any of the three site copies. This can be done by:

A. Creating a single DNS entry and including all three IP addresses

B. Creating three separate entries with the name of the Web server as an alias

C. Creating virtual directories on two of the servers that link back to a central IIS server

D. Writing an Active Server page redirector

UNIT

4

Integration and Interoperability

Test Objectives: Integration and Interoperability

- **Configure IIS to connect to a database. Tasks include:**

  - Configuring ODBC

- **Configure IIS to integrate with Index Server. Tasks include:**

  - Specifying query parameters by creating the `.IDQ` file

  - Specifying how the query results are formatted and displayed to the user by creating the `.HTX` file

NOTE Exam objectives are subject to change at any time without prior notice and at Microsoft's sole discretion. Please visit Microsoft's Training & Certification Web site (www.microsoft.com/Train_Cert) for the most current exam objectives listing.

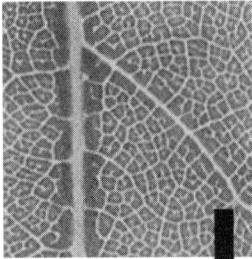

In this unit, you will learn about connecting IIS to an ODBC compliant data source, such as Microsoft Access or SQL Server. Additionally, we'll cover how to index your Web site for searching using Microsoft Index Server.

ODBC Connections

IIS provides the Web developer with many methods of connecting to various databases from within a Web site. The Microsoft Data Access Components (MDAC) provide the newest and most advanced technologies to effect this integration. MDAC 1.5, which ships with the NT Server Option Pack, contains:

- ActiveX Data Objects (ADO)
- Remote Data Services (RDS)
- Object Linking and Embedding (OLE) DB Provider for ODBC
- Open Database Connectivity (ODBC) Driver Manager
- ODBC Drivers for:
  - Microsoft Access
  - Microsoft SQL Server
  - Oracle

In addition, IIS supports older legacy methods to provide backwards compatibility with existing sites, such as:

- Advanced Data Connector (ADC)
- Joint Engine Technology (Jet) through Data Access Objects (DAO)

- Remote Data Objects (RDO)

- Internet Database Connector (IDC)/Internet Database Query (IDQ)

Given the numerous options, ADO provides the most dynamic and flexible model available, and most significantly, it is designed to integrate seamlessly with the Active Server Pages technology.

ADO is essentially a collection of ActiveX controls that use the OLE DB specification to provide fast, low-level access to various data sources. Similarly, RDS is the client-side complement to ADO. Essentially a feature of ADO, RDS components are the ActiveX controls that use HTTP or DCOM to communicate with ADO on the server. RDS 1.5 is implemented with Internet Explorer 4.0.

You can use ADO to write scripts for connecting to ODBC-compliant databases and OLE DB compliant data sources. Microsoft Access can easily write ADO applications for you from simple queries, reports, and forms by using the HTML export capabilities in Access 97. These capabilities, while simple in nature, allow the simple sites to publish data to the Web in a quick and easy manner.

Configuring ODBC

While ADO is beyond the scope of the IIS exam, the concept of establishing database connections must be mastered. Before creating database scripts for your Web page, you need to provide a way for the drivers to locate, identify, and communicate with your database. These "database drivers" pass information from your Web application to an ODBC compliant database, such as Oracle or SQL Server. These drivers require a Data Source Name (DSN) to locate and identify the ODBC compliant database your Web page wants to access. Typically, the DSN contains database configuration, user security, and database server location information.

With ODBC drivers, the following types of DSN can be specified:

- **User:** The User and System DSN are both stored in the Windows NT registry and therefore are subject to the limitations of the Windows NT registry. The User DSN limits database connectivity to a specific user with appropriate security credentials.

- **System:** The System DSN enables all users logged on to a particular server to access a database.

- **File:** Unlike the System and User DSNs, the File DSN is stored in a text file. It provides access to multiple users and is easily transferable from one server to another by copying DSN files.

While the DSN type selection affects the scope of the users who will have access to the database and should be evaluated on a case-by-case basis, most of the time a System DSN is selected.

It is strongly recommended that if you are deploying a data-driven Web application in an enterprise, you use a robust client-server database engine to house your database. This means that your IIS server and your database server should be on separate machines. Although Active Server Pages works with any ODBC-compliant database, it has been extensively tested and is designed to work with client-server databases, such as Oracle or Microsoft SQL Server. Access 97's JET database engine has a maximum limit of 64 simultaneous connections, but performance will degrade as the number of connections reaches 20 or more.

To make the connection between IIS and an ODBC data source, you must first configure ODBC. The following steps outline the method for configuring a System DSN that allows all users connected to the IIS server to have access to the ODBC data source.

To configure ODBC, first open the ODBC control panel by selecting Start ➤ Settings ➤ Control Panel ➤ ODBC. A screen similar to Figure 4.1 will be displayed.

FIGURE 4.1

The ODBC Control Panel

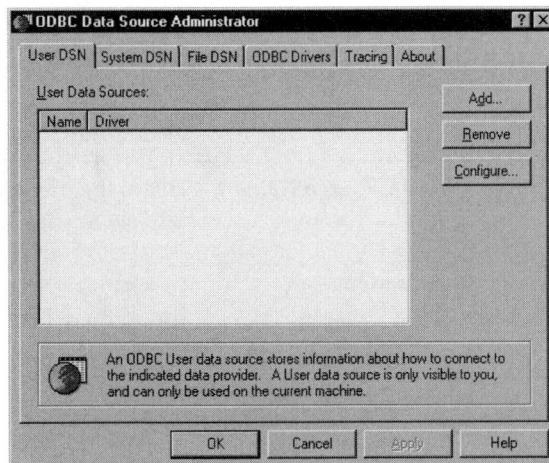

Then, follow these steps:

1. From the ODBC Control Panel Applet, select the System DSN tab.

2. Click Add.

3. Choose the database driver for your database in the Create New Data Source dialog. (Figure 4.2 shows the three default selections: Microsoft Access Driver, Microsoft ODBC for Oracle, and SQL Server.)

4. Click Finish.

5. You will see the ODBC database setup dialog box for the database driver you selected in step 3.

6. The options that can be entered in the System DSN Tab for Access and SQL Server are defined in Table 4.1.

FIGURE 4.2
The ODBC Create Data Source

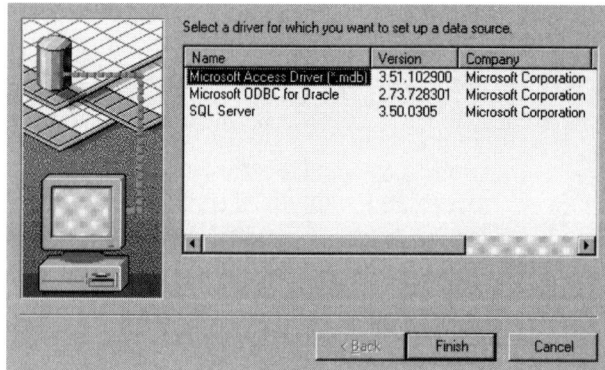

TABLE 4.1: ODBC Data Source Setup Options

Driver	Option	Description
Microsoft Access	Data Source Name	This is the name that the Web database application will use to refer to the database.
	Description	This is designed to provide useful information about the data source, for informational purposes.

T A B L E   4.1:   ODBC Data Source Setup Options *(continued)*

Driver	Option	Description
Microsoft Access	Database	This area displays the name of the file that contains your selected database. Click Select to locate the file that contains the Microsoft Access database. This file may be located on the IIS server itself, or on another share somewhere in the network.
	System Database	Enter the complete path name of the Microsoft Access system database that will be used with the Access database. In most cases, a system database is not used, so "none" is selected.
SQL Server	Data Source Name	This is the Data Source Name that the Web database application will use to refer to the database when requesting a connection.
	Description	This is designed to provide useful information about the data source, for informational purposes.
	Server	This is the name of the Windows NT Server that contains the SQL Server database. If the SQL Server is on the same NT Server, then (local) can used.

Figures 4.3 and 4.4 show the ODBC setup dialog boxes for the default Microsoft ODBC default drivers.

F I G U R E   4.3

The ODBC Microsoft Access 97 Setup

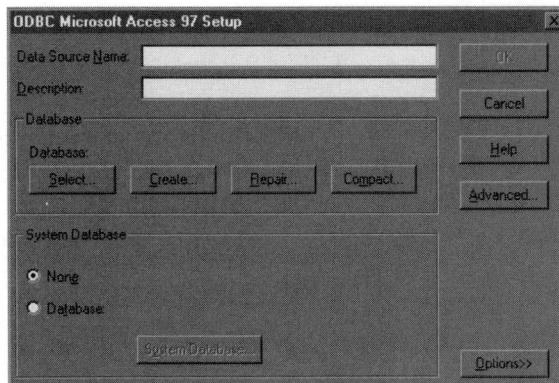

FIGURE 4.4

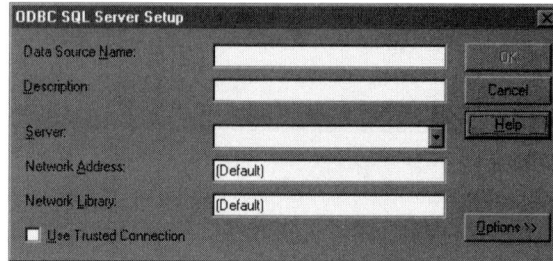

FIGURE 4.4

The ODBC SQL Server
Setup

If Microsoft Access is the database being used, consider having a development version of the data source somewhere in the network and a production (live) version of the data source located on the IIS server. Using the Briefcase as a synchronizer, the production .MDB is placed into the briefcase on the IIS server. Register the ODBC System DSN as being located in the Briefcase. Updates to the data can be done elsewhere in the network, and then "published" to the Web server by simply updating the briefcase. See the Microsoft Access documentation for more information about uses of the Briefcase with Microsoft Access.

SQL Server Connection and Security Information

If you are developing a database application intended to connect to a remote SQL Server database, you should also be aware of two issues: connection methods and security.

Remote SQL Server Connection Methods

You can choose between two methods of connecting to a remote SQL server database: TCP/IP Sockets and Named Pipes.

With Named Pipes, Windows NT must authenticate your Web application before establishing a connection to the database server. This raises the possibility that a remote computer running Named Pipes might deny access to a user who has the appropriate SQL Server access rights, but does not have an appropriate Windows NT user account on that computer.

Using TCP/IP Sockets, the application connects directly to the database server, without connecting through an intermediary computer (for authentication), as is the case with Named Pipes. And because connections made with TCP/IP Sockets connect directly to the database server, users can gain access through SQL Server authentication, rather than Windows NT authentication.

Remote SQL Server Security

If SQL Server's Integrated or Mixed security features are implemented on a remote server, users will not be able to use Windows NT Challenge/Response authentication. NT cannot forward Windows NT Challenge/Response credentials from the IIS Web server to the remote computer. This means that Basic authentication must be used, which relies on the user to provide user name and password information for authentication.

> **NOTE** To improve Web application performance, you should use TCP/IP Sockets rather than Named Pipes to connect to a remote database, such as Oracle or SQL Server.

Microsoft Transaction Server

Microsoft Transaction Server (MTS) is a new application that provides programming interfaces to support database clients.

At its basic level, MTS provides transaction guarantees. One of two things can occur:

- The transaction succeeds. All elements of the database are changed and updated.

- The transaction fails. All elements are removed from the database.

MTS does provide other features, but its primary function is to ensure that database transactions either fully complete or don't complete at all. MTS isn't automatically invoked until it is programmed to do so. Active Server Pages can cause IIS to call the MTS components.

Index Server

The Index Server that runs in IIS provides an indexing service for all documents stored on any Internet or intranet Web site that is being hosted by IIS. When a simple query is created and submitted to IIS, the Index Server is then called, and it takes the submitted data, conducts the search process, takes the returned data on completion of the query, and returns the result to the user's browser in an HTML format.

In addition to searching local Web sites, Index Server can search Internet sites and Word and Excel documents.

The Index Server must first generate an initial index before it can respond to any queries. The collection of documents to be indexed is known as the *corpus*. By defining which virtual directories are to be indexed, the *scope* of the index is set.

Index Server first generates *word lists* by reviewing the documents and passing them through several processes:

- Content Filters index documents by file types. Word and Excel filters are installed by default and others can be added.

- Word Breakers take the incoming character sequences and turn them into words based on the language specifications for treating words and word breaks.

- Normalizer resolves such language-specific treatments as capitalization, punctuation, and "noise words." Noise-word lists are used to remove words like "and", "or", and "the", which can "clog" indexes. They are language-specific and can be modified by adding specific terms as required.

The noise-word list is stored in the NOISE.ENU file, which is located in the SYSTEM32 directory.

After these three steps are completed, the output is sent to the index.

Indexes and Merges

When words enter the index, they first are sent to the *word list*, a small RAM-based list that is used to hold words until they are merged into one of two types of persistent indexes. By adjusting certain parameters in the NT registry, word-list generation can be controlled.

When the word list grows too large, it is merged into the first of two persistent indexes, the *shadow index*. The shadow index allows the quick compilation of the word lists to a disk-based form and reduces the total number of indexes in existence. Persistent indexes are disk-based and are highly compressed files. From there, another merge process combines shadow indexes into *master indexes*, which hold all of the index data from the time they are generated. The total number of persistent indexes cannot exceed 255.

The overarching unit in the Index Server is the *catalog*. It contains all the indexes and properties for all the virtual directories and servers that are defined for the site. While multiple catalogs can be created, queries cannot be run against more than one catalog.

The indexing process requires merges to combine the data into the three types of indexes in the catalog. The three types of merges are:

- Shadow, which combines word lists into shadow indexes to free up memory resources and create non-volatile indexes. Shadow merges occur when:

  - The number of words in the word list exceeds MaxWordLists as set in the Registry

  - The number of word lists exceeds MinSizeMergeWordlists

  - An annealing or master merge occurs

- Annealing, a type of shadow merge accomplished when the CPU loading is minimal and the number of persistent indexes exceeds the MaxIdealIndexes value in the Registry. Annealing merges combine shadow indexes to recover disk space and improve query speed.

- Master, which combines all existing shadow indexes and any master index into a single master. This process is very resource-intensive but results in the highest performance level for subsequent queries. Master merges can be set to automatically occur based on:

  - Server time in minutes after midnight

  - Number of changed documents since last Master merge

  - Remaining disk space and total space of Shadow indexes

  - Total disk space occupied by all Shadow indexes (a separate value from the preceding criteria)

Indexes require about 40 percent of the volume of the corpus to properly function. For a 100MB corpus, 40MB of disk space will allow indexing to occur without degradation.

While not called out as a specific learning point, it is important to understand the concepts of merges and indexes and how they affect the Index Server.

IDQ and HTX

The interface between IIS and the Index Server is accomplished by implementing a query file called an Internet Data Query File (.IDQ) and an output format called an HTML Extension file (.HTX). The IDQ file is an extension to the Internet Database Connector File (.IDC). While still in extensive use today, Microsoft's push is towards ASP and ADO. IDC/IDQ and HTX remain active technologies to ensure legacy support.

The Index Server runs as a service on an NT server (with IIS installed) but is not configured to start until it receives a query. When an .IDQ file is requested, the IDQ.DLL starts and handles the query.

Index Server is essentially a search engine of the virtual directories associated within the Web site(s). While Index Server can search more than one site, usually a separate catalog containing the index files is created for each site. The default catalog points to the wwwroot directory on the IIS server. The files Index Server needs to complete a query are listed in Table 4.2.

> **NOTE**
>
> Detailed information on these topics is available in the NT 4.0 Option Pack documentation, which was installed with Index Server. See http://localhost/iishelp/ix/htm/ixschbld.htm for more information.

T A B L E 4.2 Files Used by Index Server for Querying	**File**	**Usage**
	.HTM	The form used to collect input parameters for the query
	.IDQ	Used with form parameters to specify the query that Index Server will run. Specifies the .HTX file to use to format the results
	.HTX	Formats the results of the .IDQ file

Internet Data Query Files

Internet Data Query files (files with an .IDQ extension) for Index Server (together with the form parameters) specify the query that Microsoft Index Server will run. The .IDQ file is divided into two sections: Names and Query. The sections are defined in Table 4.3.

T A B L E 4.3:   Index Server .IDQ File Sections

Section	Description
Names	This optional section need not be supplied for standard queries. If specified, this section defines the nonstandard column names that can be referred to in a query. The columns refer to properties stored in the property cache, standard file system properties, or ActiveX properties that have been created in document files with IpropertyStorage, or in the Microsoft Office summary and custom properties.
Query	Details the four minimum parameters (CiScope, CiColumns, CiRestrictions, and CiTemplate) that must be used in a query. It can refer to form variables and can include conditional expressions to set a variable to alternative values depending upon some condition.

HTML Extension Files

HTML extension (.HTX) files for Microsoft Index Server are similar to HTML extension files for the Internet Database Connector. Index Server uses the .HTX file mainly to format the results of a query.

Sample Query Form

To create a basic query form:

1. Type the following HTML code in a file.

2. Save the file in HTML format.

```
<HTML>
<HEAD>
    <TITLE>MCSE IIS 4.0 Example Form</TITLE>
</HEAD>
<BODY>
<FORM ACTION="tinker.idq" METHOD="GET">
Search for:
<INPUT TYPE="TEXT" NAME="CiRestriction" SIZE="30"
MAXLENGTH="100" VALUE="">
<INPUT TYPE="SUBMIT" VALUE="Execute Query">
<INPUT TYPE="RESET" VALUE="Clear">
</FORM>
</BODY>
</HTML>
```

In this example, there are two very important lines of HTML code:

```
<FORM ACTION ...>
```

This line specifies the `.IDQ` file that goes with this form. Because an `.IDQ` file helps process an Index Server query form, every Index Server query form must specify a corresponding `.IDQ` file.

```
<INPUT TYPE="TEXT" ...>
```

This line defines a variable called CiRestrictions. This variable is preset to accept whatever text is typed into the query field (the Search for field, in the example). For example, if you type **cache** in this field, CiRestrictions would hold the text "cache."

When the Execute Query button is clicked, the data in the text field is sent to IIS and processed. IIS finds the specified .IDQ file and passes the query data and the .IDQ file to Index Server.

Sample `.IDQ` File

The Internet Data Query (`.IDQ`) file defines query parameters, such as the scope of your search, any restrictions, and query results sets. When the results are returned in raw format, Index Server formats the results according to the `.HTX` file specified in the CiTemplate parameter. The following example shows a basic `.IDQ` file:

```
[Query]
CiColumns=filename,size,rank,characterization,vpath,DocTitle,
➥write
CiRestriction=%CiRestriction%
CiMaxRecordsInResultSet=300
CiMaxRecordsPerPage=10
CiScope=/
CiFlags=DEEP
CiTemplate=/queryforms/form123.htx
CiSort=rank[d]
CiForceUseCi=true
```

The specifications for the parameters are further defined in Table 4.4.

T A B L E 4.4: Example IDQ Parameters Explained

Parameter	Description
[Query]	Identifies the following information as a query restriction.
CiColumns=filename,size,rank, characterization,vpath,DocTitle, write	Indicates the kind of information to return in the result set.
CiRestriction=%CiRestriction%	Indicates the query terms to search for. In this case, the CiRestriction form parameter is used.
CiMaxRecordsInResultSet=300	Sets the maximum number of results to be returned, 300 in this example.
CiMaxRecordsPerPage=10	Determines how many results are shown on each Web page returned. In this case, 10 results will be shown per Web page.
CiScope=/	Tells where to start the query. In this example, the query starts at the root of the virtual directory space. You can list more than one virtual directory in your scope by separating the directories with a comma (,). For example: CiScope=/cars,/trucks, /buses
CiFlags=DEEP	Tells the query to search all subdirectories within the scope.
CiTemplate=/queryforms/ form123.htx	Indicates what path and file to use to format the results; in this case, /queryforms/form123.htx
CiSort=rank[d]	Tells how to sort the results. This example calls for results to be listed in descending [d] rank order. In other words, the results are listed in order from the file with the most hits to the file with the fewest hits.
CiForceUseCi=true	This is an optional variable that, when set to True, forces Index Server to search the content index even if it's out of date.

Sample .HTX File

HTML Extension Files (.HTX files) control the formatted data output resulting from an index server query.

The <%begindetail%> and <%enddetail%> tags surround a section of the HTML extension file in which the results of the search will be merged. The section will be interpreted once for each record that matches the query on the page. Within the section, the column names delimited with <% and %> are used to mark the position of the returned data from the query. There can be only one detail section in the HTML extension file.

For example, the following HTML file fragment shows how query results might be displayed:

```
...
<dl>
<%begindetail%><p>
<dt>
<%CiCurrentRecordNumber%>.
<b><a href="<%vpath%>"><%filename%></a></b>
<dd>
<b><i>Document Abstract: </i></b><%characterization%><br>
<font size=-1> - size <%size%> bytes - <%write%> GMT</font>
<%enddetail%>
</dl>
...
```

This query does the following:

- Shows the name of the file where the search string comes from

- Gives a brief abstract of the file

- Shows the size of the file in bytes

- Shows when the file was last modified

NOTE If there are no records returned from the query, the <%begindetail%> section will be skipped.

Active Server Pages

Active Server Pages (.ASP files), allow you to utilize the power and flexibility of ActiveX scripting. Queries created with .ASP files allow you to leverage scripting languages, such as Microsoft Visual Basic Scripting Edition (VBScript) and Microsoft JScript, to add flexibility in displaying query results.

ASP can also be used to conduct queries. To use this capability, you need to first create the header and then the form.

Setting Up the Header

You begin by setting up header information, as you did when creating the .HTX form in the previous example. The <SCRIPT LANGUAGE> and </SCRIPT> tags turn scripting on and off. This example is turning on a Visual Basic Scripting command, option explicit.

```
<HTML>
<HEAD>
    <SCRIPT LANGUAGE="VBScript" RUNAT="Server">
    <!--
        option explicit
      -->
    </SCRIPT>
    <TITLE>Index Server Search Form</TITLE>
    <META NAME="DESCRIPTION" CONTENT="Example ASP Index
    ➥Server Query">
    <META NAME="KEYWORDS"   CONTENT="query, content, hit, asp">
    <META NAME="MS.LOCALE" CONTENT="EN-US">
    <META HTTP-EQUIV="Content-Type" CONTENT="text/html;
                charset=Windows-1252">
<%
NewQuery = FALSE
UseSavedQuery = FALSE
QueryForm = Request.ServerVariables( "PATH_INFO" )
SearchString = ""
if Request.ServerVariables("REQUEST_METHOD") = "POST" then
    SearchString = Request.Form("SearchString")
```

```
        pg = Request.Form("pg")
        if pg <> "" then
            NextPageNumber = pg
            NewQuery = FALSE
            UseSavedQuery = TRUE
        else
            NewQuery = SearchString <> ""
        end if
    end if
%>
</HEAD>
```

The Meta Tags in the above example are identified in Table 4.5.

T A B L E 4.5	Meta Tag	Description
Server Query ASP Meta Tag Descriptions	Description	Sets the abstract that a client sees in the query results
	Keywords	Lists keywords a client can search for in a query
	MS.Locale	Sets the language code for this form. EN–US stands for American English
	Content Type	Determines the character set (charset) used. In this example, the Roman alphabet as opposed to Kanji.

The next section turns form variables into server-side VBScript variables. The actual query form appears later in the file. Positioning the form data here allows the form fields to be pre-initialized, which causes the text of your query to reappear in the form field after the query results are displayed.

Setting Up the Form

Next, you need to create the HTML search form. The following HTML code fragment demonstrates the necessary sections to include.

```
<TABLE>
    <TR>
        <TD><H1>Index Server ASP Example</H1></TD>
    </TR>
```

```
</TABLE>
<HR WIDTH=75% ALIGN=center SIZE=3>
<p>
<TABLE>
  <TR>
    <TD ALIGN=LEFT>Enter your query below:</TD>
  </TR>
  <TR>
    <TD>
      <FORM ACTION="<%= QueryForm%>" METHOD=POST>
        <TABLE>
          <TR>
            <TD><INPUT TYPE="TEXT" NAME="SearchString"
SIZE="60" MAXLENGTH="100" VALUE="<%=SearchString%>"></TD>
            <TD><INPUT TYPE="SUBMIT" NAME="Action"
            ➥VALUE="New Query"></TD>
          </TR>
        </TABLE>

      </FORM>
    </TD>
  </TR>
</TABLE>
```

As with the .HTX form, the two most important lines are the FORM ACTION and the INPUT TYPE lines.

```
<FORM ACTION ...>
```

Instead of naming an .IDQ file, this line names the current file, where the .IDQ processing code is located.

```
<INPUT TYPE="TEXT" ...>
```

Notice the different syntax in the .ASP file. Here the variable SearchString, rather than CiRestriction, is preset to accept whatever text is typed in the "Enter your query below" field. For example, if you type **cache** in this field, SearchString will hold the text "cache".

```
<INPUT TYPE="SUBMIT" ...>
```

This line creates the button that executes your query. In this example, the button is called New Query.

Little Known Facts

The query and format files (`.IDQ` and `.HTX`) must both be located in directories that have Execute permissions assigned. Furthermore, you can't store `.IDQ` files on a virtual server if that server is mapped to a remote UNC share.

Wrapping It Up

With the push to more powerful tools to harness databases for use on the Internet, ODBC still provides the best connectivity method for storing, manipulating and retrieving records from most sources. While the strength of Active Server Pages and ActiveX Data Objects has now outdistanced IDC/IDQ/HTX files, these methods are still in widespread use today and are handled in IIS 4.0. While most of the coding examples are past the level of knowledge for the exam, they provide good background data for understanding Index Server concepts.

Now it's time to check your knowledge on database connections!

ODBC Connections

1.   Microsoft Access can easily write _____ applica-
tions for you from simple access queries, reports, and forms by using its HTML export
capabilities.

2.   The "database drivers" pass information from your Web application to a(n)
_____-compliant database.

3.   The "database drivers" require a _____ _____ Name to
locate and identify the _____-compliant database
your Web page wants to access.

4.   The File DSN stores information in a _____ format.

5.   The two methods of connecting to a remote SQL server database are _____
Sockets and _____ _____.

6.   Using _____ _____ , the remote application connects
directly to the database server.

7.   True or False. You can forward Windows NT Challenge/Response credentials from the IIS
Web server to the remote computer.

8.   To improve Web application performance, you should use _____
_____ rather than _____ _____ to connect
to a remote database.

STUDY QUESTIONS

Index Server

9. The interface between IIS and the Index Server is accomplished by creating an interface with an Internet _____ _____ file and a(n) _____ extension file.

10. The _____ _____ files control the format of the data output resulting from an Index Server query.

11. True or False. If there are no records returned from the query, the <%begindetail%> section of your HTML file will be skipped.

12. In a(n) _____ query, you need to first create the header and then the form.

13. The <_____> and </SCRIPT> tags turn scripting on and off.

14. With the .HTX form, the two most important lines in your HTML file are the _____ _____ and the _____ _____ lines.

15. The .IDQ and .HTX files must be stored in a directory that has the _____ permission assigned.

16. IIS 4.0 supports _____ index catalogs per site.

17. To properly execute indexing, disk space needs to exceed corpus size by at least _____ percent.

18. True or False. Multiple connections can be made to ODBC databases through the ODBC Control Panel.

19. True or False. An ODBC connection can be made to existing mainframe systems, such as the IBM AS/400.

```
SAMPLE TEST
```

4-1   When connecting IIS to an external data source via ODBC, which type of ODBC DSN must be used?

    A. System

    B. User

    C. File

    D. None is required

4-2   The default ODBC drivers that come with IIS are (choose all that apply):

    A. Access

    B. FoxPro

    C. SQL Server

    D. Oracle

4-3   How do you force Index Server to execute a Master Merge more frequently?

    A. Manually start a Master Merge

    B. Send a Master Merge Query from the Index Server Manager

    C. Set the MasterMergeTime Registry key to a smaller value

    D. Set the MaxIndexes Registry key to a smaller value

4-4   What are the three types of Data Source Names available when establishing an ODBC connection? (Choose all that apply.)

    A. User

    B. File

    C. Server

    D. System

4-5 You want to prevent users from querying certain words via the Index Server. You should:

    A. Add the word to the dirty word list stored in the system registry

    B. Edit `%SYSTEMROOT%\system32\noise.ENU` to add the word to the noise list

    C. Create a file called `NOISE.WORDS` in the virtual root for the directory, and add the words to that file

    D. You cannot disable searching for words using Index Server

4-6 What are the main component sections of an `.IDQ` file?

    A. Name

    B. File

    C. Query

    D. Form

4-7 What is the total disk space required for a 150MB corpus that is to be indexed?

    A. 150MB

    B. 210MB

    C. 300MB

    D. 450MB

4-8 Query results formats are based on files with which of the following extensions?

    A. `.HTM`

    B. `.IDC`

    C. `.IDQ`

    D. `.HTX`

4-9 Which of the following indexes are persistent (choose all that apply):

    A. Noise Word lists

    B. Shadow

    C. Query

    D. Master

4-10 A Master Merge will start under which of the following conditions (choose all that apply):

    A. When executing a Master Query

    B. Assigned time in Registry (minutes after midnight)

    C. Total number of changed documents since last Master Merge exceeds a determined value

    D. When IIS is stopped and restarted

4-11 Users trying to connect to an ODBC database through a Web application report that they are getting an error message that includes things like `"MS OLE ERROR 48 0005: ODBC Driver"` and `"Login Failure"`. What is the most likely cause of this occurrence?

    A. The users have insufficient permissions to access the database.

    B. The users have insufficient permissions to access the resources in the database.

    C. Recent revisions of the database changed the connection method from Named Pipes to TCP/IP.

    D. The database was recently moved to another database server.

4-12   Users trying to connect to an ODBC database through a Web application report that they are getting an error message that includes things like `"MS OLE ERROR 48 0005: ODBC Driver"` and `"General Network Error"`. What is the most likely cause of this occurrence?

  A. The users have insufficient permissions to access the database.

  B. The users have insufficient permissions to access the resources in the database.

  C. Recent revisions of the database changed the connection method from Named Pipes to TCP/IP.

  D. The database was recently moved to another database server.

4-13   Users trying to connect to an ODBC database through a Web application report that they are getting an error message that includes things like `"MS OLE ERROR 48 0005: ODBC Driver"` and `"Cannot find Name Space"`. What is the most likely cause of this occurrence?

  A. The users have insufficient permissions to access the database.

  B. The users have insufficient permissions to access the resources in the database.

  C. Recent revisions of the database changed the connection method from Named Pipes to TCP/IP.

  D. The database was recently moved to another database server.

UNIT

5

Running Applications

Test Objectives: Running Applications

- Configure IIS to support server-side scripting.

- Configure IIS to run ISAPI applications.

NOTE Exam objectives are subject to change at any time without prior notice and at Microsoft's sole discretion. Please visit Microsoft's Training & Certification Web site (www.microsoft.com/Train_Cert) for the most current exam objectives listing.

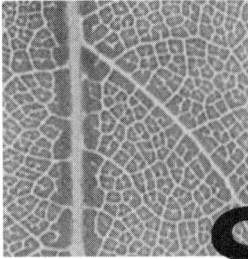

Several years ago, Web pages that displayed text and graphics in a static format were considered acceptable. The fact that a company, let alone an individual, had a Web site that consisted of a static page or pages put them at the cutting edge of the technology curve. Just a few short years later, static pages are passé. Users want Web pages that are dynamic and can be modified to their individual requests and needs. IIS supports dynamic Web page creation in several forms, but the most commonly utilized are server-side scripting and ISAPI application execution. Using IIS to support these Web technologies is an increasingly critical aspect of NT Server.

Using server-side scripting has allowed the Webmaster to improve site dynamics while at the same time ensuring that:

- Proprietary executables or controls that may not be supported by all Web browsers are not required. Despite Internet Explorer's market share, there are lots of other browsers out there.

- Program scripts never have to be revealed to the end user.

- Browsers are not required to perform all the scripting execution, instead sharing the processing burden with the server.

Server-Side Scripting

Server-side scripting is as simple in concept as it sounds. IIS, as the Web server, creates the dynamic Web page based on the generated, or scripted, response to a request from the browser or a server-side include.

IIS has the capacity to support scripts of several types, allowing the site designer to mix and match scripting languages in order to optimize content creation and delivery. IIS supports all of the most common scripting mechanisms today.

This section will cover how IIS handles:

- Active Server Pages (ASP)
- Common Gateway Interfaces (CGIs)

Active Server Pages

Internet Information Server (IIS) contains a feature, called Active Server Pages (ASP), that allows server-side scripting. ASP is Microsoft's multi-language environment that allows various scripting languages (currently JScript and VBScript) and ActiveX controls to be used in parallel to expand dynamic HTML. Whereas Java, JavaScript, VBScript, and the ActiveX controls on HTML pages used to be interpreted and rendered only by the client-side browser, Active Server Pages scripting is processed by an engine on the Web server, creating an HTML page that is sent to the browser.

An ASP script begins to run when a browser requests an .ASP file from your Web server. Your Web server then calls the ASP.DLL, which reads through the requested file entirely, executes any script commands, and sends a Web page to the browser.

Because scripts are run on the server rather than on the client, IIS does all the work involved in generating the HTML pages that are sent to client browsers. IIS transmits standard HTML to the browser, so compatibility issues are minimized. Server-side scripts cannot be readily copied because only the result of the script is returned to the browser. Additionally, users cannot view the script commands that created the page they are viewing.

You can use Active Server Pages to write server pages (.ASP files) that can be referred to as URLs from any Internet browser. These pages are composed of text, HTML tags, and scripting language commands. The script commands consist of Visual Basic code embedded within the <% and %> tags.

In IIS 4.0, ASP has been enhanced with new features, including the following major improvements:

- Microsoft Script Debugger, to improve .ASP file debugging
- Transactional scripting, to reduce data failure and corruption from uncompleted events
- Support for Internet Explorer Channels and Webcasting
- HTTP 1.1 protocol support

Processing Server Script

Script in an .ASP file is not event-driven. Instead, when the page is requested, the server reads the page and processes all server script from top to bottom. This also includes script that is inline with HTML text. Because all script in the .ASP file is processed as soon as the page is requested, both syntax errors and runtime errors are caught immediately.

Creating ASP Pages

An Active Server Pages (ASP) file is a text file with the extension .ASP that contains any combination of the following:

- Text
- HTML tags
- ASP script commands

It's easy to create an .ASP file. For any HTML file to which you want to add scripts, rename the file by replacing the existing .HTM or .HTML file name extension with .ASP. To make the .ASP file available to Web users, save the new file in a directory on your Web site (be sure that the directory has Script or Execute permission enabled). When you view the file with your browser, you will see that ASP processes and returns an HTML page. You can now add script commands to the .ASP file.

> **NOTE** By default, the primary scripting language is VBScript. You can change to a different scripting language, such as JScript, if required.

Active Server Support

IIS 4.0 requires little or no setup to support Active Server Pages. The ASP.DLL, which is called by the .ASP file suffix in the URL, parses the scripting language text from the rest of the HTML page. The ASP.DLL then delivers the HTML tags to the browser. Several items must be kept in mind when setting up ASP pages:

- The ASP.DLL is loaded with IIS, and the .ASP extension is registered in the metabase.

- ASP applications can be run in the same memory space as IIS or placed in a separate memory space. This improves the server stability in the event of an ASP crash.

With an ever-lengthening list of features, Active Server Pages are becoming one of the most frequently used methods for developing dynamic HTML output. Nevertheless, the majority of pages are still developed using CGIs, the topic of the next section.

Common Gateway Interface (CGI)

The first and oldest method of building dynamic Web pages was implemented by the use of Common Gateway Interfaces or CGIs. These scripts and programs, which evolved from UNIX Web servers, are often written in a common interpreted language, usually Perl, but also in other compiled languages, such as C. IIS supports CGI applications, making the migration from other Web servers easier.

The CGI applications and scripts are basically written the same for any Web server, regardless of the operating system involved. The process follows the same basic steps:

1. The Web server recognizes the `.CGI` extension in the URL as one registered in the metabase.

2. IIS recovers the path and filename to the associated executable.

3. IIS then builds the program memory space and establishes system-level settings and variables to support the application. Some of these variables include:

   - Remote IP Address

   - Server Port

   - Server Protocol

4. IIS then starts the associated executable. This application is run in a separate memory space as a stand-alone application. Command-line parameters for the executable are also sent if required.

5. The executable runs in the memory space, generates the associated HTML output, passes it to IIS for further processing, and then completes execution. Once completed, it passes program control back to the IIS.

CGI Support

Like Active Server Pages, IIS needs very little configuration to run CGI associated scripts and applications. In essence, CGI (called WIN-CGI to differentiate it from the UNIX and Mac OS variations) is ready to be supported right out of the box. Configuring the scripting languages and executables are the only remaining requirements:

- No default CGI scripting language is supplied with NT Server or IIS. In order to support Perl, for example, a Perl interpreter must be installed.

- The ScriptMap Registry key and the metabase must reflect the registration of the scripting language application.

- The first command line passed in the CGI script must be the translated path identifying the NT filing system location of the CGI executable. The second command line is the executable parameters or switches.

CGI applications have one major drawback when implemented in IIS. They consume a larger amount of system resources and process more inefficiently as the number of sessions increases. As each new client request starts another process, NT creates a separate memory space and set of system resources. Given that NT is optimized for multithreaded applications, this can result in a large number of separate threads occurring, which precludes NT from effectively managing them, and therefore, system resources can quickly be used up and even exhausted.

CGI Configuration

Like Active Server Pages support, CGIs are fairly straightforward in implementation. To configure IIS for CGI program support, follow these guidelines:

- Create a directory for your CGI programs or use the existing `CGI-BIN` directory.

- Keep executable files in a separate directory from content files.

- Install a script interpreter to support script execution, if required.

- The executable files must always be in a directory that has Execute permissions enabled. Do not enable Read access for this directory unless absolutely essential (see Figure 5.1).

- Directories containing scripts must have either the Execute or Script permission enabled.

- Mark the Script Interpreter files as Script Engines so that they will execute correctly.

- Create the Application Mapping between the script file extension and the script interpreter.

- Set appropriate NTFS permissions for the directories that contain the Interpreter and those that will be accessed by the CGI.

- Ensure that the CGI programs will access only directories that are safe for them to read and write to.

FIGURE 5.1

Directory tab of the CGI-BIN Properties dialog box

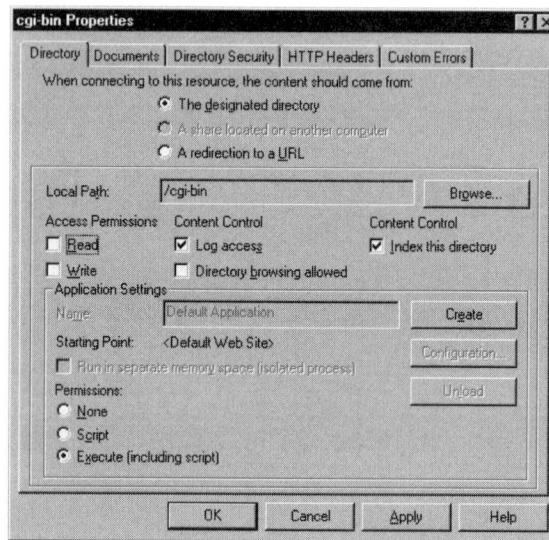

ISAPI Applications

Internet Server Application Programming Interface (ISAPI) provides a set of interfaces that you can use to create extensions and filters for IIS. Microsoft developed the ISAPI model as an alternative to CGI. The ISAPI model provides a number of advantages over the CGI model, including low overhead, fast loading, and better scaleability.

Known collectively as ISAPI programs, filters and extensions are written to take advantage of the ISAPI interface that was developed, a more robust and integrated interface specification than those available to CGI applications. Using ISAPI, you can add to the functionality of IIS and create Web-based applications that have as much functionality as any desktop application. ISAPI applications can run as much as 20 times faster than an equivalent CGI executable.

ISAPI programs are divided into two types:

- *ISAPI extensions* are loaded on demand to provide extended functionality to a Web application. The samples provided here range from the basic extension outline to a complex ISAPI program that deals with threads and keep-alives.

- *ISAPI filters* are loaded with the server, and you can use them to customize and enhance the services provided by the server.

ISAPI Extensions

ISAPI extensions are in the form of a dynamic link library and can either coexist in the same space as IIS or in a separate one. Unlike a CGI executable, an ISAPI DLL runs only once, regardless of the number of client requests. While this is more efficient than CGIs in terms of thread management, it also highlights the ISAPI vulnerability.

Since ISAPI DLLs execute only once, an execution failure will disrupt all sessions that are actively invoking it. Furthermore, if the ISAPI DLL is running inside the IIS program space, the failure may cause the server itself to become unstable and crash.

IIS 4.0 allows ISAPI extensions to be selectively run in or out of process. DLLs that are undergoing testing or require their own memory space to run or execute can be stopped and started independently, and can even automatically restart following a crash. This also helps retain the NT Security integrity, since access to the DLL space won't necessarily allow access to the IIS space.

ISAPI Filters

ISAPI filters are programs that are linked to IIS and respond when the Web server receives an HTTP request. They are driven by Web server events rather than by client requests as ISAPI extensions are. Filters can be used to add additional features to IIS. Triggered by being associated to a server event, the filter is then notified every time its associated event occurs. For example, a filter could be notified when a read event occurs and then could conduct a formatting of the raw data to be returned to the client.

ISAPI filters can be best considered as value-added processors for IIS. They are usually loaded when the IIS service starts, and they then intercept the server events. The filter can then decide to act on the event, pass it to another filter, or pass control directly to the server.

In this section, you will learn about:

- ISAPI filter types

- Adding ISAPI filters

- Caching ISAPI extensions

- Configuring ISAPI filter's properties

ISAPI Filter Types

Filters can be set for every Web site on an IIS server (global filters), and specific filters can also be set for individual sites. If both global filters and site filters are installed, the two filter lists are merged for the site.

Unlike ISAPI applications, ISAPI filters are always run in the server process, so they share memory space with it. Inefficient filters then drag down the entire Web site. Worse yet, filters that crash can easily take down the entire server.

Adding ISAPI Filters

To add an ISAPI filter to a Web server or Web site, you would take the following steps to configure the filter through the ISAPI Filters tab of the WWW Properties dialog box (see Figure 5.2):

1. Start Internet Service Manager

2. Select the Web server or Web site where the filter is to be installed.

3. Right-click on the site and select Properties.

4. Click the ISAPI Filters tab.

5. Click the Add button.

6. Enter the name of the filter in the Filter Name box.

7. Enter the DLL file in the Executable box.

8. Click OK.

9. Change the load order of the filter using the up and down arrow keys, if required.

FIGURE 5.2

ISAPI Filters tab of the
WWW Properties
dialog box

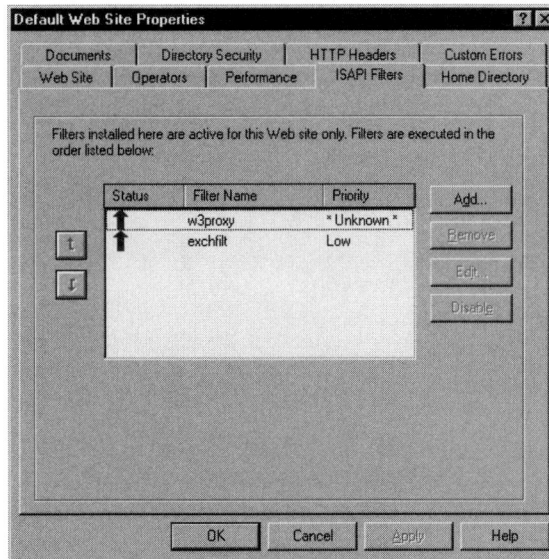

> **WARNING**
>
> If you are adding filters to a Web site, you will not see any global filters inherited from the Web server's master properties. You will see only the filters installed for the Web site, even though both sets of filters are run.

If you have added or changed a global filter, you must stop and restart the Web server to load the new global filters into memory. A filter added at the Web Site level is automatically loaded when you add it.

> **NOTE**
>
> If an HTTP request triggers an event for which the filter is registered, the filter will receive the data contained in the request regardless of whether the request is for a file, a CGI application, or an ISAPI application.

Caching ISAPI Extensions

ISAPI DLLs can be loaded and cached in memory so that future requests can be processed without having to call them again. If they are not cached, the DLLs are unloaded after execution. While caching reduces the time a process waits for a DLL to load, it does consume memory resources. However, the resource cost is always worth the performance gain. Most ISAPI applications (including Active Server Pages) benefit from caching. You should clear this option only in special circumstances, such as ISAPI application development.

To enable caching from the ISAPI Application directory configuration (see Figure 5.3):

1. In Internet Service Manager, select the Web site or the starting-point directory of an application.

2. Open the directory's property sheets, and then click the Home Directory, Virtual Directory, or Directory tab.

3. Click the Configuration button.

4. Click the App Mappings tab, and then select the Cache ISAPI applications check box.

FIGURE 5.3

Cache ISAPI Applications check box in the App Mappings tab of the Application Configuration dialog box

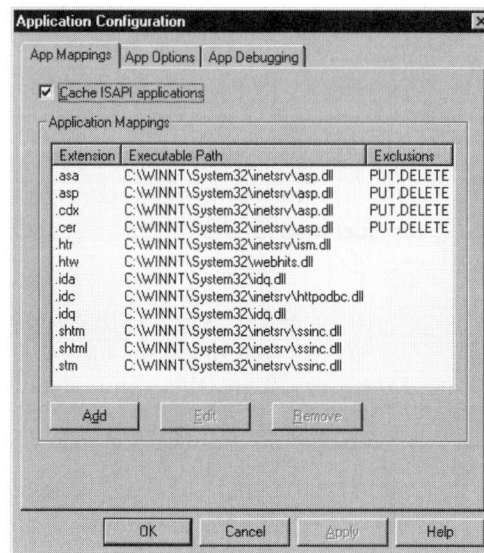

Configuring ISAPI Filter's Properties

As previously shown in Figure 5.2, you can use the property sheet to set options for ISAPI filters.

Through the ISAPI Filters property sheet, you can configure the following:

- Status of each filter (loaded, unloaded, or disabled)

- Name of the filter

- Priority rating of the filter (high, medium, or low) set inside the DLL

By clicking the Add, Remove, and Edit buttons in the windows, you can modify filter mappings. Likewise, clicking the Enable or Disable buttons modifies the status of filters. The loading order of the filters can be set by selecting a filter and clicking the arrows to change the position it occupies in the list. Filters are loaded in the order listed, from top to bottom.

The filter details box (refer back to Figure 5.2) is used to list:

- Status of the selected filter

- Filter name

- Priority rating of the filter

All Web sites on a server inherit the global filters configured in the Web service's master properties. When filters are added to an individual site, the filter lists are merged, but only the individual site filters will be listed. The filters set by the master properties do not appear on this tab.

When several filters are registered for the same browser event, they are called sequentially by filter priority. If several filters have the same priority, the following selection criteria are applied:

- Global filters are run before site filters.

- Filters with the same priority at the same inheritance level are run according to the order in which they were loaded.

Configuring IIS for ISAPI

Installing an ISAPI DLL for a Web site is fairly simple. Unlike previous versions of IIS, Registry Entries are no longer required. The following steps install the DLL:

1. In Internet Service Manager, select the Web site or the starting-point directory of an application.

2. Open the directory's property sheets, and then click the Home Directory, Virtual Directory, or Directory tab.

3. Click the Configuration button.

4. Click the App Mappings tab (refer back to Figure 5.3).

5. Add the extension and file pathname.

6. Click OK.

With that completed, the DLL is now registered with the site.

That covers the IIS application support topic. Start the review questions to see what you learned.

Server-Side Scripting

1.   True or False. Server-side scripting is a more efficient way of developing static HTML documents than just straight static coding.

2.   IIS server-side scripting primarily utilizes _____ and _____.

3.   The ASP script begins running when a(n) _____ requests a(n) _____ file from your Web server.

4.   The Web server does all the _____-_____ processing, transmitting standard _____ to the browser.

5.   Proprietary code from _____ _____ scripts cannot be readily copied because only the result of the code is returned to the browser.

6.   Users cannot view the script _____ that created the page they are viewing.

7.   Active Server Pages allows _____-_____ scripting, whereas VBScript and ActiveX render _____-_____ browsing.

8.   Script in an .ASP file is not _____-driven.

9. Because all script in the .ASP file is processed as soon as the page is requested, both

_____ errors and _____

errors are caught immediately.

10. It's easy to create an .ASP file. For any _____ file to

which you want to add scripts, rename the file by replacing the existing

_____ or _____

file name extension with .ASP.

11. Unlike HTML tags, which simply format text or read in a graphic, video, or sound file, a script

command instructs the Web server to perform a(n) _____.

12. Script commands are differentiated from text by the _____

symbols.

13. Commands enclosed by _____ are called primary

script commands.

14. The primary scripting language for IIS is _____.

15. True or False. VBScript, JScript, and JavaBeans are the scripting languages available to ASP

by default.

16. True or False. Active Server Pages can be scripted in any language that has an ActiveX Script-

ing Engine available.

17. The major CGI scripting language used today is _____ .

18. CGI executables are usually stored in the Web site _____ directory.

19. Repeated instances of CGI executables will run in _____ memory spaces.

20. True or False. IIS does not have any CGI interpreters pre-installed for running CGI scripts.

21. CGI interpreters require the _____ or _____ permission to be assigned to directories that they are installed in.

ISAPI Applications

22. The ISAPI model provides a number of advantages over the CGI model, including low overhead, fast loading, and better _____ .

23. ISAPI programs are divided into two types: ISAPI _____ and ISAPI _____ .

24. You can install filters for all sites on a server (global filters), and you can install filters for individual Web sites. If you install both global filters and site filters, the two filter lists are _____ for the site.

25. Unlike ISAPI applications, ISAPI filters are always run in the _____ process.

26. ISAPI DLLs can be loaded and _____ so that further requests can be processed without calling them again.

27. All Web sites on a server inherit the filters configured in the _____ properties for the Web service. When several filters have registered for the same event, they are executed in a(n) _____ order.

28. If several filters have the same priority, global filters set in the _____ properties are run before filters set at the _____ level.

29. True or False. The ISAPI DLL recognizes only the .ASP suffix as an Active Server page.

30. ISAPI filters extend the basic functionality of the _____ service in IIS.

5-1 Which of the following server-side scripting technologies does IIS support? (Choose all that apply.)

    A. JScript

    B. VBScript

    C. JavaBeans

    D. Perl

5-2 Internet users report that they are unable to access certain features of your Web site that you have created through CGI scripts. Intranet users seem to have full functionality. The IIS server is using NTFS security. What is the most likely cause of this problem?

    A. The Execute permission on the CGI script directory is not selected.

    B. The IUSR_*computername* account does not have access to the CGI directories.

    C. The Internet users aren't using the proper version of Internet Explorer.

    D. The CGI directories can't be located in an NTFS directory for anonymous users.

5-3 You have developed an ISAPI DLL that needs to be beta tested on an IIS 4.0 Web server in a production environment. How can you implement the DLL to minimize risk to the IIS service and the entire server?

    A. Set up a separate IIS server and run the DLL in a stand-alone Web site.

    B. Run multiple copies of IIS.

    C. Check the Run in Separate Memory Space option in the Home Directory tab of the Web site.

    D. There is no way to isolate the DLL into a separate memory space from IIS. Only ISAPI filters can be run in a separate space.

SAMPLE TEST

5-4 After migrating your Intranet server from a UNIX-based system to IIS on an NT Server, you discover that none of your Perl scripts execute properly. What is the probable cause for this failure?

    A. All of the Perl scripts must be renamed to have the .PL extension.

    B. IIS will only support JScript and VBScript programs.

    C. A Perl interpreter must be installed and the .PL extension must be registered.

    D. The Perl script directory does not have the appropriate permissions set to allow the scripts to run.

5-5 You are planning your company's Web site, which will be run from existing NT Servers. Most of your programmers have experience in CGI and Perl, but only a few have Active Server Pages or ActiveX experience. What is the best reason to persuade management to adopt Active Server Pages over CGI?

    A. Active Server Pages has more scripting functions available than CGI.

    B. Active Server Pages scripts run as much as an order of magnitude faster than CGI scripts.

    C. Active Server Pages script interpreters are included with IIS, while CGI interpreters are not.

    D. CGI executables run each instance in their own memory space while Active Server Pages runs only one instance in a single space to allow for true multithreading.

5-6 You have written an ISAPI DLL that you want to install in your Web site. How do you set up IIS to accomplish this?

    A. In the Home Directory tab of the Web site, select Configuration and add the extension and file path name in the App Mappings tab.

B. Use the Registry Editor to add an extension and a path to the ScriptMap key.

C. In the ISAPI Filters tab of the Web site, select Configuration and add the extension and file pathname in the App Mappings tab.

D. Use the Registry Editor to add an extension and a path to the ISAPI Map key.

5-7   Which ISAPI elements may run in either the IIS memory space or in a separate one?

A. ISAPI filters only

B. ISAPI extensions only

C. ISAPI filters and extensions

D. Neither ISAPI filters or extensions

5-8   How would you install an ISAPI DLL so that it runs in a separate memory space?

A. Rebuild the ISAPI DLL as a CGI script.

B. Start IIS from the DOC command line using the `/sep` switch.

C. Select the Run in a Separate Memory Space option in the Home Directory tab.

D. Start another instance of IIS.

5-9   ISAPI filters are used to extend the basic WWW service. Filters can be used to:

A. Preprocess or postprocess HTTP requests

B. Elaborate access control mechanisms above the NT Security model

C. Encrypt or compress data

D. Support HTTP commands not yet supported by IIS

UNIT

6

Monitoring and Optimization

Test Objectives: Monitoring and Optimization

- **Maintain a log for fine-tuning and auditing purposes. Tasks include:**
  - Importing log files into a Usage Import and Report Writer database
  - Configuring the logging features of the WWW service
  - Configuring the logging features of the FTP service
  - Configuring Usage Import and Report Writer to analyze logs created by the WWW service or the FTP service
  - Automating the use of Usage Import and Report Writer

- **Monitor performance of various functions by using Performance Monitor. Functions include HTTP and FTP sessions.**

- **Analyze performance. Performance issues include:**
  - Identifying bottlenecks
  - Identifying network-related performance issues
  - Identifying disk-related performance issues
  - Identifying CPU-related performance issues

- **Optimize performance of IIS.**

- **Optimize performance of Index Server.**

- **Optimize performance of Microsoft SMTP Service.**

- **Optimize performance of Microsoft NNTP Service.**

- **Interpret performance data.**

- **Optimize a Web site by using Content Analyzer.**

NOTE Exam objectives are subject to change at any time without prior notice and at Microsoft's sole discretion. Please visit Microsoft's Training & Certification Web site (www.microsoft.com/Train_Cert) for the most current exam objectives listing.

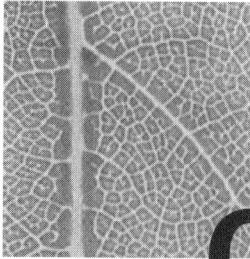

Once a Web site is up and running on IIS, the Webmaster's and network technician's jobs are just beginning. In addition to the myriad of changes in content that will be made over the course of time, IIS must be monitored and tuned to ensure that all requests are filled and delivered as quickly as possible. While IIS is inherently a self-tuning service, several utilities and methodologies exist to ensure that maximum performance is achieved and maintained.

Maintaining Log Files

One of the basic, tried and true methods for tracking performance and analyzing trends is by logging key data points and variables. Most NT-based services have multiple logging formats to facilitate this type of data capture, and IIS is no exception. However, unlike previous versions of IIS, 4.0 uses a new application to assist in the analysis of site usage logs: Site Server Express. A subset of the full production BackOffice version of Site Server, Site Server Express is a multipurpose application that allows usage analysis as well as content publication and management.

In this section, you will learn to configure the logging properties of WWW and FTP. You will also learn how to import the log files to Usage Import and Report Writer and to analyze the data that is extracted from the log files.

Configuring Logging Features of WWW and FTP

Within your Web Site or FTP Site property tab (the Web Site tab is shown in Figure 6.1), you can specify whether or not logging will be enabled or disabled, the log format you will choose, and the properties of the log file.

FIGURE 6.1

Web Site tab of the
WWW Properties
dialog box

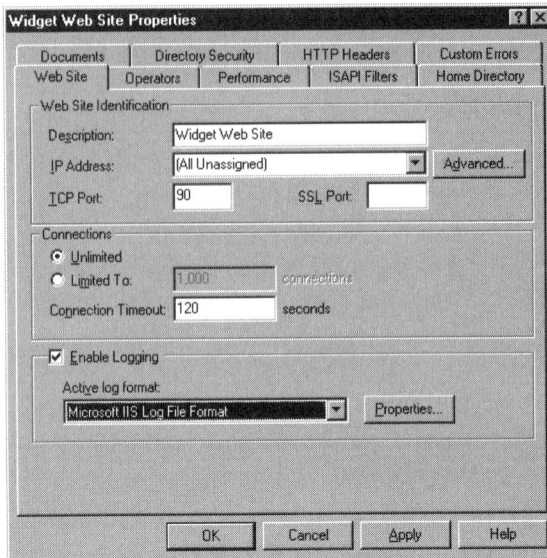

Log Formats

If you enable logging, you can choose from the following log formats:

- Microsoft IIS Log Format

- NCSA Common Log File Format

- W3C Extended Log File Format

- ODBC Logging

These formats are covered in the following subsections.

Microsoft IIS Log Format

If you choose to log with Microsoft IIS Log Format, the log is created using a predefined ASCII format. Each item is separated by commas, which makes this format easy to port into spreadsheets or databases. The information included within this log type includes:

- User's IP address

- User name

- Date and time the request is made (time is local)

- HTTP or FTP status code

- Number of bytes received

- Number of bytes sent

- Elapsed time connected

- Action carried out

- Source or target file that was uploaded or downloaded

NCSA Common Log File Format

The NCSA (National Center for Supercomputing Applications) Log follows the standard defined by NCSA. This log format also uses ASCII and is not customizable. Items within this log are separated by spaces. The following information is recorded in the NCSA log file:

- Remote host name

- User name

- Date (local)

- Time (local)

- Request type

- HTTP status code

- Bytes received by the server

NCSA logging can be defined for WWW sites, but not FTP sites.

W3C Extended Log File Format

The W3C Extended Log File Format also produces an ASCII file. The main difference between this format and the others that have been defined is that this format is customizable. This means that you decide what you want to log and what you don't want to log. W3C extended logging uses spaces to separate log fields, and time is recorded as GMT (Greenwich Mean Time) as opposed to local time.

When you select W3C Extended Log File Format and click Properties, you will see a tab called Extended Properties as shown in Figure 6.2. The options that can be logged are defined in Table 6.1.

FIGURE 6.2

W3C Extended
Logging Properties
dialog box

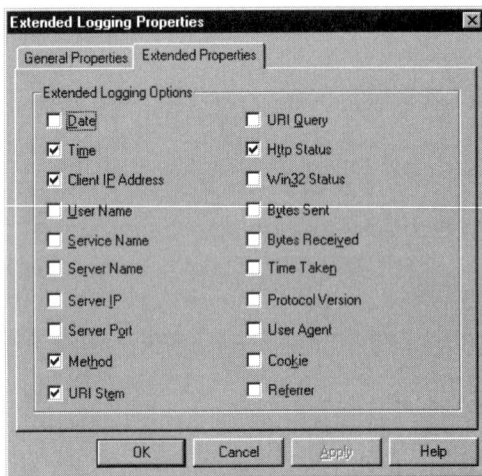

TABLE 6.1: W3C Extended Logging Properties Defined

Extended Logging Option	Description	Enabled or Disabled by Default
Date	The date at which the activity was initiated.	Disabled
Time	The time at which the activity was initiated.	Enabled
Client IP Address	The IP address of the computer that is accessing your site.	Enabled
User Name	The name of the user accessing your site. With anonymous access this will most likely be IUSR_*computername*.	Disabled
Service Name	The Internet service the client is using.	Disabled
Server Name	The name of the server that is hosting the log file.	Disabled

T A B L E 6.1: W3C Extended Logging Properties Defined *(continued)*

Extended Logging Option	Description	Enabled or Disabled by Default
Server IP	The IP address of the server that is hosting the log file.	Disabled
Server Port	The port number on the server that the client is connecting to.	Disabled
Method	The action that the client is using to access your site, for example, using the GET command.	Enabled
URI Stem	The type of resource that is being accessed. This could be a CGI script, an HTML page, or an ISAPI application.	Enabled
URI Query	Query, including search string that client used if attempting a search.	Disabled
Http Status	HTTP status of the action being performed.	Enabled
Win32 Status	NT status of the action being performed.	Disabled
Bytes Sent	Number of bytes the server has sent.	Disabled
Bytes Received	Number of bytes the server has received.	Disabled
Time Taken	How long the action being performed took.	Disabled
Protocol Version	HTTP or FTP version of the client software.	Disabled
User Agent	The browser software that the client is using.	Disabled
Cookie	If cookies were used, the content of the cookie sent or received.	Disabled
Referrer	Link (if any) that was used to refer the client to this site.	Disabled

ODBC Logging

ODBC stands for Open DataBase Connectivity. ODBC Logging allows you to log fixed data to an ODBC compliant database, for example, Microsoft SQL Server or Microsoft Access.

In order to log to an ODBC database, you must take the following steps:

1. You must create an ODBC database with the following fields:

   - ClientHost
   - Username
   - LogTime
   - Service
   - Machine
   - ServerIP
   - ProcessingTime
   - BytesRecvd
   - BytesSent
   - ServiceStatus
   - Win32Status
   - Operation
   - Target
   - Parameters

2. On the IIS computer that hosts the WWW or FTP site, configure Control Panel ➤ ODBC to give the database a Data Source Name (DSN).

3. Specify that the WWW or FTP site will use ODBC Logging. This allows you to click Properties, which brings up the dialog box shown in Figure 6.3.

4. From this box you can configure:

   - **ODBC Data Source Name:** DSN for the database you will send log entries to.
   - **Table:** Name of the database table you will log to.
   - **User Name and Password:** This allows you to specify a user name and password that allows you to connect to the database.

FIGURE 6.3

ODBC Logging
Properties dialog box

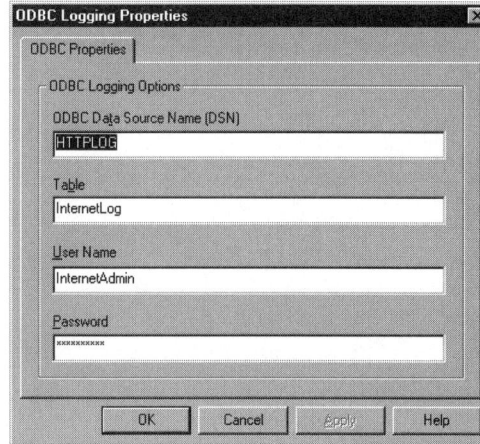

Log Properties

If you select Microsoft IIS Log File Format, NCSA Common Log File Format, or W3C Extended Log File Format, you can configure general properties that define the log period and log file directory.

New Log Time Period

New Log Time Period defines when new log files are created. The options include:

- Start log daily
- Start log weekly
- Start log monthly
- File size can be unlimited
- Start new file when file size reaches threshold you define (in MB)

Log File Directory

Log file directory allows you to define the folder that log files will be stored in. By default this is: %winntroot%\System32\LogFiles.

Usage Import and Report Writer

When the logging features are turned on for an IIS Web or FTP site, the server records information each time a user interacts with the site in a single line of a log file. This data could be extremely cumbersome to read and analyze, so the Windows NT 4.0 Option Pack provides software to help you analyze the data you collect within your log files.

One of the most helpful utilities is Microsoft Usage and Import Writer, which is part of the Microsoft Site Server utility. This information can then be used to evaluate performance, identify trends, and gain usage information for the Web or FTP site.

The Usage Import utility is used to access the data from your log file and configure it into a format that Report Writer will understand.

The Report Writer utility is used to take the data that was extracted through Usage Import and display it in one of 21 predefined reports to allow you to see how Web and FTP sites are being accessed.

Analyzing Logs through Usage Import and Report Writer

Once log files are created, you can import the log files through a utility called Usage Import. After the files are imported, you can view the data through predefined reports in the Report Writer utility. You will learn more about these utilities in the following subsections.

Usage Import

In this section, you will learn how Usage Import is organized through an overview, then see how to import an existing log file through Usage Import.

Overview of Usage Import

Before any log files that contain usage data can be imported into the database, the servers and sites that produce the data must be configured through the Usage Import Server Manager utility that exists within Site Server Express. The Server Manager utility (not to be confused with the NT Server Manager utility) is designed to import log files from the server environment you use into the database, which can then be analyzed through Report Writer.

In order to import data through the Usage Import Server Manager utility, you must configure three levels of the log import. The levels are hierarchical in nature and are as follows:

- **Log data source:** The log data source is the log file format you specified when logging was enabled on your site. For IIS this could be Microsoft IIS Log File Format, NCSA Common Log File Format, W3C Extended Log File Format, or ODBC logging. In addition, Usage Import Server Manager supports other common logging formats. The log data source is required so that the data can be properly extracted, based on the format and fields specified by the log data source.

- **Server:** Every log data source contains data from at least one server. Within almost any Internet-based environment, multiple servers can be logged to one log file. In these cases, there can be multiple servers per log data source, but there are exceptions. For example, a Netscape server produces its own log file, thus there is one log data source per server.

The term *server,* as used here, does not refer to a physical hardware server but to an application program or service that responds to a request from a client browser. A site has one software server for each type of content—HTTP, FTP, or other newer ones—that it publishes.

- **Site:** A site is a collection of content. It can be replicated across several servers, and likewise, different components of a site can be spread across several servers. Every server handles the content from at least one site and every site has content on at least one server.

In the next section, you will learn how to use the Usage Import Server Manager to add sources, servers, and sites.

Configuration of Usage Import

Once log files have been generated, you would take the following steps to extract the data using the Usage Import Utility.

1. Start the Usage Import utility from Start ➤ Programs ➤ Windows NT 4.0 Option Pack ➤ Microsoft Site Server Express 2.0 ➤ Usage Import.

2. The first time you run this utility, you will see a dialog box stating `"There are no Internet Sites configured in this database. Please use Server Manager to configure your Internet sites now. "` Click OK to continue.

3. A dialog box will appear, asking you to select the type of log file you will import. The log type can be IIS Site Server Log File Format, IIS W3C Extended Log File Format, IIS Log File Format, or IIS NCSA Common Log File Format. This selection will be based on the log type you specified for your Web or FTP site logging.

4. The Server Manager (different from the Server Manager in NT) will appear as shown in Figure 6.4. From this dialog box, you will configure:

- Server Type, from IIS this will be FTP or WWW
- Any directory index files that will be included
- IP address if the server is multihomed
- Local time zone and domain name

Once you have configured these options, click OK.

FIGURE 6.4

Usage Import Server Properties dialog box

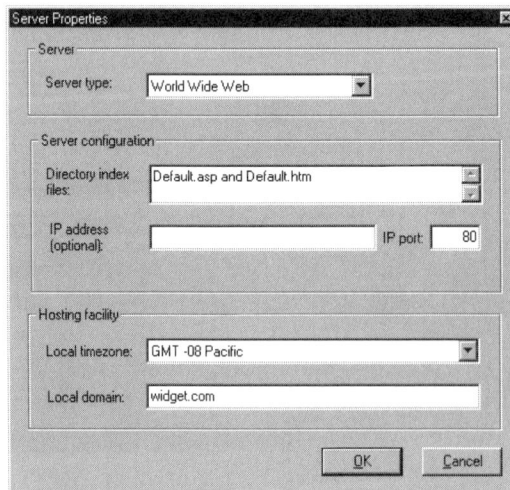

5. The Log Service Manager will then appear so that you can configure the log that will be imported, as shown in Figure 6.5. Within this dialog box, specify the location of the log file you will import.

FIGURE 6.5

Usage Import Log File
Manager dialog box

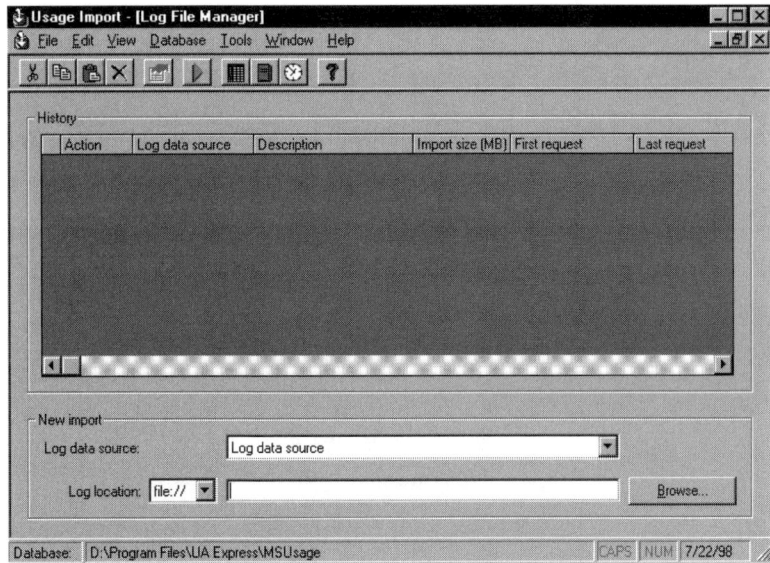

FIGURE 6.5

Usage Import Log File
Manager dialog box

6. From the Usage Import main dialog box, select File ➤ Start Import.
This will complete the Site Server Analysis process.

Once the log file has been imported through Usage Import, you can see
predefined reports through the Report Writer utility.

Report Writer

In this section, you will learn about Report Writer and how to create a predefined report or a customized report.

Overview of Report Writer

Once Usage Import has been configured to import the log data from a log
data source associated with an IIS or other server, the Report Writer application can be used to create reports.

Report Writer can be used with any of the 21 predefined reports, a new
custom report, or a previously created custom report. The 21 supplied
reports are subdivided into two major groups:

- Detail Reports, which provide comprehensive analysis

- Summary Reports, which summarize site activity

Examples of what can be tracked through the reports include:

- Bandwidth usage

- Browser and operating systems used to access your site

- Geographical information about who is accessing your site

- Hit summaries for your site

- Referral information identifying sites used to link to your site

- User visits to your site, including new and repeat visitors

Creating Predefined Reports

To run any of the predefined reports:

1. Start Report Writer from Start ➣ Programs ➣ Windows NT 4.0 Option Pack ➣ Microsoft Site Server Express 2.0 ➣ Report Writer.

2. Select Open One of Your Own Creations and then click the report name that was previously defined through Usage Import. Click OK.

3. Select File ➣ Create Report Document.

4. Designate a report name and select a report format (HTML, Word, Excel). Click OK.

Once the report is generated, it will be displayed on your screen.

Creating Custom Reports

In addition to using the predefined reports, any number of customized reports can be created. The following steps outline the process as a sample:

1. Start Report Writer.

2. Select the From the Report Writer Catalog. Click OK.

3. Expand the Detail or Summary Reports entry.

4. Select a report type. Click Next.

5. Accept the Every Request You've Imported option. Click Next.

6. At the Filter dialog box, click Finish.

7. To specify a database, from the Database menu select the Change option.

8. Select an .MDB file and click the Open button.

9. Select Create Report Document from the File menu.

10. Enter the report name. Click OK twice.

These defined and custom reports can be used to gather and analyze critical data on your sites. To further automate the analysis process, the logs and reports can be scheduled to run automatically.

Automating Use of Usage Import and Report Writer

Usage Import and Report Writer enable the collection and analysis of IIS log files from a single server. By regularly extracting this usage information, you can identify trends and gain valuable insights for making more informed Internet business decisions. But manually running these processes on a routine basis is boring and inefficient. The data can automatically be imported by scheduling these events.

For example, if the log file closes at 3:00 a.m. for the previous day, the data import can be scheduled to start at 3:05 a.m. The Scheduler, which creates Jobs and Tasks, is used to automate Site Server Express events. Tasks are the individual events, and Jobs are the collections of related Tasks linked together by time. To schedule a Usage Schedule automated event, follow these basic guidelines:

1. Start Usage Import.

2. Select Tools ➤ Scheduler.

3. Right-click on All Jobs and select New Job.

4. Check the Active (NT only) box.

5. Select the periodicity and time that will define when your automated task will occur. Click OK.

6. Right-click on New Job and select New Task.

7. Select the appropriate Task type, such as Import Log File.

8. Enter associated information, such as Log Data Source information and Log Path. Click OK.

You would then need to schedule Report Writer events in the same manner.

Monitoring IIS Performance through Performance Monitor

Performance Monitor in Windows NT can be used to monitor the Web site connection activity on IIS. By monitoring of the number of current and attempted connections, the popularity of the site content can be assessed. More importantly, you can determine whether the bandwidth is adequate for the client load. For example, Performance Monitor counters can reveal that a Web site has had many more connection attempts than current connections. This performance information can then be used to help identify the bottlenecks and then you can decide what to do about increasing the bandwidth for the site.

Overview of Performance Monitor

Performance monitoring in IIS builds on the concepts created in Windows NT, the difference in IIS being the addition of new Objects, Counters, and Instances. This section will cover the organization and views available through Performance Monitor.

Organization of Performance Monitor

The basic conceptual units in Performance Monitor are:

- Objects, which are major groupings or families of system metrics that can be measured, such as Processor, Network, Physical Disk, etc. IIS adds its own Object set of the same name—Internet Information Services Global.

- Counters, which are specific service or mechanism metrics that can be directly utilized to determine range and rate of function. IIS has over 40 counters available for collecting data. These are largely grouped into those that measure bandwidth parameters, ISAPI/CGI parameters, Active Server parameters, and IIS cache parameters.

- Instances, which are individual counters applied to more than one occurrence of the same metric. For example, if you are hosting more than one Web site, Performance Monitor could have two instances of the Current Anonymous Users counter, one instance for each site.

Views Available through Performance Monitor

Performance Monitor can display any number of counters in several formats:

- Chart provides a (default) time-based graph that can display several counters in real time. Chart is a good option if you are tracking information in real-time and are using a small number of counters.

- Alert gives notification (to include the starting of an application or running a specific executable) if a threshold is exceeded.

- Log specifies the logging of object counters at a predetermined rate (the default is every 15 seconds) to a designated log file. Logs are typically used to create baselines.

- Report provides snapshot screen text reporting on selected counters that updates at a default rate of every five seconds.

Monitoring the Internet Information Services Global Object

IIS 4.0 adds an object called Internet Information Services Global, which is used to track global usage of the IIS server.

The commonly used counters of this object are defined in Table 6.2.

T A B L E 6.2 Performance Monitor Internet Information Services Global Counters	**Internet Information Services Global Counter**	**Description**
	Cache Hits	The number of times a file or folder that a user requested was able to be serviced from memory.
	Cache Hits %	Ratio of requests as a percentage that are serviced from cache, as opposed to being serviced from hard disk requests.
	Cache Misses	The number of times a file or folder that a user requested was not able to be serviced from memory and had to be serviced from disk.

TABLE 6.2 *(cont.)* Performance Monitor Internet Information Services Global Counters	**Internet Information Services Global Counter**	**Description**
	Cached File Handles	This is the number of file handles that have been allocated for IIS.
	Current Blocked Async I/O Requests	Lists the number of requests that are refused because of bandwidth throttling limitations.
	Objects	The number of all objects that are being cached by IIS.

Monitoring HTTP Sessions

When you install IIS, you will notice a new object through Performance Monitor called Web Service. The Web Service is used to monitor HTTP sessions and includes a large number of counters to help you see how resources are being used.

Some of the commonly used counters are defined in Table 6.3.

TABLE 6.3 Performance Monitor Web Service Counters	**Web Service Counter**	**Description**
	Bytes Received/Sec	Shows the number of bytes the Web site receives per second
	Bytes Sent/Sec	Shows the number of bytes the Web site was sent per second
	Bytes Total/Sec	Shows the number of bytes the Web site received and sent per second
	Current Blocked Async I/O Requests	Lists the number of requests that are refused because of bandwidth throttling limitations
	Current Connections	Displays how many users are currently connected to the Web service
	Files/Sec	The speed at which files are transferred by the Web service

TABLE 6.3 (cont.)	Web Service Counter	Description
Performance Monitor Web Service Counters	Maximum Connections	Defines the maximum number of concurrent connections that have been established since the Web service was started
	Not Found Errors/Sec	The errors per second that are mainly generated from HTTP 404 error codes (requested document not available)

If your IIS server hosts multiple virtual servers, you can monitor the Web service as a whole, or you can monitor each virtual site individually, by choosing to monitor the specific virtual server as an instance counter.

Monitoring FTP Sessions

When you install IIS 4.0, you will see a new object in Performance Monitor called FTP Service. Through this object, you can see how the FTP Service is functioning.

Common FTP Service counters are defined in Table 6.4.

TABLE 6.4	FTP Service Counter	Description
Performance Monitor FTP Service Counters	Bytes Received/Sec	Shows the number of bytes the FTP site received per second
	Bytes Sent/Sec	Shows the number of bytes the FTP site sent per second
	Bytes Total/Sec	Shows the number of bytes the FTP site received and sent per second
	Current Connections	Displays how many users are currently connected to the FTP service
	Maximum Connections	Defines the maximum number of concurrent connections that have been established since the FTP service was started

Configuring Performance Monitor

To set up Performance Monitor to record an IIS counter (such as Bytes Total/Sec), you would complete the following steps:

1. Start Performance Monitor from Start ➤ Programs ➤ Administrative Tools (Common) ➤ Performance Monitor.

2. The Performance Monitor dialog box will appear.

3. From the Edit menu, select Add to Chart.

4. The Add to Chart dialog box will appear.

5. Select an Object from the Object list (such as FTP Service or Web Service).

6. In the Instance list, if applicable, select the Web or FTP site that you wish to monitor. Select Total if you want to monitor all Web sites or FTP sites together.

7. In the Counter list, select the counters you wish to record. See Table 6.2, Table 6.3, or Table 6.4 for common counters.

8. Click Done after selecting the counters to be tracked.

Analyzing General Performance Problems

Many performance problems are related to a lack of computer resources. The most common source of performance problems can be traced to:

- Memory bottlenecks
- Network bottlenecks
- Disk bottlenecks
- CPU bottlenecks

These potential bottlenecks are reviewed in the following subsections.

Memory Bottlenecks

Memory is one of the most common system bottlenecks. To determine how your system is utilizing memory, you should check the usage of physical memory and the usage of your page file (virtual memory). Specific counters that should be tracked through Performance Monitor are listed in Table 6.5.

T A B L E 6.5 Performance Monitor Memory Object Counters Defined	Memory Counter	Description
	Available Bytes	This counter shows the memory that is available for system use. This value should be more than 4.2MB at all times.
	Pages/Sec	This counter shows the number of pages that are being written between memory and the page file. This number must be below 20.
	Committed Bytes	This counter shows the number of bytes of memory that have been committed to servicing applications. This number should be lower than the amount of physical RAM installed on your server.

If Performance Monitor indicates that you have a memory bottleneck, the best solution is always to add more physical RAM.

Network Bottlenecks

On a moderately busy site, IIS can completely saturate a 10MB Ethernet card. To prevent the server from becoming network bound, use either multiple 10MB Ethernet cards, or install a 100MB Ethernet or FDDI network card. You should also install 32-bit network cards as opposed to 16-bit network cards.

To check for network saturation, check the %Network Utilization counter. This should typically be below 40 percent for Ethernet networks and 80 percent for Token Ring networks.

You can also monitor network utilization through the Network Monitor utility.

Disk Bottlenecks

Hard disk bottlenecks are most often seen on sites with a very large set of files that is accessed randomly. If the bottleneck is in disk access, the percentage of the CPU utilized remains low, the network card is not saturated, and the Physical Disk % Disk Time is high.

To improve disk access in this kind of situation, use a Redundant Array of Independent Disks (RAID). This includes disk mirroring and striped sets with parity. Table 6.6 lists some of the counters that you should track through Performance Monitor to analyze disk utilization.

T A B L E 6.6 Performance Monitor Logical Disk Object Counters Defined	**Logical Disk Counter**	**Description**
	%Disk Time	This is the percent of time that the disk is busy responding to read or write operations. This number should not be above 90 percent on average.
	Average Disk Queue Length	This is the average number of read or write requests that have been queued (as opposed to being serviced right away) during the sample period. If this average is 2 or higher during the sample period, a disk bottleneck may be indicated.

Be aware that insufficient memory can sometimes cause a disk bottleneck, due to the requirements placed on the page file when RAM is low. Check memory before determining that the disk is a bottleneck.

> **NOTE** By default, disk counters are not enabled. To enable disk counters, type DISKPERF –y (or DISKPERF –ye on a RAID-enabled system) from a command prompt; then restart your computer.

CPU Bottlenecks

CPU bottlenecks are characterized by very high %Processor Time counter values while other system counters are below capacity. If the %Processor Time counter is consistently above 80 percent, you can upgrade the CPU, add additional CPUs to the same computer, or add additional computers which you replicate, and then distribute the traffic across each. If you are running other CPU-intensive applications on the Web server, such as a database application, you should move the application to another computer.

The counters defined in Table 6.7 will help you track CPU utilization.

T A B L E 6.7: Performance Monitor Processor Object Counters Defined

Processor Object Counter	Description
%Processor Time	This counter indicates how busy a processor is. It shows the percentage of elapsed time that a processor has been busy executing system and application threads. During some operations (such as initialization of an application, a compile, or a worksheet recalculation), the system might experience spikes that approach 100 percent. As long as the processor averages a utilization below 80 percent, the processor is probably not a bottleneck in your system. If more than a couple of processes are contending for the majority of the processor time, a faster processor or an additional processor in an SMP (Symmetric MultiProcessor) machine should be considered.
Interrupts/Sec	This is also an important processor counter, measuring the rate of service requests from I/O devices. A dramatic increase in this counter value, without a corresponding increase in system activity, indicates a hardware problem.

Another important counter for CPU utilization is the System object, Processor Queue Length counter. This counter lists the number of requests that are queued and waiting to be processed by the processor. If this counter lists two or more requests, a processor bottleneck is indicated.

Optimizing Performance of IIS

You can optimize the performance of IIS in many ways. The following list provides some suggestions:

- Replace or convert CGI applications to ASP or ISAPI applications. CGI applications are more memory- and processor-intensive than ASP and ISAPI applications.

- Logically organize your data so that related documents are kept on the same logical disks. Defragment your disks to further improve performance.

- Optimize application code. This includes performance-testing code once it is written, not inserting comment information, and avoiding interspersing HTML and Script code.

- Avoid placing large numbers of graphics, or complex graphics, on each Web page. This can reduce bandwidth requirements for your site.

- Use disk striping or disk mirroring to improve read access time from disks.

- To optimize bandwidth, enable HTTP keep-alives.

- Don't require SSL services on folders that do not require high security.

Other IIS optimization suggestions include setting bandwidth limits and connection limits, monitoring memory, and making sure you have an appropriate Internet connection, each of which are discussed in turn.

Bandwidth Limits

IIS 4.0 now allows selective bandwidth limiting. Limits can be placed on the Web sites in aggregate and also on individual sites. This allows other services to share a maintained data pipe at least equal to the total bandwidth minus the IIS limit. As a rule of thumb, start by limiting the bandwidth to 50 percent of the total connection bandwidth and adjust from there. Configure bandwidth limitations through bandwidth throttling.

Connection Limits

By limiting the total number of connections, the data throughput increases while sacrificing the total number of clients that can be handled. Too many connections result in timeout errors and slower data rates. This may lead to reduced traffic at the Web site—the death knell!

Memory and Response Speed

If Performance Monitor indicates that an ISAPI or Active Server process is running a large number of threads and is requiring enormous memory resources to execute, it will drag IIS performance down if it shares the same memory space. Set up the executable to run in a separate memory space.

Internet Connection

Although increasing dramatically in the past several years, telephony-based data rates have languished far behind network rates. While most network backbones have remained at about 10 Mbps for several years, common Internet data rates have gone from 14.4 Kbps modem speeds to as high as 10 Mbps (through cable modems for read access) for business and even home use. Typically, the Internet connection is the limiting factor in Internet communications, rather than the network backbone. As a general rule, a T1 line is typically the fastest WAN data line that is used on a 10 Mbps Ethernet backbone.

Optimizing Performance of Index Server

There are two ways to check Index Server and the overall indexing status:

- Windows NT Performance Monitor
- Any Web browser

Both can be used to provide complementary data that can help identify bottlenecks and ensure efficient operation.

Windows NT Performance Monitor Method

Index Server installs a number of performance counters to monitor the state of Index Server from Microsoft Performance Monitor. Table 6.8 defines the counters used by Index Server.

	Index Server Counter	Description
T A B L E 6.8 Windows NT Performance Monitor Index Server Counters	# of Documents Filtered	The number of documents that have been filtered by the system.
	Files to Be Filtered	Specifies how many files have been edited or created and still need to be filtered.
	Index Size	Specifies the size of the index in MB.
	Merge Progress	Lets you know whether or not an index optimization is taking place. If a merge is taking place, it shows the progress during optimization. A reading of 100 means the merge is complete.
	Persistent indexes	Specifies the number of indexes stored on the disk. This number is ideally 1. As indexes are built, the system may create several, simultaneous indexes. As time passes, these indexes are merged together to optimize system performance.
	Running Queries	Lists how many concurrent queries are being processed by the server.
	Total # of Documents	Specifies how many objects are currently indexed by the system.
	Unique Keys	Specifies how many unique words have been identified through the index.

TABLE 6.8 *(cont.)*	Index Server Counter	Description
Windows NT Performance Monitor Index Server Counters	Wordlists	Shows how many temporary word lists have been created. Word lists are created when objects are indexed. After 14–20 wordlists are created, they are merged into a persistent index and cleared from memory. Once a certain number of persistent indexes have been created, they are merged into a single persistent index, the master index.

Web Browser Method

Index Server can publish its indexing status on the World Wide Web. Index Server does this through a special query generated by the Index Server Manager (HTML) page. This query lets any computer with a Web browser check the status of Index Server.

To create and view an Indexing Status page:

1. From Start ➤ Programs ➤ Windows NT 4.0 Option Pack ➤ Microsoft Index Server ➤ Index Server Manager (HTML). Open the Index Server Manager (HTML) Web page.

2. The browser will display the Index Server Manager (HTML) page.

3. Index Server displays the cache and index statistics as shown in Figure 6.6.

After compiling data on the Index Server, the balance between resources spent on merges and the length of time to perform queries can be reviewed. If necessary, the registry values controlling Index Server merges can be adjusted.

If you host multiple Web sites on your IIS server, and users complain that they are getting numerous non-pertinent hits from their queries, you can create multiple catalogs and link them to the virtual servers.

FIGURE 6.6

HTML Index Server
statistics

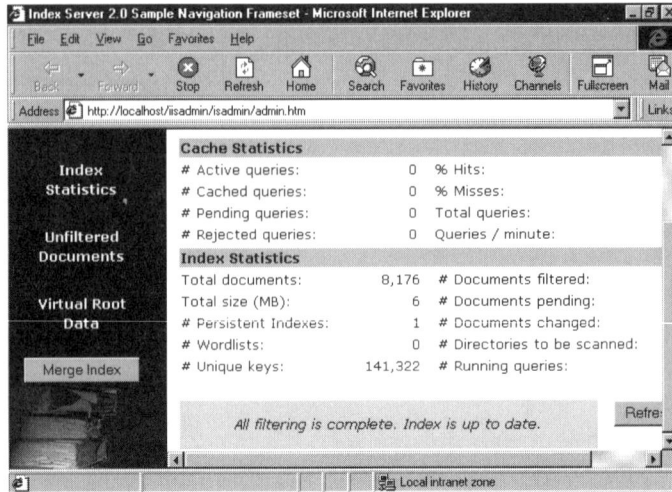

FIGURE 6.6

HTML Index Server
statistics

Optimizing Performance of SMTP

The SMTP Service has a specialized object in Performance Monitor called SMTP. The SMTP Server object has three key counters that should be used to monitor performance, as shown in Table 6.9.

TABLE 6.9	SMTP Objects	Description
Performance Monitor SMTP-Related Counters Defined	Local Queue Length	Specifies the number of messages in the queue. A number of more than 0 indicates that the server is receiving more messages locally than it can process.
	Remote Queue Length	This number specifies the number of messages in a remote queue. A number of more than 0 indicates that the server is receiving more messages remotely than it can process.
	Inbound Connections Current	Specifies the number of concurrent inbound connections. A number greater than 0 for an extended time can indicate a hung connection

Optimizing Performance of NNTP

The performance counters included with Microsoft NNTP Service enable you to build charts and reports that show performance data including activity, security, and overall performance. They also allow trend analysis.

The NNTP Service includes two objects in Performance Monitor: the NNTP Server Commands object, which contains counters for client commands, and the NNTP Server object, which contains over 40 counters for service performance. In refining the performance of the NNTP Service, use the objects described in Table 6.10.

T A B L E 6.10	Object	Counter	Description
Performance Monitor NNTP-Related Counters Defined	NNTP Server	Bytes Total/Sec	Total number of bytes sent and received by the NNTP service.
	NNTP Server	Current Connections	Total number of active connections using the NNTP service.
	NNTP Commands	Logon Attempts & Failures	Logon attempts, including successful logons and login failures. Failures should be a very small percentage of Attempts.
	NNTP Server	Maximum Connections	Specifies the largest number of simultaneous connections to the NNTP server.

Optimizing Web Sites with Content Analyzer

Content Analyzer is a critical piece of the Site Server Express package. It enables the Webmaster to create a visual database of the site(s), called the WebMap, and to create graphic reports to indicate content, layout, links, and properties of the sites.

Keeping Maps Current

Once you've made some changes and corrections to your site, it's a good idea to use the Remap Site command (on the Mapping menu) to make a revised map. This allows you to keep your WebMap current as a database of objects and links. Rather than creating a new map from scratch, you can quickly regenerate a map and reports for the latest version of your site. Content Analyzer will use the same filename for the new and old maps by changing just the file extension. (It renames the old map to `filename.bak.wmp`.)

If you start from the default settings, Content Analyzer remaps the site in this way:

- Explores the entire site, including all previously explored pages

- Re-imports any pertinent META tag data (that is, for author, date, notes, and so on) from the site's pages into the Annotations tab of the Properties dialog box

- Retains all your previous settings for display, labels, and mapping options

- Retains any usage data you've imported into your map

- Generates a results window showing what's new and what has changed

- Closes the previous version of the map and saves the new version with the same name

> You can use Content Analyzer to identify all resources over 32KB in size. This allows you to minimize the number of large documents published by your site, consequently improving performance.

Comparing and Updating WebMaps

Even though you can use the Remap Site command when you need a new map of your site, there may occasionally be times when you already have two maps that you want to compare to each other. If that's the case, use the Compare and Update command. Like Remap Site, Compare and Update generates results windows for what's new and changed in your site, as well as for what has been "orphaned."

Each map window can have a single associated results window, displaying either the results of a map comparison or the results of a search. The Orphaned Objects window is associated with the source map, and the Changed and New Objects window is associated with the target map.

Interpreting Performance Data and Log Files

You can study the log files from your Web or FTP server by viewing them in a text editor. You can also use Microsoft Usage Import and Report Writer to help you analyze the data.

You can access the current log file only after stopping the site (that is, by starting Internet Service Manager, selecting the site, and clicking the Stop button).

Maintaining Log Files

1. List the four log formats that are used to track WWW activity.

\
\
\
\

2. Which log type allows you to define the fields that you want to track?

\

3. True or False. You must configure a Data Source Name through Control Panel, ODBC before you can use ODBC Logging.

4. Which logging method typically requires the most overhead?

\

5. True or False. NCSA logging can be defined for WWW or FTP sites.

6. What is the default directory that is used to store IIS log files?

\

7. What utility is used to extract data from IIS log files so that the data can be used by Site Server Express Report Writer?

_____

8. True or False. You can configure logging properties so that a new log file is opened on a daily basis.

9. The _____ utility allows you display the data that was collected through the log files in one of 21 predefined reports.

10. True or False. You can directly access the data that is collected through IIS logging in Report Writer.

11. True or False. You can specify that Report Writer create reports in HTML, Word, or Excel format.

12. True or False. You can create customized reports through Report Writer.

Monitoring IIS Performance through Performance Monitor

13. List the three conceptual units that are used to organize Performance Monitor in a hierarchical format.

_____

_____

_____

14.   What are the four views available through Performance Monitor?

_____

_____

_____

_____

15.   What object is added to Performance Monitor to track general IIS counters?

_____

16.   What counter is added to Performance Monitor to track WWW site usage?

_____

17.   What counter is added to Performance Monitor to track FTP site usage?

_____

18.   Which Web Service Performance Monitor counter would allow you to track how many errors are generated each second because the documents that are being requested are unavailable?

_____

19.   Which FTP Service Performance Monitor counter would allow you to track how many bytes are sent and received by the FTP service each second?

_____

20. Which FTP Performance Monitor counter would you use if you wanted to see if any connections were being refused due to bandwidth throttling?

_____

21. To fine-tune the tracking and increase administrator response time to events, you can set Performance Monitor to generate a(n) _____ whenever a counter exceeds or drops below a measurement you specify.

Analyzing General Performance Problems

22. List the four most common sources of general performance problems.

_____

_____

_____

_____

23. True or False. If you were checking the Available Bytes counter of the Memory object in Performance Monitor, and it showed at least 2MB, then a memory bottleneck would not be indicated.

24. What is the best way to overcome a problem related to insufficient RAM?

_____

25. Which Performance Monitor counter allows you to see how busy your processor is?

_____

26. Which Performance Monitor counter allows you to see how busy your network segment is?

_____

27. If the %Disk Time Logical Disk counter is above _____ percent, as an average, a disk bottleneck may be indicated.

28. True or False. If a disk bottleneck is indicated, you can improve performance by using disk striping or disk mirroring.

Optimizing Performance of IIS

29. True or False. CGI applications are less memory- and CPU-intensive than ISAPI applications.

30. Which option allows you to specify how much of the total bandwidth is available for each IIS service site?

_____

31. True or False. Enabling HTTP keep-alives will help optimize IIS bandwidth requirements.

32. True or False. You can improve IIS performance by placing related Web documents on the same logical disk.

Optimizing Performance of Index Server

33. What Index Server counter allows you to track how many documents have been indexed through Index Server?

_____

34. True or False. You should have at least three persistent indexes stored on disk in order to improve performance.

35. True or False. You can see the status of Index Server through Index Server (HTML version) and through Performance Monitor.

36. True or False. Index server has several Registry Keys that control the conduct of a Master Merge.

Optimizing Performance of SMTP

37. Which SMTP Performance Monitor counter allows you to track the number of local messages waiting to be processed?

_____

38. Which SMTP Performance Monitor counter allows you to track the number of remote messages waiting to be processed?

_____

Optimizing Performance of NNTP

39. Which two objects are added to Performance Monitor to allow you to track the NNTP Service?

_____

_____

40. Which NNTP Performance counter would you track if you wanted to see the total number of bytes that were sent or received by the NNTP server?

_____

41. Which NNTP Performance counter would you track if you wanted to see the total number of active connections to your NNTP server?

_____

Optimizing Web Sites with Content Analyzer

42. When renaming maps, Content Analyzer will use the same name for the new map as for the old, and rename the old map to _filename_.bak._____.

43. Although you can use the Remap Site command when you need a new map of your site, there may be times when you already have two maps that you want to compare to each other. If that's the case, use the Compare and _____ command.

44. True or False. The Content Analyzer can identify objects that have file sizes over 16KB, 32KB, or 64KB.

SAMPLE TEST

6-1   Your NT server functions as both an in-house application server and also hosts your IIS server. Your users are complaining that your Web site is so popular that it's taking a long time to print or save files to the server. How can you best improve performance in this situation?

    A. Move the IIS Service to another NT server.

    B. Move the IIS server outside of the network firewall.

    C. Enable Bandwidth Throttling on the default Web site.

    D. Limit the Number of Connections to the default Web site.

6-2   You want to know whether or not your IIS Service requests are being serviced from memory or from disk. How can you track this information?

    A. Use the Chart view to track the Internet Information Services Global to monitor the Cache Hits counter.

    B. Use the Alert view to track the Internet Information Services Global to monitor the Cache Hits counter.

    C. Use the Report view to track the TCP: Cache Hits counter.

    D. Use the Alert view to track the IIS Service: %Cache Hits counter.

6-3   You have multiple IIS servers on your network. Monitoring network utilization, you note that the IIS servers are using 60 percent of the bandwidth. How can you improve the performance of the network?

    A. Subnet the network and install routers between the IIS servers.

    B. Place firewalls between the IIS servers and the rest of the network.

    C. Consolidate the Web sites on a smaller number of servers.

    D. Increase the network backbone capacity.

6-4   In order to optimize the Web site pages, you want to verify that no image files are greater than 32KB. What tool can you use to accomplish this?

    A. Site Server Express Report Writer

    B. NT Explorer

    C. Index Server

    D. Site Server Express Content Analyzer

6-5   Your users complain that they are getting numerous non-pertinent hits from their queries. You have three sites hosted on the server. How do you resolve this problem?

    A. Add non-pertinent words to the Noise List.

    B. Create Catalogs for each site.

    C. Create multiple catalogs for each site.

    D. Create multiple catalogs and link them to the virtual servers.

6-6   You want to minimize the processing time that IIS logging uses. Where should you direct the output?

    A. Log to an ODBC SQL file format.

    B. Log to an NCSA format file.

    C. Log to a Microsoft IIS log file format.

    D. There is no significant difference between performance based on file types.

6-7   Which logging feature allows you to log data directly to an SQL database?

    A. Microsoft IIS Log Format

    B. NCSA Common Log File Format

    C. W3C Extended Log File Format

    D. ODBC Logging

6-8   You have specified that all virtual directories use digital certificates for access. How can you best increase the performance of the IIS Web Server from the following choices?

    A. Only require SSL on folders that require secure services.

    B. Disable HTTP keep-alives.

    C. Enable the ServerSideIncludes registry key.

    D. Add more RAM.

6-9   You are running CGI applications on your IIS server. Which of the following options will help you improve performance?

    A. Disable the memory cache.

    B. Disable the object cache scavenger.

    C. Convert your CGI applications to ISAPI applications.

    D. Increase the bandwidth of the connection to the network.

6-10   On one server you have IIS, SQL, SSL, and a SSL ISAPI filter installed. How can performance be best increased?

    A. Add more RAM.

    B. Add another CPU.

    C. Add a faster hard disk drive.

    D. Move some of the services to another computer for load balancing.

6-11 The IIS server is running a single ISAPI application that has begun to consume excessive resources. How can the number of threads be reduced?

A. Add more RAM.

B. Run each occurrence of the ISAPI application in a separate memory space.

C. Execute the ISAPI application in the IIS memory space.

D. Execute the ISAPI application by using an Active Server page.

6-12 The IIS computer is configured with 64MB of RAM and 64MB of virtual memory. In attempting to improve the performance of Index Server, you increase the cache. Performance actually decreases because:

A. The cache is not optimized for more than 32MB.

B. A Master Merge must be accomplished before the additional cache can be utilized.

C. The cache is now using virtual memory, which is slower.

D. The cache cannot use virtual memory.

6-13 Which of the following objects are added to Performance Monitor in order to track IIS, HTTP, and FTP performance? Choose all that apply.

A. Internet Information Services Global

B. IIS Service

C. HTTP Service

D. Web Service

E. FTP Service

6-14   What Performance Monitor counter allows you to track the number of all objects that are cached by IIS?

    A. Internet Information Services Global object, Objects counter

    B. IIS Service object, Cache Hits counter

    C. Internet Information Services Global object, Cache Hits% counter

    D. IIS Service object, %Objects Cached counter

6-15   The two principle advantages of using Content Analyzer to optimize a Web site are:

    A. Identifying "Not Found" Objects

    B. Identifying files with load sizes over 64KB

    C. Identifying broken Web links

    D. Identifying all `.GIF` files

UNIT

7

Troubleshooting

Test Objectives: Troubleshooting

- Resolve IIS configuration problems.

- Resolve security problems.

- Resolve resource access problems.

- Resolve Index Server query problems.

- Resolve setup issues when installing IIS on a Windows NT Server 4.0 computer.

- Use a WebMap to find and repair broken links.

- Resolve WWW service problems.

- Resolve FTP service problems.

Exam objectives are subject to change at any time without prior notice and at Microsoft's sole discretion. Please visit Microsoft's Training & Certification Web site (www.microsoft.com/Train_Cert) for the most current exam objectives listing.

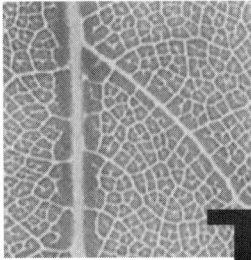

his section will cover common issues that relate to configuration errors. Some of the issues that will be addressed are IIS configuration errors (through the WWW and FTP services), security and resource access errors, Index Server query errors, installation errors, and using WebMap to identify broken links. In addition, you will also learn how to interpret ODBC connection errors.

Troubleshooting IIS Configuration Problems

IIS configuration problems can involve a variety of settings. This section will review configuration problems that relate to the WWW and FTP services. In addition, you will learn how to resolve virtual server access.

Resolving WWW Service Problems

WWW service problems can involve a variety of settings. Possible errors include:

- You have configured the WWW service to use a port other than port 80. This requires the client to specify the port that has been assigned.

- You have configured the WWW service to use SSL, and the client is not using SSL or does not provide the correct digital certificate for authentication.

- The number of connections is limited, and the maximum has been exceeded, preventing new connections.

- The connection timeout value has been set too low, and connections are being dropped too quickly.

- Correct permissions have not been applied to the WWW objects that users need to access.

- A valid default document has not been defined.

- Access control has been set and the user cannot access resources. This could result from the authentication method used, SSL being enabled, or IP address restrictions.

- You have used file types that do not have valid MIME mappings defined.

> **NOTE** See Unit 2 for more information on configuring the WWW service.

Resolving FTP Service Problems

FTP service problems, like WWW service problems, have many possible causes. They include:

- You have configured the FTP service to use a port other than port 21. This requires the client to specify the port that has been assigned.

- The number of connections is limited, and the maximum has been exceeded, preventing new connections.

- You have limited anonymous access, and the client has no valid NT account and password.

- The client browser does not support the directory listing style you have specified.

- The client does not have correct permissions to access the FTP site directory, or the NTFS permissions have not been applied, or they are too restrictive.

- IP address restrictions have been applied that prevent the client from accessing the FTP site.

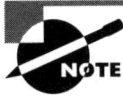

See Unit 2 for more information on configuring the FTP service.

Resolving Virtual Server Problems

With IIS 4.0, you can create multiple virtual servers on a single IIS computer, all sharing a single IP address. In order for users to properly access the correct virtual server, you must ensure that the following configuration is correct:

- A virtual home directory that contains the documents for the site must be defined for each virtual server.

- You must install and configure a DNS server. As an alternative, you could configure a HOSTS file. However, each client would need to copy the HOSTS file to their computer.

- You must edit the property sheet of each virtual server to use host header names.

Resolving Security and Resource Access Problems

Security and resource access problems also can have many causes. Some of the issues that come into play include:

- Logon access and authentication

- Access control by IP address

- Access permissions applied

These items are covered in the following subsections.

Logon Access and Authentication

When you install and configure IIS, you can specify which users can access your IIS services. You can allow anonymous access (for public sites) or you can force users to authenticate using valid NT user accounts and passwords (for private sites).

Logon access can be configured to support:

- Anonymous access
- Basic authentication
- Windows NT Challenge/Response

These options are defined in Table 7.1.

T A B L E 7.1 Logon authentica- tion options	**Logon Authentication Option**	**Description**
	Allow anonymous access	This specifies that users should be allowed anonymous access to your site. This uses the IUSR_*computername* NT account that is created when IIS is installed.
	Basic authentication	This option requires that users access your site with a valid NT user account and password. This option is not secure, as it sends the user name and password without any encryption. The advantage is that it is widely supported by most Web browsers.
	Windows NT Challenge/ Response	This authentication method requires that users access your site with a valid NT user account and password. It is the most secure authentication method, as it uses a cryptographic exchange. This authentication method requires that clients use Internet Explorer 3.0 or higher.

Access Control by IP Address

You can also control who accesses your site by granting or denying access based on IP address. Access control based on IP address can be configured for a specific site or a specific folder within the Web site.

Controlling access by IP address can be specified through:

- A specific IP address

- A specific IP network (including subnet mask)

- A domain name (this requires reverse DNS lookup capabilities)

Access Permissions Applied

Access permissions come in two flavors, NTFS and Web server permissions. NTFS permissions allow you to take advantage of NT security, and Web server permissions allow you to apply security to folders on non-NTFS folders. If both sets of permissions are applied, the more restrictive will be the effective permission.

NTFS Permissions

If the folder you are using for your Web site is on an NTFS partition, you can apply NTFS permissions as an additional layer of security. The five standard NTFS permissions include:

- Read: allows a user to read files or run executable files.

- Change: allows a user to view and modify the content of files. A user who has Change permission can also delete files.

- Full Control: a very powerful permission that allows a user to read, write, or delete files. In addition, a user with Full Control is able to modify NTFS permissions and take ownership of NTFS objects.

- Special Access: used to customize which permissions a user has.

- No Access: used to deny any access to a folder or file, even if the user has permissions applied through user or group membership.

Web Server Permissions

Web server permissions can be applied to Web sites and folders. Web permissions differ from NTFS permissions in that NTFS permissions can be applied to specific users and groups, whereas Web server permissions are applied to all users who access the Web site.

Web server access permissions include:

- Read: allows users to read or download files located in your home folder. This is used if your home folder contains HTML files. If your home folder contains CGI applications or ISAPI applications, you should uncheck this option so that users cannot download your application files.

- Write: allows users to modify or add to your Web content. This access should be granted with extreme caution.

- Script: allows you to run script engines to be executed, even if no Execute permissions have been set. This permission should be used for folders that contain ASP scripts or IDC scripts.

- Execute: includes Script permission and specifies that you can run script engines and NT binary files which include .EXE and .DLL extensions.

Resolving Index Server Query Problems

Index Server is used to track and index Web content so that users can query the index and find the information they need quickly and easily. This section will review the steps required to implement Index Server. This will provide a foundation for your troubleshooting, if an error occurs.

1. IIS must first be installed. See Unit 2 for more information on installation of IIS.

2. You can specify whether Web content contained in virtual root folders will be included within the index. This is configured through the WWW site Home Directory property tab as shown in Figure 7.1. If the virtual folder is on a remote server, then you must configure a domain account that has the user right Log on Locally specified, and the user account must have access permissions to all of the folders that will be indexed.

F I G U R E 7.1

Home Directory tab of
the WWW Properites
dialog box

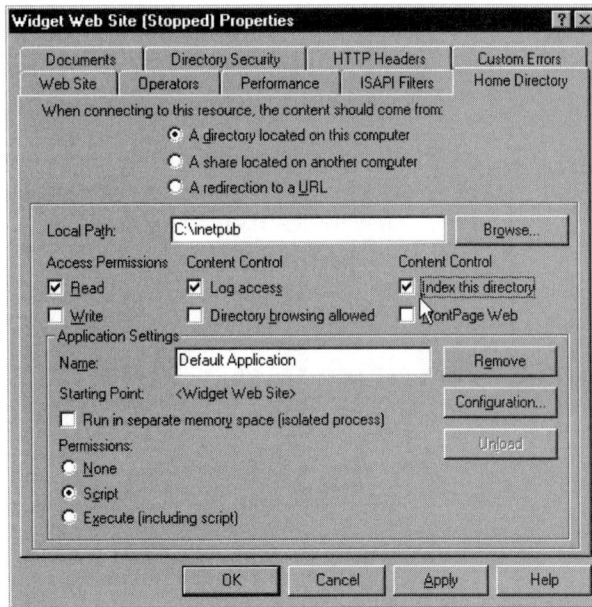

3. Install and configure Index Server. For more information on Index
   Server, see Unit 4.

4. Create and publish Web content in the folders that have been configured so that they are included in the index.

5. When a query is issued, Index Server will begin the index process. The
   index is then automatically updated. Users submit queries, and Index
   Server then accesses the index and produces an HTML file with links
   to the specified query subjects.

Setup Issues for IIS Installation

Before IIS 4.0 can be installed onto NT Server, the following issues
must be taken into consideration:

- You must be running NT 4.0 with Service Pack 3 installed.

- You must be running Internet Explorer 4.01 or later.

- If you were running Alpha or Beta versions of IIS 4.0, they must be removed prior to installation of the current release of IIS 4.0.

- The Netlogon, Server, and Computer Browser services must be running on the computer. Netlogon requires Workstation service also.

- ODBC connection errors will occur if there are any other applications using the ODBC connector. You should stop the offending applications for the IIS installation. They can be restarted after installation is complete.

Troubleshooting with WebMap

A typical Web site contains pages that are local to the Web site, and pointers to other Web sites, which are called links.

WebMap is used to create a graphical map of your Web site. The map includes Web pages that can involve a wide variety of media. You can create a WebMap through Site Server Express using the Content Analyzer feature.

WebMap allows you to graphically view your site through two different views: the tree view and the cyberbolic view. The tree view displays information in a hierarchical format that is similar in nature to Windows Explorer. The cyberbolic view shows the Web site as a series of interrelated links.

Resolving ODBC Connection Errors

IIS can be linked to ODBC databases. If there are problems with the connection, you will receive an error message. This section will cover ODBC error messages and their possible causes.

ODBC Error #1

Error Message

```
Microsoft OLE DB Provider for ODBC Drivers error "80004005"
[Microsoft] [ODBC Microsoft Access 97 Driver] The Microsoft Jet
database engine cannot open file "(unknown)". It is already
opened exclusively by another user, or you need permission to
view its data.
```

Cause

This message is caused by the user account (usually IUSR_*computername*) having insufficient NT access rights to the ODBC database. You should check NTFS and share permissions.

ODBC Error #2

Error Message

```
Microsoft OLE DB Provider for ODBC Drivers error "80004005"
[Microsoft] [ODBC Driver Manager] Data source not found and no
default driver specified.
```

Cause

This message is most commonly caused by the GLOBAL.ASA file not being properly executed. Check that this file is in the Application Root for IIS 4.0 and that users have Execute permission for this folder.

ODBC Error #3

Error Message

```
Microsoft OLE DB Provider for ODBC Drivers error "80004005"
[Microsoft] [ODBC Microsoft SQL Driver] Logon Failed
```

Cause

This message is caused by the SQL server denying access to the account that is attempting to authenticate and access the SQL server. Check that the SQL account and NT user account (used by IIS) and password match. Make sure that the IIS connection to the SQL server maps the user's name properly.

ODBC Error #4

Error Message

```
Microsoft OLE DB Provider for ODBC Drivers error "80004005"
[Microsoft] [ODBC Microsoft Access 97 Driver] Couldn't use
"(unknown)"; file already in use.
```

Cause

The database file you are attempting to access is configured for single-user use only, and the file is already open.

ODBC Error #5

Error Message

```
Microsoft OLE DB Provider for ODBC Drivers error "80004005"
[Microsoft] [ODBC Microsoft SQL Driver] [dbnmpntw] ConnectionOpen
(create file)
```

Cause

This message is usually caused by incorrect permissions being applied. This is especially common if the database is remote and you are trying to access it via a UNC path, particularly when accessing the database with the IUSR_*computername* account. This account is local to the IIS server, and one solution is to create this account on the remote computer that contains the remote database. In addition to duplicate user names, the passwords must match on both accounts.

Troubleshooting IIS Configuration Problems

1. By default, the WWW service is configured to use port _____.

2. By default, the FTP service is configured to use port _____.

3. What is the purpose of MIME mapping?

_____

4. True or False. In order to access a Web site without referencing a specific document, you must create a default document called DEFAULT.HTM.

5. How do clients specify that they want to use SSL services?

_____

6. What would cause the following error:

HTTP Error 403

403.6 Forbidden: IP address rejected

_____

7. True or False. If you are using virtual servers in IIS that all share a single IP address, you must use the services of WINS or create a LMHOSTS file that will be used for IP address resolution.

8. You are using multiple virtual servers that all share a single IP address on a single IIS computer. What must be configured for each virtual server to allow proper access?

_____

9. What file is required for IP to domain name resolution if DNS is not installed, and where is the file located?

_____

_____

Resolving Security and Resource Access Problems

10. True or False. If you allow Anonymous access to your Web site, then no NT user account will be used.

11. Your Web site has a home folder called WebDocs that has Read permission applied to it. This folder is on an NTFS folder that specifies the Everyone group has Full Control permission. What permissions will Web users have when accessing this folder?

_____

_____

12. True or False. If you require the Windows NT Challenge/Response authentication method, then all of your clients must use Internet Explorer 3.0 or later as their Web browser.

13. When would the Execute permission be applied to a WWW virtual directory?

_____

_____

14. When would the Script permission be applied to a WWW virtual directory?

_____

_____

Resolving Index Server Query Problems

15. What user right is required for the user account that will be used to access a remote folder that will be included in an index using Index Server?

_____

16. What is the easiest way to specify whether or not a Web folder is included or is not included within an index?

_____

Setup Issues for IIS Installation

17. In order to install IIS, you must be running NT version _____ or later.

18. In order to install IIS, you must be using Service Pack version _____ or later.

19. In order to install IIS, you must be running Internet Explorer version _____ or later.

20. True or False. IIS 4.0 can be successfully upgraded from IIS 4.0 Alpha or Beta versions.

21. List the four services that must be running in order for IIS to be successfully installed.

_____

_____

_____

_____

22. True or False. ODBC connection errors will occur if there are any other applications using the ODBC connector. You should stop the offending applications for the IIS installation. They can be restarted after installation is complete.

Troubleshooting with WebMap

23. List the two views available through WebMap.

_____

_____

24. What utility is used to create a WebMap?

_____

Resolving ODBC Connection Errors

25. What would cause the following ODBC error message:

Microsoft OLE DB Provider for ODBC Drivers error "80004005" [Microsoft] [ODBC Microsoft Access 97 Driver] The Microsoft Jet database engine cannot open file "(unknown)". It is already opened exclusively by another user, or you need permission to view its data.

_____

_____

26. What would cause the following ODBC error message:

Microsoft OLE DB Provider for ODBC Drivers error "80004005" [Microsoft] [ODBC Driver Manager] Data source not found and no default driver specified.

_____

_____

27. What would cause the following ODBC error message:

Microsoft OLE DB Provider for ODBC Drivers error "80004005" [Microsoft] [ODBC Microsoft SQL Driver] Logon Failed

_____

_____

STUDY QUESTIONS

28. What would cause the following ODBC error message:

```
Microsoft OLE DB Provider for ODBC Drivers error "80004005" [Microsoft] [ODBC
Microsoft Access 97 Driver] Couldn't use "(unknown)"; file already in use.
```

_____

_____

29. What would cause the following ODBC error message:

```
Microsoft OLE DB Provider for ODBC Drivers error "80004005" [Microsoft] [ODBC
Microsoft SQL Driver] [dbnmpntw] ConnectionOpen (create file)
```

_____

_____

7-1 A client calls you complaining that when they attempt to access your Web site, they get the following error:

`HTTP Error 403`

`403.4 Forbidden: SSL required`

The client states that they were told that their computer has been configured to use SSL, but they are not sure how to implement SSL. What needs to be done?

    A. The client needs to check the Use SSL Protocol box in the Advanced Configuration tab of their Web browser.

    B. The client needs to access the SSL resources by typing `HTTPS://` before the URL they are specifying.

    C. The client needs to access SSL resources by calling the `.SHTML` extension, instead of the `.HTML` extension.

    D. The client needs to access the SSL resources by typing `SHTTP://` before the URL they are specifying.

7-2 A client calls you complaining that when they attempt to access your Web site, they get the following error:

`HTTP Error 403`

`403.6 Forbidden: IP address rejected`

What needs to be done to fix this problem?

    A. You have restricted the IP addresses that can access your site. This client's IP address needs to be granted access.

    B. The client is attempting to access your Web site with an IP address that is already in use. The client needs to pick a non-conflicting IP address.

    C. The client is not using a proper NT account name and password to access your Web site. The client needs to be assigned a valid NT account and password.

    D. The Web site is configured to require SSL services, and the client needs to be configured to use SSL.

7-3   You want to index a folder that exists on a remote server. What must be configured? Choose all that apply.

    A. You must configure the folder as a remote virtual folder to the Web site.

    B. The user account used to access the folder must have the user right Log on Locally on the computer that contains the remote resource.

    C. The user account used to access the folder must have the user right Access Network Resources.

    D. The user account used to access the remote virtual folder must have access permission to the folder that will be indexed.

7-4   Which of the following requirements must be met before IIS can be installed? Choose all that apply.

    A. You must be running NT 3.51 or later.

    B. You must be running NT 4.0 or later.

    C. You must be using Service Pack 3 or later.

    D. You must be using Service Pack 4 or later.

    E. You must be using Internet Explorer 3.01 or later.

    F. You must be using Internet Explorer 4.01 or later.

SAMPLE TEST

7-5   Which of the following services must be running in order to successfully install IIS? Choose all that apply.

    A. Netlogon

    B. Server

    C. Workstation

    D. Computer Browser

7-6   Which of the following authentication methods would require the user to present a valid NT user account and password?

    A. Anonymous

    B. Basic

    C. Secure

    D. Windows NT Challenge/Response

7-7   You have configured your IIS server to host multiple virtual WWW sites. Users complain that when they attempt to access virtual WWW sites, they are connecting to the default WWW site. You cannot use a DNS server for other reasons. What must you configure?

    A. You must configure a HOSTS file on the IIS server.

    B. You must configure a HOSTS file on each client computer.

    C. You must configure a LMHOSTS file on the IIS server.

    D. You must configure a LMHOSTS file on each client computer.

7-8   Which utility can be used to create a graphical representation of your Web site?

    A. WebMap

    B. WebMapper

    C. Web Site Mapper

    D. SiteMap

7-9   Users are having trouble accessing ASP scripts and IDC scripts. Which access permission should you verify as being applied?

    A. Read

    B. Write

    C. Script

    D. Execute

7-10   Users are having trouble running script engines that include .EXE and .DLL extensions. Which access permission should you verify as being applied?

    A. Read

    B. Write

    C. Script

    D. Execute

UNIT

8

Final Review

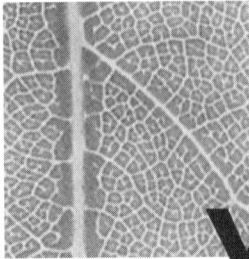

ou'll notice that this exam uses a different testing format than the core MCSE exams. Instead of using all multiple choice questions, some questions will use an MMC simulator that asks you to perform specific tasks. For example, you may be asked to configure the FTP service to use MS-DOS style directory listings or configure a WWW site to only allow 100 concurrent connections. This means that you should definitely get some hands-on experience with MMC before you take this exam. You can expect 8-10 questions out of 55 to be simulative in nature.

The rest of the questions will be the same old multiple choice questions you are used to. So, if you think you're ready, try your hand at the following questions. If you want to time yourself, the real test allows you an hour and a half to complete all the questions.

1   You host a Web site that is accessed by users with different Web browsers. You have configured directory security exclusively with Basic authentication required. Based on this configuration, which of the following statements are true? Choose all that apply.

    A. Anonymous users can still log on.

    B. Only users with valid NT accounts can log on.

    C. Passwords will be encrypted before they are sent to the IIS server.

    D. Data will be encrypted before it is sent to the IIS server.

2   You host a Web site that contains very sensitive data. You decide to use SSL and configure the Web site to require digital certificates. You create the digital certificates through Microsoft Certificate Server, and all clients install the digital certificate. One client calls and complains that when he attempts to access a folder that has been secured, he gets the following error:

```
403.4 Forbidden: SSL required.
```

What should be done so that this user can access the secured folder?

    A. You should make sure this user has NTFS permissions to the secured folder.

B. The user should access the URL using HTTPS.

C. The user should access the default document by referencing .HTMS as opposed to .HTM.

D. The user should access the URL using SHTTP.

3 Your computer is configured so that it supports a Web site, an FTP site, and an e-mail server. Users are complaining that it is very hard to access the FTP site and e-mail because the Web site is using most of the available bandwidth. You cannot move the Web site to another computer for at least 30 days. What can you do to the Web site in the meantime to specify the maximum bandwidth it will be able to use?

A. In the Performance tab of the WWW site properties, disable HTTP keep-alives.

B. In the Performance tab of the WWW site properties, set Performance Tuning for your Web site so that it is tuned for fewer than 10,000 users.

C. In the Performance tab of the WWW site properties, check the Limit Bandwidth Used by this Site and specify the maximum bandwidth the site can use in KB.

D. In the Performance tab of the WWW site properties, check the Enable Bandwidth Throttling option and specify the maximum bandwidth the site can use in KB.

4 You have decided to host a Web site on your internal corporate network as a way of improving corporate communications. You want to make this as easy for users to use as possible. Which of the following services is used to resolve NetBIOS names to IP addresses?

A. DNS

B. DHCP

C. WINS

D. HTML

5   Your company wants to improve corporate communications. Three departments want to host Web sites that will be accessed by up to 20 users at any given time. The requirements you face are that the Web sites will require NTFS security and the ability to connect to an SQL database. What is the minimum platform that the IIS server could be installed on?

   A. NT 4.0 Server

   B. NT 4.0 Workstation

   C. Windows 95 computer

   D. Windows 98 computer

6   You have many users who access your Web site with slow modems, so you want to minimize the number of large documents stored on your Web site. Which utility would you use to see which of your Web site documents were over 32KB in size?

   A. Microsoft Index Server

   B. Microsoft Transaction Server

   C. Microsoft Site Server Express

   D. Microsoft SNMP Service

7   You have a Web site that is configured so that logging is enabled and written to an ODBC log stored on your SQL database. You want to take all of the data that is gathered through the log file and present it as a single page. Which of the following do you implement?

   A. Create an Active Server Page script.

   B. Use an ISAPI script.

   C. Use a CGI script.

   D. Use a Perl script.

8   You are attempting to access an FTP server that has had the default port changed and is configured to use port 1234. From the FTP client, you attempt to access the FTP server and you get the following error message:

    ftp:connect:connection refused.

What is the most likely problem?

   A. The client is attempting to use the default FTP port.

   B. The client does not have access permission to the FTP site.

   C. The client's browser does not support FTP ports above 1000.

   D. When accessing the FTP site, the client should specify FTPS as opposed to FTP.

9   You recently installed the NNTP service on your IIS server. The NNTP service is used to host newsgroups for your corporation. Some connections are local, and others are supported through the Internet. You run Performance Monitor to see the effects of NNTP and find that the Processor Utilization is really low and network bandwidth is really high. What should you do to optimize performance?

   A. Add a faster processor.

   B. Segment the network by adding another network card.

   C. Increase the amount of RAM in your server.

   D. Increase the size of your page file in your server.

10   You are using Index Server to index the contents of your Web site. You currently have about 500MB of data that is being indexed. How much disk space will the index file require?

   A. 50MB

   B. 100MB

   C. 150MB

   D. 200MB

11 Your corporation consists of two subsidiary companies, and each subsidiary wants to host its own Web site. You have a computer that you will install IIS on, but you only have a single IP address. You want to install both Web sites on this computer. What needs to be done to support this configuration? Choose two.

    A. You need to get an extra IP address assigned.

    B. You need to install and configure a DNS server.

    C. You need to install and configure a WINS server.

    D. You need to configure each Web site to use Host Header information.

12 You want to create five Web sites on a single server running IIS. Each virtual server will use the same basic configuration. What is the most efficient way of creating these Web sites?

    A. Use Internet Server Manager.

    B. Use Internet Service Manager (HTML version).

    C. Use WSH.

    D. Create and implement the sites using an ASP script.

13 You are using Index Server to index your Web site. You want to be able to specify which folders are included within the index and which folders are excluded from the index. How do you accomplish this?

    A. Create a catalog that specifies which folders should be indexed.

    B. Create an `.IDQ` file that specifies which folders should be indexed.

    C. Create a master index list that specifies which folders should be indexed.

    D. Create a `.CAT` file that specifies which folders should be indexed.

14   You want users of your FTP site to be able to download files, but not be able to upload files. What permission should be assigned to the FTP site directory?

        A. Read

        B. Write

        C. Execute

        D. List

15   Which of the following configuration options are stored in the metabase? Choose two answers.

        A. Location and configuration of virtual directories

        B. Components that should be loaded into MMC

        C. Logging properties for your Web site

        D. The size and positioning of windows configured for MMC

16   You have a CGI application that has been written with the Perl scripting language. This application has been tested and was run successfully on a test Web site. After you copy the application to the production Web site, it no longer executes properly. What is the most likely cause?

        A. You need to recompile the script.

        B. You must install a Perl interpreter on the production Web site.

        C. You must install a CGI interpreter on the production site.

        D. The client software you are using does not support CGI.

17 Which of the following software options would you use if you wanted to see a graphical map of your Web site and also verify that all of the links were working properly?

    A. Microsoft Index Server

    B. Microsoft Transaction Server

    C. Microsoft Site Server Express

    D. Microsoft SNMP Service

18 You are using SMTP to send and receive e-mail messages through the Internet. Your local domain name is configured as `CORP.COM`, but you want mail messages that are sent from this domain to appear as if they are from the `WIDGET.COM` domain. How do you configure SMTP?

    A. In the Security properties of SMTP, use the Alias option and specify `WIDGET.COM`.

    B. In the Security properties of SMTP, use the Masquerade Domain option and specify `WIDGET.COM`.

    C. In the Security properties of SMTP, use the Smart Alias option and specify `WIDGET.COM`.

    D. In the Security properties of SMTP, use the Masquerade Alias option and specify `WIDGET.COM`.

19 Which of the following configuration options are stored through Microsoft Management Console (MMC) `.MSC` configuration files? Choose all that apply.

    A. Location and configuration of virtual directories

    B. Components that should be loaded into MMC

    C. Logging properties for your Web site

    D. Size and positioning of windows configured for MMC

20   Your Web site is heavily accessed and has been performing sluggishly. You want to minimize the number of open connections to your Web site. How do you configure the Web site?

   A. Disable bandwidth throttling.

   B. Adjust performance tuning to support under 10,000 connections.

   C. Adjust performance tuning to support under 100,000 connections.

   D. Disable HTTP keep-alives.

21   You want to install the SMTP service. Which of the following requirements must be met? Choose all that apply.

   A. You must have a FAT partition.

   B. You must have an NTFS partition.

   C. The SMTP service must be installed on Windows NT Server.

   D. The SMTP service must be installed on Windows NT Workstation.

22   You want to manage your IIS server from your desktop NT Workstation. You have installed Internet Service Manager (HTML). Which of the following requirements must be met in order to remotely administer the IIS server?

   A. You must provide the correct port number for the Administration Web site.

   B. You must use SSL and provide the correct SSL port number that has been configured for the Administration Web site.

   C. You must use secure NetBIOS and provide the correct NetBIOS port that has been configured to support remote communications.

   D. You must use secure TCP/IP and provide the correct TCP/IP port that has been configured to support remote communications.

23   You are running Index Server and want to include a share that is located on a Net-Ware server. You have a NetWare redirector installed. The NetWare share is called \\NWServer\SYS\data. You want to access the NetWare share as a user called Web-Dude. When you try to index the NetWare share, the index fails. What is the most likely problem? Choose two answers.

    A. You must configure the NetWare server as a virtual server in order to index it.

    B. You must create a user on the NetWare server called WebDude who has Read permission to the folder to be indexed.

    C. In order to index this folder, you will be required to have administrative rights to the NetWare server.

    D. You must configure the NetWare folder as a virtual directory in your WWW site in order to index it.

24   You have a computer in the domain CORP called SERVERCORP. SERVERCORP is running IIS and has Index Server installed. There is another computer called SERVERSALES in the SALES domain that contains a share called \\SERVERSALES\SalesData that you want to index. Which of the following requirements must be met? Choose all that apply.

    A. Configure domain CORP to trust domain SALES.

    B. Configure domain SALES to trust domain CORP.

    C. Configure \\SERVERSALES\SalesData as a virtual directory on the Web site located on SERVERCORP.

    D. You cannot index a remote share.

25   You have two folders that contain information that should be published on your Web site. The first folder is C:\InetPub\Wwwroot and the second folder is D:\WebDocs. Users can access pages stored under C:\InetPub\Wwwroot, but cannot access any of the documents stored in D:\WebDocs. What should you do?

    A. Make sure that the anonymous user has permission to access the D:\WebDocs folder.

    B. Create a virtual directory for D:\WebDocs.

    C. Specify that D:\WebDocs be the Web site's home directory.

    D. Create a virtual server for D:\WebDoc.

26   You are attempting to access your corporate Web site. You have a valid NT user name and password, but when you attempt to access the Web site, you receive an error stating that your Web browser does not support the required encryption. What is the most likely problem?

    A. The Web site has been configured to use Windows NT Challenge/Response, and you are using a Web browser other than Internet Explorer 3.0 or higher.

    B. IP address restrictions have been defined, and your IP address is restricted.

    C. You are attempting to log on using the anonymous user account.

    D. You have not installed SSL on your client browser.

27   Which SMTP option allows you to specify which server should be used to route outgoing mail messages?

    A. Masquerade server

    B. Smart host

    C. Default gateway

    D. Default host

28   You are the administrator of your SMTP site. Users complain that it takes too long to receive error messages if the e-mail is undeliverable. Which options should you configure to minimize this problem?

    A. Within SMTP Delivery options, configure Maximum retries.

    B. Within SMTP Delivery options, configure Minimum retries.

    C. Within SMTP Delivery options, configure Retry interval.

    D. Within SMTP Delivery options, configure Smart host.

29   You are using NNTP to host several newsgroups, and you want to maximize access to the newsgroup files. Which of the following configurations offers the best performance?

    A. The newsgroup files should be stored on a single disk.

    B. The newsgroup files should be configured so that they span multiple physical disks.

    C. The newsgroup files should be stored on the same disk that stores the home directory.

    D. The newsgroup files should be stored on a different disk than the disk that stores the home directory.

30   You have just installed a new Web site that is designed for public access via the Internet. You want to track how many hits you have the first day. What is the easiest way to track hits to your site?

    A. Track hits through Performance Monitor counters.

    B. Track hits through Network Monitor counters.

    C. Create an ISAPI filter that tracks hits to your Web site.

    D. Use the ASP Page Counter component to track hits to your Web site.

31 Which of the following services would be used to support newsgroups and the ability to post and moderate news items over the Internet?

    A. News Server

    B. NNTP

    C. POP3

    D. SMTP

32 How is the configuration information for IIS stored?

    A. Through MMC

    B. Through the registry

    C. Through the metabase

    D. Through HTMLA

33 You have created a document called `welcome.htm`. You want this to be the document that is returned if a client accesses your Web site without requesting a specific document. How do you configure this?

    A. In the Web site Document property tab, add `welcome.htm` to the Default Document section.

    B. Delete the `default.htm` document and rename `welcome.htm` to `default.htm`.

    C. Delete the `index.htm` document and rename `welcome.htm` to `index.htm`.

    D. In the Web site Defaults property tab, add `welcome.htm` to the Default Document section.

34   You have configured the Directory Security of your Web site so that IP restrictions are set as follows:

- The Granted Access button is selected.
- You add the following IP address: 162.48.6.21.
- You add the following IP network: 172.54.32.0 (255.255.255.0).

Which of the following statements are true?

A. The IP address 162.48.6.21 is restricted from accessing your Web site.

B. The IP address 162.48.6.21 is granted access to your Web site.

C. The IP network 172.54.32.0 is restricted from accessing your Web site.

D. The IP network 172.54.32.0 is granted access to your Web site.

35   Users access your FTP site through anonymous access. The anonymous access account uses the NT account IUSR_WebServer. The user password for IUSR_WebServer has been changed through User Manager for Domains, and now users cannot access your FTP site. What would you do to fix this problem and avoid it in the future?

A. Edit the IUSR_WebServer account through ISM to reflect the new password.

B. Edit the IUSR_WebServer account through ISM (HTML version) to reflect the new password.

C. In the Security Accounts property tab of the FTP site, check the Enable Automatic Password Synchronization option.

D. In User Manager for Domains within IUSR_WebServer's user properties, check the Enable Automatic Password Synchronization option.

36   What folder is used to store SMTP messages that are returned because they are undeliverable?

   A. Badmail

   B. NDRmail

   C. Errormail

   D. NDRsmtp

37   Which software component would you install if you wanted to build reliability into your database transactions?

   A. Microsoft Index Server

   B. Microsoft Transaction Server

   C. Microsoft Transaction Tracking Server

   D. Microsoft SMTP Service

38   You have a Web site that contains highly sensitive corporate data. You want to specify that data be encrypted as it is transmitted across the Internet. Which option must be configured?

   A. You must configure the C2 authentication option.

   B. You must configure the Windows NT Challenge/Response authentication method.

   C. You must configure SSL encryption.

   D. You must configure C2/E2 encryption.

39 You have configured your FTP site to allow only Read access. The FTP site also allows anonymous access through the IUSR_WebServer user account. You notice that the following NTFS permissions have been applied:

Everyone: Full Control

IUSR_WebServer: Change

Guests: Write

What access will users to your FTP site have?

    A. Read

    B. Write

    C. Change

    D. Full Control

40 You want to require that user passwords are encrypted when they are transmitted over the Internet to access your Web site. Which authentication methods support this? Choose all that apply.

    A. Basic

    B. DES

    C. Public key

    D. Windows NT Challenge/Response

41 Which of the following options can be used to specify which users can access your FTP site?

    A. The IP address of a user

    B. The network IP address and subnet mask for a specific range of IP addresses

    C. The NetBIOS computer name of a user

    D. The domain name the user is from

42   Your IIS server hosts multiple virtual servers. The IIS server is configured to use a single IP address. Each virtual server is configured to use Host Header information. You do not use DNS. What must be configured?

   A. You must configure a HOSTS file.

   B. You must configure a LMHOST file.

   C. You must configure a DOMAIN file.

   D. You must configure a DNS file.

43   Which of the following utilities can be used to manage IIS? Choose all that apply.

   A. ISM

   B. ISM (HTML)

   C. WSH

   D. WSH (HTML)

44   You want to configure a virtual directory for your WWW site that points to a share located on a Windows 95 computer. What information is required?

   A. The IP address of the Windows 95 computer

   B. A valid user name and password

   C. The URL of the Windows 95 computer

   D. You cannot create virtual directories on Windows 95 computers.

45   You have a Web site that has been running for three months. You have recently had security problems and have implemented Windows NT Challenge/Response for authentication and SSL for data encryption. Users are complaining that access is now very slow. What do you do?

    A. Add RAM

    B. Upgrade to a faster processor

    C. Increase the size of your page file

    D. Get a faster disk I/O channel

46   You manage a Web site that has both public and private data stored on it. The private data requires data encryption when it is sent over the Internet. However, you don't want to degrade performance any more than is necessary. What do you do?

    A. Require SSL services on the folders that contain the private data.

    B. Require SSL services for the entire Web site.

    C. Require DES services on the folders that contain the private data.

    D. Require DES services for the entire Web site.

47   You want to apply an ISAPI filter file called TEST.DLL. What permission should be applied so that users can properly access the .DLL file?

    A. Read

    B. Execute

    C. Script

    D. Write

48   You copy an ASP script file from another server. The ASP script file does not properly execute on your Web site. What permission should be applied?

    A. Read

    B. Execute

    C. Script

    D. Write

49   Which of the following services are supported by IIS 4.0? Choose all that apply.

    A. WWW

    B. Gopher

    C. FTP

    D. NNTP

50   Which of the following IIS services is used to transfer files between a server and a client?

    A. WWW

    B. Gopher

    C. FTP

    D. NNTP

51   Your IIS server has a virtual folder that resides on an SQL server. When you try to access a document located on the virtual folder, you get the following error message:

```
Microsoft OLE DB Provider for ODBC Drivers error "80004005" [Microsoft] [ODBC
Driver Manager] Data source not found and no default driver specified.
```

What is the most likely cause of this error?

    A. Proper permissions have not been defined for SQL access.

    B. The file is configured for single-user access and is already in use.

    C. There is not a valid local account that can be used to log on to the SQL server.

    D. The ODBC driver you are using is missing or corrupt.

FINAL REVIEW

52 Your IIS server has a virtual folder that resides on an SQL server. When you try to access a document located on the virtual folder, you get the following error message:

```
Microsoft OLE DB Provider for ODBC Drivers error "80004005" [Microsoft] [ODBC
Microsoft SQL Driver] Logon Failed
```

What is the most likely cause of this error?

   A. Proper permissions have not been defined for SQL access.

   B. The file is configured for single-user access and is already in use.

   C. There is not a valid local account that can be used to log on to the SQL server.

   D. The ODBC driver you are using is missing or corrupt.

53 Your IIS server has a virtual folder that resides on an SQL server. When you try to access a document located on the virtual folder, you get the following error message:

```
Microsoft OLE DB Provider for ODBC Drivers error "80004005" [Microsoft] [ODBC
Microsoft SQL Driver] [dbnmpntw] ConnectionOpen (create file)
```

What are the two most likely causes of this error?

   A. Proper permissions have not been defined for SQL access.

   B. The file is configured for single-user access and is already in use.

   C. There is not a valid local account that can be used to log on to the SQL server.

   D. The ODBC driver you are using is missing or corrupt.

54 Your IIS server has a virtual folder that resides on a SQL server. When you try to access a document located on the virtual folder, you get the following error message:

```
Microsoft OLE DB Provider for ODBC Drivers error "80004005" [Microsoft] [ODBC
Microsoft Access 97 Driver] The Microsoft Jet database engine cannot open file
'(unknown)'. It is already opened exclusively by another user, or you need per-
mission to view its data.
```

What is the most likely cause of this error?

    A. Proper permissions have not been defined for SQL access.

    B. The file is configured for single-user access and is already in use.

    C. There is not a valid local account that can be used to log on to the SQL server.

    D. The ODBC driver you are using is missing or corrupt.

55   You are testing a new ISAPI DLL. What is the best way to test this on IIS 4.0 without affecting other services and applications?

    A. Install another instance of IIS on the computer and run the ISAPI DLL on the secondary instance of IIS.

    B. Rename the `.DLL` extension to `.SAF`. This will cause the file to run in a protected memory area.

    C. Check the Run in Separate Memory Space option in the Home Directory tab of the Web site.

    D. Since everything runs in the same memory space, you should install IIS on a separate computer and test the ISAPI DLL on the separate computer.

56   How do you configure the IIS Web site to use ISAPI DLLs?

    A. In the Home Directory tab of the Web site, select Configuration and add the extension and file pathname in the App Mapping tab.

    B. Add the mapping for the ISAPI DLL through the metabase.

    C. Add the mapping for the ISAPI DLL through the registry.

    D. Add the mapping for the ISAPI DLL through the ISAPI Manager.

57   How do you configure Index Server so that Master Merges are executed with higher frequency?

   A. Decrease the MasterMergeTime value in the registry.

   B. Decrease the MaxIndexes value in the registry.

   C. Increase the MasterMergeTime value in the registry.

   D. Increase the MaxIndexes value in the registry.

58   When you execute a query in Index Server, what extension is used on the query output file?

   A. `.HTM`

   B. `.IDC`

   C. `.IDQ`

   D. `.HTX`

59   What are the three possible locations for a virtual directory?

   A. A directory located on the IIS server computer

   B. A directory located on another computer referenced through a UNC path

   C. A redirection to a URL

   D. A directory located on a UNIX server using an FQDN

60   What three items make up a Web site's unique identity?

   A. IP address

   B. Subnet mask

   C. Port number

   D. Host header name

APPENDIX

Study Question and Sample Test Answers

Unit 1 Answers

Study Questions

Microsoft Internet Services

1. WWW Service

    FTP Service

    SMTP Service

    NNTP Service

2. Microsoft Management Console

3. Microsoft Certificate Server

4. Microsoft Transaction Server

5. SMTP Service

6. True

7. 40

    Explanation: Although the typical index size is around 30 percent, it can be as large as 40 percent.

8. NNTP Service

9. Site Server Express—Content Analyzer

10. Site Server Express—Report Writer

Implementation of Internet Services

11. False

Explanation: When you install IIS on a Windows 95 computer, you do not have full functionality of IIS, and you are actually using Peer Web Services. Index Server is not supported on the Windows 95 platform at all.

12. False

Explanation: ODBC logging is only available if IIS is installed on NT Server.

13. Windows NT Server

Windows NT Workstation

Windows 95

14. Peer Web Services

15. Use DNS or a HOSTS file to resolve host names to IP addresses.

Configure each virtual server by specifying, within the property-sheet configuration box, which Host Header Name it will use.

IIS Security Strategies

16. IUSR_*computername*

17. False

Explanation: Only clients using Internet Explorer 3.0 or later can authenticate to an IIS Server that has been configured to use the Windows NT Challenge/Response authentication method.

18. Anonymous

Basic

Windows NT Challenge/Response

Client Certificate Mapping

19. Client Certificate Mapping

20. True

21. False

22. True

23. public, private

Sample Test

1-1 B

1-2 C, E

1-3 D

1-4 C

1-5 B, C

1-6 B

1-7 B

1-8 D

1-9 B

1-10 B

1-11 B

> **Explanation:** Because you have a mixture of client software, you cannot use Windows NT Challenge/Response, so the next level of authentication security would be Basic.

Unit 2 Answers

Study Questions

IIS Installation

1. TCP/IP

2. True

3. IUSR_*computername*

4. metabase

5. False

   Explanation: In order to take advantage of NTFS security features, it is recommended that you use NTFS, but it is not required.

6. Microsoft Management Console

7. Content Index
   FTP Publishing Service
   IIS Admin Service
   Microsoft NNTP Service
   Microsoft SMTP Service
   MSDTC
   World Wide Web Publishing Service

8. Performance Monitor

9. Microsoft Windows NT 4.0 Option Pack

10. True

    Explanation: The SMTP protocol requires that it be installed onto an NTFS partition to add security to mail messages.

11. Minimum

    Typical

    Custom

Managing FTP

12. True

    Explanation: Hosting multiple FTP sites on a single installation of an IIS is referred to as using virtual servers.

13. Internet Service Manager

14. False

    Explanation: If you customize a specific FTP site, the specific configuration will overwrite the configuration specified by master properties.

15. UNIX

    MS-DOS

16. True

17. A virtual directory is a directory that is not a part of the site home directory. A virtual directory can be referenced as a local path, a UNC name, or a URL.

18. You create virtual servers when a single IIS server hosts more than one FTP or WWW site. This is transparent to external users.

19. Specific IP address

    IP network address and subnet mask

    Domain name

20. Welcome message

Exit message

Maximum connections message

21. Administrators

22. Read

Write

Log Access

23. True

Managing WWW

24. Bandwidth throttling

25. HTTP Header

26. Local directory

Local network share through UNC

Redirection to a URL

27. Home Directory (configuration button)

28. Read

Explanation: The most restrictive permission will be applied.

29. Read

Explanation: The most restrictive permission will be applied.

30. From the Home Directory property tab, you can specify Application Settings. One of the Application Settings options allows you to specify that you want to Run Applications in Own Memory Space.

31. From the Home Directory property tab, you can specify Access Permissions and Content Control. One of the Content Control options allows you to specify Index This Directory.

32. Users will be required to specify a document when accessing your Web site.

33. WWW Site Property, Connection Timeout value

34. WWW Site Property, Enable Logging

35. False

    Explanation: Performance tuning is based on the number of hits your Web site is expected to receive each day.

36. HTTP keep-alives are used to maintain client connections by maintaining an open connection to your server. This allows clients to make new requests without having to reestablish a new connection.

37. ASP or IDC scripts

38. NT binary files including `.EXE` and `.DLL` files.

39. Allow anonymous access

    Basic authentication

    Windows NT Challenge/Response

40. You would use Basic authentication if you were not using anonymous access and you were not sure what client browsers would be used.

41. True

Using Microsoft Management Console

42. True

Administration Methods of IIS

43. Internet Service Manager snap-in

Internet Service Manager (HTML)

Windows Scripting Host

44. SSL

45. Windows Scripting Host

Installing and Configuring Certificate Server

46. True

Installing and Configuring SMTP Service

47. False

Explanation: You can specify the maximum number of retries, but this is a finite number and cannot be configured for unlimited.

48. The Delivery property tab allows you to specify maximum hop count, which determines the maximum number of hops a message can take.

49. Smart host

Installing and Configuring NNTP Service

50. Through NNTP Settings, limit post size

51. Directory security

52. False

Explanation: You can configure the NNTP site to allow other servers to pull articles, but you cannot specify that articles be forwarded.

Installing and Configuring Site Server Express

53. Content Analyzer

54. Posting Acceptor

55. Report Writer

Sample Test

2-1   B

2-2   D

2-3   B, D

2-4   B, C

2-5   C

2-6   B, D

2-7   A

2-8   B

2-9   C

2-10   A

2-11   A

2-12   B

2-13   A

2-14   B

2-15   C

2-16   A, B

Unit 3 Answers

Study Questions

Creating and Sharing Directories

1. NTFS

2. False

   Explanation: In the case that a resource defined through IIS is located on an NTFS partition, the more restrictive permission will apply. In this case, NTFS permissions and IIS permissions must be defined.

3. Read

   Explanation: In the case that a resource defined through IIS is located on an NTFS partition, the most restrictive permission applies, in this case the IIS permission.

4. False

   Explanation: Auditing can only be implemented on NTFS partitions.

5. True

6. False

   Explanation: You can create a remote virtual directory on a FAT or NTFS folder.

7. Read

8. Administrators

   Server Operators

Virtual Directories

9. False

   Explanation: IIS supports an unlimited number of virtual directories.

10. A directory on the local IIS computer

    A remote directory referenced through a UNC path

    A redirection to a URL

11. True

12. A valid user account and password for the remote computer

13. False

    Explanation: The home directory must be a local directory to your computer.

14. Read, which allows a user to read or download files

    Write, which allows Web clients to modify or upload files to your Web site

15. In the virtual directory content control, check the Directory Browsing Allowed box.

16. In the virtual directory content control, you can check the Index this Directory box, which would cause the directory to be included within an Index Server index.

17. None

    Script

    Execute

18. Execute

19. Script

20. True

21. False

    Explanation: If you were pointing to a virtual directory, you would use a UNC name as opposed to a URL.

22. `rootdrive:\InetPub\wwwroot`

Virtual Servers

23. HOSTS

24. Fully Qualified Domain Names (FQDN)

25. IP address

Port number

Host header name

26. A virtual server exists when multiple Web sites exist on a single server running IIS.

27. LMHOSTS

28. False

Explanation: If you use host header names, you can use a single IP address with multiple virtual servers.

29. The Web browser must be HTTP 1.1 compliant.

Scripts with WWW and FTP Services

30. WSH allows you to automate common tasks through a script file, as opposed to using Internet Service Manager.

31. Cscript

32. Wscript

Microsoft Content Analyzer

33. True

34. Tree view

Cyberbolic view

35. Map from a URL

Map from a file system

36. True

37. Object statistics

Status summary

Map statistics

Server summary

Microsoft NNTP Service

38. The NNTP service is used to support client-server newsgroups.

39. True

40. Microsoft Internet Mail and News

41. True

42. Expiration date that defines how old articles can be before they are deleted

How much disk space a newsgroup can use

Certificate Server and Certificates

43. CertReq

44. True

Index Server and Web Sites

45. 40MB

Explanation: The index can take between 30 and 40 percent of the size of the corpus.

46. Add more memory

Upgrade the processor

47. True

MIME Types

48. To tell a Web browser which application should process a file, based on the file's extension.

Sample Test

3-1 D

3-2 D

3-3 D

3-4 B

3-5 A

3-6 A, B, D

Explanation: You can only reference a remote computer using an existing share. If the folder has not been shared, you cannot reference it with a direct path.

3-7 D

3-8 B

3-9 A, C, D

3-10 D

3-11 C

3-12 A, B

Explanation: All servers can point to the same directory, and the host header is only necessary if two servers share the same IP and port numbers.

3-13 A, B, C

3-14 B

3-15 C

> **Explanation:** In cases A, B, and D, the user will never get to the 404 stage. The browser will be unable to find the destination system.

3-16 B

> **Explanation:** SSL will always add an additional load on the IIS, but only because of encryption on the server side.

3-17 A

3-18 C, D

3-19 C

3-20 B

> **Explanation:** All three servers must be able to answer for the domain name by linking the IP address to them. Otherwise, the three servers won't share the load.

Unit 4 Answers

Study Questions

ODBC Connections

1. ADO

2. ODBC

3. Data Source
    ODBC

4. Text

5. TCP/IP

   Named Pipes

6. TCP/IP Sockets

7. False

   Explanation: Only clear text user names and passwords will be forwarded to a remote server.

8. TCP/IP Sockets

   Named Pipes

Index Server

9. Data Query

   HTML

10. HTML extension

11. True

    Explanation: If no records are returned, there is no data for the detail section to process.

12. ActiveX

13. SCRIPT LANGUAGE

14. FORM ACTION

    INPUT TYPE

15. Execute

16. unlimited

17. 40

18. True

Explanation: ODBC can handle unlimited connections.

19. False

Explanation: Most legacy computers are not ODBC compliant.

Sample Test

4-1 A

4-2 A, C, D

4-3 D

4-4 A, B, D

4-5 B

4-6 A, C

4-7 B

Explanation: The optimal disk space for an index server is 40 percent of the corpus size, or 60MB, for a total disk requirement of 210MB.

4-8 D

4-9 B, D

Explanation: Persistent indexes are disk based, and only B and D are stored on disk.

4-10 B, C

4-11 B

4-12 C

4-13 D

Unit 5 Answers

Study Questions

Server-Side Scripting

1. False

2. Active Server Pages (ASP)
   Common Gateway Interface (CGI)

Active Server Pages

3. a browser
   an .ASP

4. server-side
   HTML

5. Active Server

6. source

7. server-side
   client-side

8. event

9. syntax
   runtime

10. HTML
    .HTM
    .HTML

11. an action

12. <% %>

   Explanation: The delimiter symbols mark the script commands for the scripting engine.

13. delimiters

14. VBScript

15. False

   Explanation: Only VBScript and JScript are installed by default.

16. True

   Explanation: Active Server uses the module concept. If a scripting engine is added, the language can then be supported. VBScript and JScript are the defaults.

Common Gateway Interface (CGI)

17. Perl

18. CGI-BIN

19. separate

20. True

21. Script

   Execute

ISAPI Applications

22. scaleability

23. extensions

   filters

24. merged

25. server

26. cached

27. master

a sequential

28. master

site

29. False

Explanation: This is configured by IIS, not the DLL. IIS can specify that the ASP ISAPI DLL is responsible for other file extensions.

30. WWW

Sample Test

5-1 A, B

Explanation: IIS does not support Perl without the additional installation of a Perl Interpreter.

5-2 B

5-3 C

5-4 C

5-5 D

Explanation: While all of these are compelling reasons, Active Server's multithreading in a single memory space gives it the best scaleability.

5-6 A

5-7 B

5-8 C

5-9 A, B, C, D

Explanation: ISAPI filters can be used for many functions. The applications are only limited by programming ability.

Unit 6 Answers

Study Questions

Maintaining Log Files

1. Microsoft IIS Log Format

   NCSA Common Log File Format

   W3C Extended Log File Format

   ODBC Logging

2. W3C Extended Log File Format

3. True

4. ODBC Logging

   Explanation: Because ODBC Logging requires a connection to an ODBC database, this method of logging requires more overhead than the other logging methods.

5. False

   Explanation: You can use NCSA logging on WWW sites, but it is not supported for FTP sites.

6. `%winroot%\System32\LogFiles`

7. Usage Import

8. True

9. Report Writer

10. False

    Explanation: Before you can access data in Report Writer, the data must first be extracted through Usage Import.

11. True

12. True

Monitoring IIS Performance through Performance Monitor

13. Object

    Counter

    Instance

14. Chart

    Alert

    Log

    Report

15. Internet Information Services Global object

16. Web Services object

17. FTP Services object

18. Not Found Errors/Sec

19. Bytes Total/Sec

20. Current Blocked Async I/O Requests

21. Alert

Analyzing General Performance Problems

22. Memory

    CPU

    Disk access

    Network access

23. False

    Explanation: This counter should be at least 4.2MB. If Available Bytes shows 2MB of memory available, then you might have a memory bottleneck.

24. Add more physical memory to the computer

25. %Processor Time

26. %Network Utilization

27. 90

28. True

Optimizing Performance of IIS

29. False

    Explanation: ISAPI applications are less memory- and CPU-intensive than CGI applications.

30. Bandwidth throttling

31. True

32. True

Optimizing Performance of Index Server

33. Total # of documents

34. False

Explanation: You should only have one persistent index for optimal performance.

35. True

36. True

Optimizing Performance of SMTP

37. Local Queue Length

38. Remote Queue Length

Optimizing Performance of NNTP

39. NNTP Commands

NNTP Server

40. Bytes Total/Sec

41. Current Connections

Optimizing Web Sites with Content Analyzer

42. wmp

43. Update

44. False

Explanation: The Content Analyzer can only identify objects over 32KB.

Sample Test

6-1   A

6-2   A

6-3   D

6-4	D
6-5	D
6-6	B
6-7	D
6-8	A

Explanation: Of the listed options, SSL data encryption techniques cause the greatest resource consumption and therefore the largest performance loss.

6-9	C
6-10	D
6-11	B
6-12	C

Explanation: When using virtual memory, the process of paging to the disk actually slows the Index Server, as it would any application.

6-13	A, D, E
6-14	A
6-15	A, C

Explanation: Content Analyzer is best suited for graphical views of Web sites, including page links and linked objects.

Unit 7 Answers

Study Questions

Troubleshooting IIS Configuration Problems

1. 80

2. 21

3. By specifying MIME maps, you configure Web browsers so that they can view files that have been configured with different formats (extensions).

4. False

Explanation: You can configure any document to be the default document that is returned through the Web site Document property tab.

5. By starting the request with HTTPS:// instead of HTTP://

6. A client with a restricted IP address would see this message if you configured IP address restrictions and he or she attempted to access your Web site.

7. False

Explanation: If you are using multiple virtual servers in IIS that all share a single IP address, you must use a DNS server or a HOSTS file for IP address resolution.

8. Each virtual server must be configured to use host header names.

9. The HOSTS file is used for IP to domain name resolution and it is located on each client computer that requires IP to domain name resolution.

Resolving Security and Resource Access Problems

10. False

Explanation: This is a trick question. Even though the users will not be prompted for a user name and password, they are still using an NT account to authenticate. By default, this user account is called IUSR_*computername*.

11. Read

Explanation: Users will be bound by the most restrictive permission that has been applied, either to the Web folder or to the NTFS permissions.

12. True

13. Execute (includes Script permission) specifies that you can run script engines and NT binary files which include `.EXE` and `.DLL` extensions. You would apply Execute to folders with these types of files.

14. Script permission allows you to run script engines, even if no Execute permissions have been set. This permission should be used for folders that contain ASP scripts or IDC scripts. It is also used to allow scripts to be executed via installed script engines without allowing executables and/or DLLs to be executed.

Resolving Index Server Query Problems

15. Log on Locally

16. In the Home Directory tab of the WWW site, there is a check box that, if checked, includes the folder in an index. If this box is not checked, then the folder is excluded from the index.

Setup Issues for IIS Installation

17. 4.0

18. 3

19. 4.01

20. False

    Explanation: If you were running Alpha or Beta versions of IIS 4.0, they must be removed prior to installing the current release of IIS 4.0.

21. Netlogon

    Server

    Workstation

    Computer Browser

22. True

Troubleshooting with WebMap

23. Tree view

Cyberbolic view

24. Site Server Express using the Content Analyzer feature

Resolving ODBC Connection Errors

25. This message is caused by the user account (usually IUSR_*computername*) having insufficient NT access rights to the ODBC database. You should check NTFS and share permissions.

26. This message is most commonly caused by the GLOBAL.ASA file not being properly executed. Check that this file is in the Application Root for IIS 4.0 and that users have Execute permission for this folder.

27. This message is caused by the SQL server denying access to the account that is attempting to authenticate and access the SQL server. Check that the SQL account and NT user account (used by IIS) and password match. Make sure that the IIS connection to the SQL server maps the user's name properly.

28. The database file you are attempting to access is configured for single-user use only, and the file is already open.

29. This message is usually caused by incorrect permissions being applied. This is especially common if the database is remote and you are trying to access it via a UNC path. This is most common if you access the database with the IUSR_*computername* account. This account is local to the IIS server, and one solution is to create this account on the remote computer that contains the remote database. In addition to duplicating the user names, the passwords must match on both accounts.

Sample Test

7-1   B

7-2   A

7-3   A, B, D

Explanation: If the virtual folder is on a remote server, then you must configure a domain account that has the user right Log on Locally, and the user account must have access permissions to all of the folders that will be indexed.

7-4   B, C, F

7-5   A, B, C, D

7-6   B, D

7-7   B

7-8   A

7-9   C

Explanation: Script allows you to run script engines, even if no execute permissions have been set. This permission should be used for folders that contain ASP scripts or IDC scripts.

7-10   D

Explanation: Execute (includes script permissions) specifies that you can run script engines and NT binary files which include `.EXE` and `.DLL` extensions.

Unit 8 Answers

Final Review

1.   B

Explanation: In this case, you have to use Basic authentication, since you support multiple types of Web browsers. The Windows NT Challenge/Response authentication method would require that all users use Internet Explorer 3.0 or later as their Web browser. A valid NT user account name is required because it has been specified that this is the only authentication method (you would need to enable Allow Anonymous Access to permit anonymous users to log on). With the Basic authentication method, passwords and data are sent as clear text.

2.   B

Explanation: The client must use a Web browser that supports SSL services. The HTTPS protocol is then used to provide SSL support that is not available through the HTTP protocol.

3.   D

Explanation: Performance tuning is used to maximize performance of your Web site. You can do this based on how many hits you expect, through Bandwidth Throttling, or HTTP Keep-Alives. Bandwidth Throttling is used to specify the maximum bandwidth that can be used by the Web site. This option is useful if your server hosts other sites or services that also can consume high bandwidth. HTTP Keep-Alives are used by clients to keep open connections so that connections do not have to be reopened with each new client request. The C answer is a made-up option.

4.   C

Explanation: WINS is used to dynamically map NetBIOS computer names to IP addresses. DNS is used to resolve IP addresses to domain names that are used when connecting to the Internet (but could also be used on an intranet). DHCP would be used for automatic IP assignment. HTML is the protocol used to produce Web documents that will be accessed through HTTP.

5.   A

Explanation: You have to use NT since it is the only operating system that supports NTFS security. You must use NT Server in this case, because you require ODBC connectivity, and NT Workstation only supports 10 concurrent connections.

6.   C

Explanation: Through the Content Analyzer component of Site Server Express, you can perform a quick search to find all resources on your Web site that are over 32KB in size.

7.   A

Explanation: ASP is used to provide dynamic Web content. A benefit of ASP is that it allows access to ODBC data sources.

8.   A

Explanation: The client needs to specify that they will use port 1234 to access the FTP site. Through Internet Explorer, you would type `ftp://path:1234`.

9.   B

Explanation: If network bandwidth is saturated, you should add another network adapter card.

10.   D

Explanation: The index file can require up to 40 percent of the corpus size. The corpus is the sum of all documents that will be included within the index.

11.   B, D

Explanation: With IIS 4, you are able to create virtual servers on a single computer using a single IP address. In order for this to be properly configured, you must provide address resolution through DNS and configure each Web site to use Host Header information. Host Headers are used for host name to IP address resolution.

12.   C

Explanation: You could create the Web sites through ISM or ISM (HTML version), but Windows Scripting Host (WSH) lets you automate the creation of virtual servers through the use of script files.

13.   B

Explanation: There are two ways to specify which folders should be indexed through Index Server. The first way is to use Internet Service Manager and, in the virtual directories property box, check the Index this Directory option. The second method is to use an Internet Data Query (IDQ) file to specify the parameters of your index.

14.   A

Explanation: FTP offers two permissions, Read and Write. Read allows you to download files and Write allows you to upload files. This assumes that more restrictive NTFS permissions have not been applied.

15.   A, C

Explanation: The metabase is used to store IIS configuration information. It is used instead of the registry as it is faster and more scaleable. Information stored in the metabase includes Web site properties, FTP and HTTP properties, logging properties, virtual server and virtual directory properties, and configuration, file, filer, and SSL properties.

16.   B

Explanation: No default CGI scripting language is supplied with NT Server or IIS. In order to support Perl, a Perl interpreter must be installed.

17.   C

Explanation: You can use the Content Analyzer option within Site Server Express to map the contents of your Web site. You can also see which links have been defined and verify that all links are in working order.

18.   B

Explanation: Masquerade domains specify that you want the local domain name to be replaced in the Mail From line with the domain name that you specify as the masquerade domain.

19.   B, D

Explanation: MMC console files do not contain any data. They simply contain preference items for the MMC interface, such as MMC snap-ins, which are used and screen preferences. This makes them small in size.

20. D

Explanation: HTTP keep-alives are used by clients to maintain open connections to your server. This allows a client to make new requests more quickly, but degrades performance on the Web site by maintaining excessive client connections.

21. B, C

Explanation: In order to provide a secure environment for SMTP, you must use an NTFS partition. The SMTP service requires that it be installed onto an NT Server running IIS 4.0.

22. A

Explanation: When Internet Service Manager (HTML) is used, it accesses a Web site called Administration Web site. This site is assigned a random port number between 2,000 and 9,999. In order to access the Web site for remote administration, you must first specify the correct port number that was randomly assigned, then be able to authenticate as an administrator or Web site operator.

23. B, D

Explanation: NetWare folders can be included within an index as long as you can access the NetWare folder (through a NetWare user account with valid folder permissions), and as long as the folder is configured as a virtual directory within your Web site.

24. B, C

Explanation: In order to index the remote share, you must first create virtual directories for the remote share. You must also configure the proper trust relationship.

25. B

Explanation: If you want to publish from a folder that is not part of the home directory, you must create a virtual directory.

26. A

Explanation: If you specify that you will use the Windows NT Challenge/Response authentication method, then users must use Internet Explorer 3.0 or higher as their Web browser and be able to authenticate using a valid NT user account and password.

27. B

Explanation: To configure the server that will be used for routing outgoing SMTP messages, you access the Delivery tab of the SMTP site and configure smart host.

28. A, C

Explanation: Before a message is considered undeliverable, the system will attempt to deliver it based on the maximum retries and retry interval that have been defined. By default, SMTP is configured to retry sending the message 40 times at an interval of every 60 minutes. By decreasing these numbers, an NDR (non-delivery report) will be generated more quickly.

29. B

Explanation: By placing the NNTP files on multiple physical disks, you are able to take advantage of multiple disk I/O channels, thus improving performance. It doesn't make any difference if the newsgroup files are on the same disk that the home folder is on.

30. D

Explanation: Install the ASP Page Counter as a quick and easy method to track hits to your Web site.

31. B

Explanation: NNTP is Microsoft's software for creating, managing, and moderating newsgroups. Through NNTP, users can post articles, view articles, and participate in newsgroup discussions.

32. C

Explanation: The metabase is used to store all IIS configuration parameters. It is used instead of the registry because it is more efficient and uses less disk space.

33. A

Explanation: In the Documents property tab of your Web site, you can select to display a default document. If this option is not enabled, then users are required to request a specific document when accessing the Web site. You can specify any document you want.

34.   A, C

Explanation: When you select the Granted to option, you specify that all nodes are granted access to your Web site with the exception of the IP addresses you list.

35.   C

Explanation: In order to synchronize the passwords used by the NT user account and the anonymous user account used by FTP, you must check Enable Automatic Password Synchronization. If you manually change the user password through ISM, you will need to manually manage the passwords each time they are changed through ISM or User Manager for Domains.

36.   A

Explanation: By default, any mail that is returned as undeliverable is stored in the Bad-mail directory.

37.   B

Explanation: With Microsoft Transaction Server, you can break a single transaction into multiple components. If a failure occurs during a transaction and a partial transaction is in progress, the transaction is rolled back to a known checkpoint. This process is used to minimize database corruption.

38.   C

Explanation: Authentication is used to specify how passwords will be transmitted across the Internet. You use SSL to specify whether or not the data will be encrypted as it is transmitted.

39.   A

Explanation: The users will be bound by the most restrictive permission. In this case, the FTP permission of Read is the most restrictive permission.

40.   D

Explanation: You can only choose from three authentication methods: Anonymous, Basic, and Windows NT Challenge/Response. Of these three options, only Windows NT Challenge/Response offers password encryption services.

41. A, B, D

Explanation: You can grant or deny access to users of your FTP site based on IP address, IP network address, or domain name. If you specify access based on domain name, you must have DNS reverse lookup capabilities.

42. A

Explanation: The HOSTS file is used to map domain names to IP addresses. You can use this file in place of DNS.

43. A, B, C

Explanation: You can use Internet Service Manager (ISM) or ISM (HTML) to manage your IIS server. In addition, you can use Windows Scripting Host (WSH) to automate IIS tasks through the use of scripts.

44. B

Explanation: Any time you create a virtual directory using a share, you must provide a valid user name and password.

45. B

Explanation: SSL has a negative impact on performance since all data must be encrypted and decrypted. To help improve performance, you should upgrade your processor.

46. A

Explanation: In order to support data encryption for your Web site, you must use SSL. However, you should only use SSL services on folders that require data encryption. Public folders should not use this service as it impacts performance in a negative manner.

47. B

Explanation: In order to process ISAPI filters, users require Execute permission.

48. C

Explanation: In order to process ASP scripts, users require Script permission.

49. A, C, D

Explanation: The Gopher service was supported by earlier implementations of IIS, but because it is obsolete, support for it was dropped in IIS 4.0

50. C

Explanation: FTP is used to transfer files between an FTP server and an FTP client.

51. A

Explanation: This message is most commonly caused by the GLOBAL.ASA file not being properly executed. Check that this file is in the Application Root for IIS 4.0 and that users have Execute permission for this folder.

52. C

Explanation: This message is caused when the SQL server denies access to the account that is attempting to authenticate and access the SQL server. Check that the SQL account and NT user account (used by IIS) and password match. Make sure that the IIS connection to the SQL server maps the user's name properly.

53. A, C

Explanation: This message is usually caused by a denial of access. This could be from incorrect permissions being applied. Another common cause is if the database is remote and you are trying to access it via a UNC path. This might happen if you access the database with the IUSR_*computername* account. This account is local to the IIS server, and one solution is to create this account on the remote computer that contains the remote database. In addition to having duplicate user names, the passwords must match on both accounts.

54. A

Explanation: This message is caused by the user account (usually IUSR_*computername*) having insufficient NT access rights to the ODBC database. You should check NTFS and share permissions.

55. C

Explanation: Within the home directory tab of your Web site, you can configure ISAPI DLLs to run in their own memory space. This can be used to provide fault tolerance when the ISAPI DLL has not been tested. This does require additional memory overhead.

56. A

Explanation: You set up mappings for ISAPI DLLs through the Home Directory tab of your Web site. This does not require you to edit the registry or the metabase.

57. B

Explanation: This is configured through the registry. You specify that MaxIndexes use a smaller value to force Master Merges more frequently.

58. D

Explanation: The file that is generated when a query is issued has an .HTX extension.

59. A, B, C

Explanation: Virtual directories can be local to the computer (for example, in another folder besides the home folder), they can be on a remote computer on the same network using a UNC path (you would need to specify a user account that is local to the computer), or they can be made available through a redirection using a valid URL (again, you would have to have access permissions).

60. A, C, D

Explanation: Each Web site has a unique, three-part identity it uses to receive and to respond to requests. This is made up of an IP address, port number, and host header name. This combination allows virtual servers to be uniquely identified.

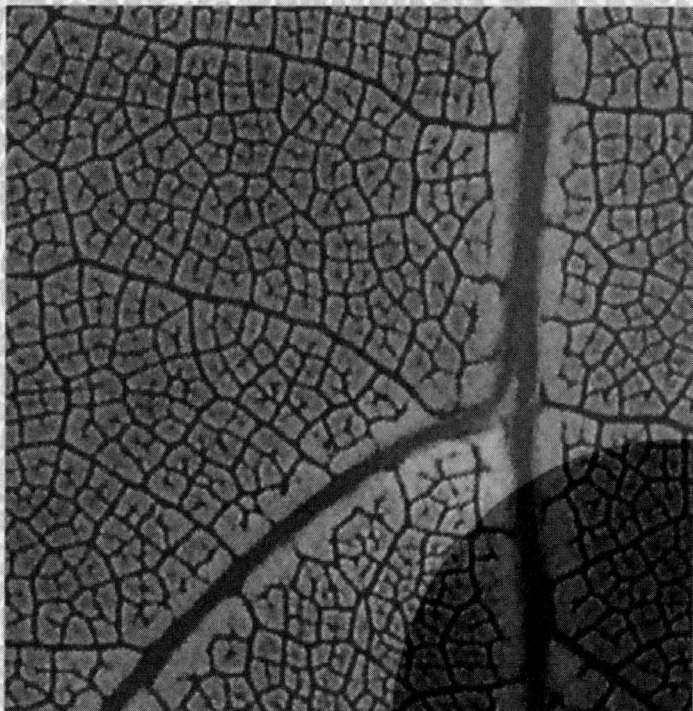

Glossary

Active Server Pages (ASP) An extension to Internet Information Server that enables you to run server-side scripts written in JScript or VBScript; those scripts return dynamically created HTML documents based on user input or other variables. See *Internet Information Server*.

ActiveX Microsoft's control plug-in technology for Web browsers that allows HTML documents to reference compiled controls and to automatically download and install them if they are not already plugged into the Web browser. ActiveX is also used on the server side with ASP.

Administrator Account A special account in Windows NT that has the ultimate set of security permissions and can assign any permission to any user or group. The Administrator account is used to correct security problems. See *Permissions*.

Alias The reference name of a virtual directory, which appears as a subdirectory in the wwwroot directory. Computers can also have alias names. See *Virtual Directory*.

Applet A small application (typically written in Java) that runs inside another application, such as a Web browser. See *Java*.

Application (IIS) Script and DLL enabled Web pages configured to run from a particular Web directory, often in memory-space isolation from other ISAPI DLLs.

Applications Large software packages that perform specific functions, such as word processing, Web browsing, or database management. Applications typically consist of more than one program. See *Program*.

ASP See *Active Server Pages*.

Authentication The process by which a user's credentials (user name and password) are verified so that the user can access a resource.

Back End The server side of a client/server application.

Bottlenecks Components operating at their peak capacity that restrict the flow of information through a system. Used singularly, the term indicates the single most-restrictive component in a system.

Browser   A Web browser application or a person using a Web browser to retrieve information from the Internet. Also refers to a computer on a Microsoft network that maintains a list of computers and services available on the network. See *Web Browser*.

Cable Modem   Ethernet-speed computer communications over cable TV coaxial wire.

Caching   A speed optimization technique that keeps a copy of the most recently used data in a fast, high-cost, low-capacity storage device rather than in the device upon which the actual data resides. Caching assumes that recently used data is likely to be used again. Fetching data from the cache is faster than fetching data from a slower, larger storage device. Most caching algorithms also copy next-most-likely to be used data and perform write-caching to further improve the speed.

Catalog   The collection of indexes maintained by Index Server.

Central Processing Unit (CPU)   The central processing unit of a computer. In microcomputers, such as IBM PC compatible machines, the CPU is the microprocessor. See *Microprocessor*.

Certificate   An encrypted electronic document that attests to the authenticity of a service, provider, or vendor of a product. Forgery of certificates is not possible, so users can trust the information the encrypted documents contain. A prerequisite to using the Secure Socket Layer is installation of a key with a valid certificate, which is then associated with SSL. See *Keys, Secure Socket Layer*.

Certificate Authority   The entity that creates a certificate (and presumably verifies that the information in the certificate is valid).

Certificate Server   A software package from Microsoft that allows you to be your own Certificate Authority.

CGI   See *Common Gateway Interface*.

Client   A computer on a network that subscribes to the services provided by a server. See *Server*.

Client/Server   A network architecture that dedicates certain computers, called *servers,* to act as service providers to other computers, called *clients,* where users do their work. Servers can be dedicated to providing one or more network services, such as file storage, shared printing, communications, e-mail, and Web response.

Client/Server Applications   Applications that split large applications into two components: computer-intensive processes that run on application servers and user interfaces that run on clients. Client/server applications communicate over the network through interprocess communication mechanisms. See *Client, Interprocess Communications, Server.*

Code   Synonymous with software, but used when the software is the object of discussion, rather than the utility it provides.

COM Port   Communications port. A serial hardware interface conforming to the RS-232 standard for low-speed serial communications. See *Modem.*

Common Gateway Interface   A standard for starting programs on the Web server computer that return dynamically created HTML documents to the HTTP service for transmission to the remote client. A new instance of the CGI application starts each time a connection is made, which can put excessive load on an Internet server.

Components   Interchangeable elements of a complex software or hardware system. See *Module.*

Compression   A space optimization scheme that reduces the size (length) of a data set by exploiting the fact that most useful data contains a great deal of redundancy. Compression reduces redundancy by creating symbols smaller than the data they represent and an index that defines the value of the symbols for each compressed set of data.

Computer   A device capable of performing automatic calculations based upon lists of instructions called programs. The computer feeds the results of these calculations (output) to peripheral devices that can represent them in useful ways, such as graphics on a screen or ink on paper. See *Microprocessor.*

Computer Name   A 1- to 15-character NetBIOS name used to uniquely identify a computer on the network.

Content Analyzer   A software tool (part of Site Server Express 2.0) that creates WebMaps from Web sites and helps you analyze site content.

Content Rating   A voluntary classification of Web site data according to the amount of violence, sex, nudity, and profanity the site contains.

Control Panel   A software utility that controls the function of specific operating system services by allowing users to change default settings for the service to match their preferences. The registry contains the Control Panel settings on a system and/or per-user basis. See *Registry*.

Cookie   A small amount of data passed to the Web browser by the Web server and then later retrieved by the Web server in order to check the last date and time of a visit to that site by the computer.

Corpus   The collection of files indexed by Index Server.

Counter   An object incremented by the operating system every time an event occurs; counters are read and graphed by Performance Monitor in order to display operating system performance.

Crystal Reports   A drill-down data-reporting tool used to extract and report on disparate information contained in many documents. A version is included with IIS to report on IIS log data. See *Report Writer*.

Database   A related set of data organized by type and purpose. The term also can include the application software that manipulates the data. The Windows NT registry (a database itself) contains a number of utility databases, such as user account and security information. See *Registry, Structured Query Language*.

Default Document   The HTML document returned when no specific page is referenced on a Web server.

Default Shares   Resources shared by default when Windows NT is installed. See *Resource, Share*.

Desktop   A directory that the background of the Windows Explorer shell represents. By default the desktop contains objects that contain the local storage devices and available network shares. Also a key operating part of the Windows GUI. See *Explorer*.

Dial-Up Connections   Data link layer digital connections made via modems over regular telephone lines. The term *dial-up* refers to temporary digital connections, as opposed to leased telephone lines, which provide permanent connections.

Digital Certificate   See *Certificate.*

Directories   In a file system, directories are containers that store files or other directories. Mass storage devices have a root directory that contains all other directories, thus creating a hierarchy of directories sometimes referred to as a *directory tree*. See *File System.*

DNS   See *Domain Name Service.*

Domain   In Microsoft networks, a domain is an arrangement of client and server computers referenced by a specific name that share a single security permissions database. On the Internet, a domain is a named collection of hosts and subdomains, registered with a unique name by InterNIC. See *Workgroup, InterNIC.*

Domain Controllers   Servers that authenticate workstation network logon requests by comparing a user name and password against account information stored in the user accounts database. A user cannot access a domain without authentication from a domain controller.

Domain Name   The textual identifier of a specific Internet Host. Domain names are in the form of *server.organization.type* (`www.microsoft.com`) and are resolved to Internet addresses by Domain Name Servers. See *Domain Name Server.*

Domain Name Server   An Internet host dedicated to the function of translating fully qualified domain names into IP addresses. See *Domain Name.*

Domain Name Service (DNS)   The TCP/IP network service that translates textual Internet network addresses into numerical Internet network addresses. See *TCP/IP, Internet, Domain Name.*

Driver   A program that provides a software interface to a hardware device. Drivers are written for the specific device they control, but they present a common software interface to the computer's operating system, allowing all devices (of a similar type) to be controlled as if they were the same.

Electronic Mail (E-mail)   A type of client/server application that provides a routed, stored-message service between any two user e-mail accounts. E-mail accounts are not the same as user accounts, but a one-to-one relationship usually exists between them. Because all modern computers can attach to the Internet, users can send e-mail over the Internet to any location that has a telephone or wireless digital service. See *Internet*.

Encryption   The process of obscuring information by modifying it according to a mathematical function known only to the sender and the intended recipient. Encryption secures information being transmitted over non-secure or untrusted media. See *Security*.

Ethernet   The most popular data link layer standard for local area networking. Ethernet implements the Carrier Sense Multiple Access with Collision Detection (CSMA/CD) method of arbitrating multiple computer access to the same network. This standard supports the use of Ethernet over any type of media, including wireless broadcast. Standard Ethernet operates at 10 megabits per second. Fast Ethernet operates at 100 megabits per second.

Exchange   Microsoft's messaging application. Exchange implements Microsoft's Mail Application Programming Interface (MAPI) as well as other messaging protocols such as POP, SNMP, and faxing to provide a flexible message composition and reception service. See *Electronic Mail, Fax Modems*.

Explorer   The default shell for Windows 95 and Windows NT 4.0. Explorer implements the more flexible desktop objects paradigm, rather than the Program Manager paradigm used in earlier versions of Windows.

FAT   See *File Allocation Table*.

Fault Tolerance   Any method that prevents system failure by tolerating single faults, usually through hardware redundancy.

Fax Modems   Special modems that include hardware to allow the transmission and reception of facsimiles. See *Exchange, Modem*.

FDDI   See *Fiber Distributed Data Interface*.

Fiber Distributed Data Interface (FDDI)   A data link layer that implements two counter-rotating token rings at 100 megabits per second. FDDI was a popular standard for interconnecting campus and metropolitan area networks because it allows distant digital connections at high speed, but ATM (Asynchronous Transfer Mode) is replacing FDDI in many sites.

File Allocation Table (FAT)   The file system used by MS-DOS and available to other operating systems, such as Windows (all variations), OS/2, and Macintosh. FAT has become something of a mass storage compatibility standard because of its simplicity and wide availability. FAT has few fault tolerance features and can become corrupted through normal use over time. See *File System.*

File Attributes   Bits stored along with the name and location of a file in a directory entry that shows the status of a file, such as archived, hidden, read-only, etc. Different operating systems use different file attributes to implement such services as sharing, compression, and security.

File System   A software component that manages the storage of files on a mass storage device by providing services that can create, read, write, and delete files. File systems impose an ordered database of files on the mass storage device, called volumes, that use hierarchies of directories to organize files.

File Transfer Protocol (FTP)   A simple Internet protocol that transfers complete files from an FTP server to a client running the FTP client. FTP provides a simple low-overhead method of transferring files between computers but cannot perform browsing functions. You must know the URL of the FTP server you wish to attach to. See *Internet, Uniform Resource Locator.*

Files   A set of data stored on a mass storage device identified by a directory entry containing a name, file attributes, and the physical location of the file in the volume.

Filter (Index Server)   A program (DLL) that can parse documents of a specific format to return a list of index terms for that document.

Filter (ISAPI)   A program (DLL) used to extend the capabilities of IIS. See *Internet Information Server, Internet Server Application Programming Interface.*

Firewall A dual-homed computer attached to both the Internet and an intranet; it protects the computers on the intranet from intrusion by blocking connections from untrusted sources and on specific protocols. Firewalls are the strongest form of Internet security yet implemented.

Form A collection of input fields processed by a scripting language or passed to a back-end service.

Format The process of preparing a mass storage device for use with a file system. There are actually two levels of formatting. Low-level formatting writes a structure of sectors and tracks to the disk with bits used by the mass storage controller hardware. The controller hardware requires this format, and it is independent of the file system. High-level formatting creates file system structures, such as an allocation table and a root directory in a partition, thus creating a volume.

Frame Relay A leased-line communications technology providing permanent links between sites using telephone lines.

Front End The client side of a client/server application.

FrontPage Microsoft's Web site organization and Web page content creation application.

FTP See *File Transfer Protocol*.

FTP Site (IIS) A manageable service providing access to files via the FTP protocol.

Gateway A computer that serves as a router, a format translator, or a security filter for an entire network.

Get A method of providing operands to a CGI script or Active Server page via the URL.

Global Group A special group that exists only on NT Server domain controllers. A global group's members must be from its own domain. See *Local Group*.

Gopher Serves text and links to other Gopher sites. Gopher predates HTTP by about a year but has been made obsolete by the richer format provided by HTTP. See *Hypertext Transfer Protocol*.

Graphical User Interface (GUI)   A computer shell program that represents mass storage devices, directories, and files as graphical objects on a screen. A cursor driven by a pointing device, such as a mouse, manipulates the objects. Typically, these are icons that can be opened into windows showing the data contained by the object.

Group Identifiers   Security identifiers that contain the set of permissions allowed to a group. When a user account is part of a group, the group identifier is appended to that user's security identifier, thus granting the individual user all the permissions assigned to the group.

Groups   Security entities to which users can be assigned membership for the purpose of applying a broad set of group permissions to the user. By managing permissions for groups and assigning users to groups, rather than assigning permissions to users, security administrators can keep coherent control of very large security environments. See *Global Group, Permissions, Security, Local Group.*

GUI   See *Graphical User Interface.*

Hardware Compatibility List (HCL)   The listing of all hardware devices supported by Windows NT. Hardware on the HCL has been tested and verified as being compatible with NT. You can view the current HCL at `http://microsoft.com/ntserver/hcl`.

HCL   See *Hardware Compatibility List.*

Home Directory   The root directory of a Web server or virtual server that contains the default document or home page. See *World Wide Web, Default Document.*

Home Page   The default page returned by a Web server from the requested Web site when a URL containing no specific document is requested. See *Hypertext Transfer Protocol, Uniform Resource Locator.*

Host   An Internet server. Hosts are constantly connected to the Internet. See *Internet.*

HotJava   A Web browser written entirely in the Java programming language designed to show the capability of the language. HotJava was the first browser to support Java applications.

HTML   See *Hypertext Markup Language.*

HTTP   See *Hypertext Transfer Protocol.*

HTTP keep-alives   A performance optimization allowing a Web browser making multiple HTTP requests to keep the original connection open rather than establishing new connections for each request.

Hyperlink   A link embedded in text or graphics that has a Web address embedded within it. By clicking on the link, you jump to another Web address. You can identify a hyperlink because it is generally a different color from the rest of the Web page. See *World Wide Web.*

Hypertext Markup Language (HTML)   A textual data format that identifies sections of a document as headers, lists, hypertext links, etc. HTML is the data format used on the World Wide Web for the publication of Web pages. See *Hypertext Transfer Protocol, World Wide Web.*

Hypertext Transfer Protocol (HTTP)   Hypertext transfer protocol is an Internet protocol that transfers HTML documents over the Internet and responds to context changes that happen when a user clicks on a hypertext link. See *Hypertext Markup Language, World Wide Web.*

IIS   See *Internet Information Server.*

Index Server   A search engine ISAPI extension to IIS that indexes all the documents stored on a Web site. Users can then query the indexes to return Web pages that match the query. See *Internet Server Application Programming Interface, Internet Information Server, Search Engine.*

Industry Standard Architecture (ISA)   The design standard for 16-bit Intel compatible motherboards and peripheral buses. The 32/64-bit PCI bus standard is replacing the ISA standard. Adapters and interface cards must conform to the bus standard(s) used by the motherboard in order to be used with a computer.

Integrated Services Digital Network (ISDN)   A direct, digital dial-up PSTN data link layer connection that operates at 64KB per channel over regular twisted pair cable between a subscriber site and a PSTN central office. ISDN provides twice the data rate of the fastest modems per channel. Up to 24 channels can be multiplexed over two twisted pairs. See *PSTN.*

Intel Architecture   A family of microprocessors descended directly from the Intel 8086, itself descended from the first microprocessor, the Intel 4004. The Intel architecture is the dominant microprocessor family. It was used in the original IBM PC microcomputer adopted by the business market and later adapted for home use.

Interactive User   A user who physically logs on to the computer where the user account resides is considered interactive, as opposed to a user who logs on over the network. See *Network User*.

Internet   A voluntarily interconnected global network of computers based upon the TCP/IP protocol suite. TCP/IP was originally developed by the U.S. Department of Defense's Advanced Research Projects Agency to facilitate the interconnection of military networks and was provided free to universities. The obvious utility of worldwide digital network connectivity and the availability of free complex networking software developed at universities doing military research attracted other universities, research institutions, private organizations, businesses, and finally the individual home user. The Internet is now available to all current commercial computing platforms. See *File Transfer Protocol, TCP/IP, Telnet, World Wide Web*.

Internet Database Connector   An extension to IIS that returns a database table formatted as an HTML document based on a query from the Web client. See *Database, Internet Information Server*.

Internet Explorer   A World Wide Web browser produced by Microsoft and included free with Windows 95/98 and Windows NT 4.0. See *Internet, World Wide Web*.

Internet Information Server (IIS)   Serves Internet higher-level protocols like HTTP and FTP to clients using Web browsers. See *File Transfer Protocol, Hypertext Transfer Protocol, World Wide Web*.

Internet Protocol (IP)   The network layer protocol upon which the Internet is based. IP provides a simple connectionless packet exchange. Other protocols such as UDP or TCP use IP to perform their connection-oriented or guaranteed delivery services. See *Internet, TCP/IP*.

Internet Relay Chat (IRC)   An informal Internet protocol for multiuser simultaneous conversation via relayed text strings between an IRC server and multiple IRC clients.

Internet Server   A server computer connected to the Internet or an intranet that serves Internet protocols such as HTTP, FTP, and Gopher based on the TCP/IP protocol suite. See *File Transfer Protocol, Gopher, Hypertext Transfer Protocol, Internet, TCP/IP.*

Internet Server Application Programming Interface (ISAPI)   A specification to which extensions to IIS are written in order to expand its functionality or the services it provides.

Internet Service Provider (ISP)   A company that provides dial-up connections to the Internet. See *Internet.*

Internetwork   A network of networks, usually based on a packet-switching scheme.

Internetwork Packet eXchange (IPX)   The network and transport layer protocol developed by Novell for its NetWare product. IPX is a routable, connection-oriented protocol similar to TCP/IP but much easier to manage and with lower communication overhead.

InterNIC   The agency that is responsible for assigning IP addresses. See *Internet Protocol, IP Address.*

Interpreter   A program that executes the commands read from a script. See *Script, Scripting Language.*

Interprocess Communications (IPC)   A generic term describing any manner of client/server communication protocol, specifically those operating in the application layer. Interprocess communications mechanisms provide a method for the client and server to trade information. See *Local Procedure Call, Mailslots, Named Pipes, Network Basic Input/Output System, Remote Procedure Call.*

Intranet   A privately owned network based on the TCP/IP protocol suite. See *Transmission Control Protocol/Internet Protocol.*

IP   See *Internet Protocol.*

IP Address   A 4-byte number that uniquely identifies a computer on an IP internetwork. InterNIC assigns the first bytes of Internet IP addresses and administers them in hierarchies. Huge organizations like the government or top-level ISPs have class A addresses, large organizations and most ISPs have class B addresses, and small companies have class C addresses. In a class A address, InterNIC assigns the first byte, and the owning organization assigns the remaining three bytes. In a class B address, InterNIC or the higher level ISP assigns the first two bytes, and the organization assigns the remaining two bytes. In a class C address, InterNIC or the higher level ISP assigns the first three bytes, and the organization assigns the remaining byte. Organizations not attached to the Internet are free to assign IP addresses as they please. See *Internet, InterNIC, Internet Protocol.*

IPC   See *Interprocess Communications.*

IPX   See *Internetwork Packet eXchange.*

ISAPI   See *Internet Server Application Programming Interface.*

ISDN   See *Integrated Services Digital Network.*

ISP   See *Internet Service Provider.*

Java   A compiled object-oriented cross-platform language based on the syntax of C++. Java uses the interpreted Java virtual machine as its machine language. Since Java applications and applets can be run on any platform, it is a natural candidate for Web-based programs.

Java Virtual Machine (JVM)   A fictitious machine architecture to which all Java applications are compiled. Java run-time environments can either interpret or compile JVM code to execute it on any computer or inside an application like a Web browser.

JavaScript   A scripting language based on the syntax of Java that can be embedded in HTML documents to provide simple client-side active content. See *Script, Scripting Language.*

JScript   Microsoft's version of JavaScript.

Key Manager   The Microsoft tool for creating and managing digital keys.

Keys   Paired codes used to encrypt data in communication streams. One part of the key is kept private on the server, while the other (public) part of the key is transmitted to Web browsers. Web browsers can then encrypt data using the public portion that must be decrypted using the private portion of the key. The process is called *public key encryption* and is used in the Secure Socket Layer mechanism. See *Encryption, Secure Socket Layer.*

LAN See *Local Area Network*.

Lightweight Directory Access Protocol (LDAP) An open standard for storing user and group information independent of the operating system that hosts the WWW service.

Local Area Network (LAN) A network of computers operating on the same high-speed, shared media network data link layer. The size of a local area network is defined by the limitations of high speed shared media networks and is generally less than 1 kilometer in overall span. Some LAN backbone data link protocols, such as FDDI, can create larger LANs called metropolitan or medium area networks (MANs).

Local Group A group that exists in an NT computer's local accounts database. Local groups can reside on NT workstations or NT servers and can contain users or global groups. See *Global Group*.

Local Procedure Call (LPC) A mechanism that loops remote procedure calls without the presence of a network so that the client and server portion of an application can reside on the same machine. Local procedure calls look like remote procedure calls (RPCs) to the client and server sides of a distributed application. See *Remote Procedure Call*.

Local Security Security that governs a local or interactive user. Local security can be set through NTFS partitions. See *Interactive User, Network Security, New Technology File System, Security*.

Localhost The standard UNIX and Internet name referring to the local computer.

Log A database of time-based security and service-related information stored in text format.

Log Off The process of closing an open session with a server. See *Log on*.

Log On The process of opening a network session by providing a valid authentication consisting of a user account name and a password to a domain controller. After logging on, network resources are available to the user according to the user's assigned permissions. See *Domain Controllers, Log Off*.

Logging   The process of recording information about activities and errors in the operating system.

Logon Script   Command files that automate the logon process by performing utility functions, such as attaching to additional server resources or automatically running different programs based upon the user account that established the logon. See *Log On*.

LPC   See *Local Procedure Call*.

Mailslots   A connectionless messaging IPC mechanism that Windows NT uses for browser requests and logon authentication. See *Interprocess Communications*.

Memory   Any device capable of storing information. This term is usually used to indicate volatile Random Access semiconductor Memory (RAM) capable of high-speed access to any portion of the memory space, but incapable of storing information without power.

Merge   The process of joining temporary indexes together (shadow merge) or of joining temporary indexes into a master index (master merge) for the purpose of speeding queries to an index service.

Metabase   An IIS storage facility for frequently updated or frequently referenced operating system, service, or application configuration data.

Microprocessor   An integrated semiconductor circuit designed to automatically perform lists of logical and arithmetic operations. Modern microprocessors independently manage memory pools and support multiple instruction lists called threads. Microprocessors are also capable of responding to interrupt requests from peripherals and include onboard support for complex floating point arithmetics. Microprocessors must have instructions when they are first powered on. These instructions are contained in nonvolatile firmware called a BIOS.

Microsoft Management Console   Microsoft's new tool for managing IIS and other Windows NT 4.0 Option Pack services.

Modem Modulator/demodulator. A data link layer device used to create an analog signal suitable for transmission over telephone lines from a digital data stream. Modern modems also include a command set for negotiating connections and data rates with remote modems and for setting their default behavior. Currently, the fastest modems run at about 56 Kbps.

Module A software component of a modular operating system that provides a certain defined service. Modules can be installed or removed depending upon the service requirements of the software running on the computer. Modules allow operating systems and applications to be customized to fit the needs of the user.

Multipurpose Internet Mail Extensions (MIME) A specification for the content types of files transmitted over the Internet. Web servers identify the type of file being sent to Web browsers using MIME types.

Named Pipes An interprocess communication mechanism that is implemented as a file system service, allowing programs to be modified to run on it without using a proprietary application programming interface. Named Pipes were developed to support more robust client/server communications than those allowed by the simpler NetBIOS.

NetBEUI See *NetBIOS Extended User Interface.*

NetBIOS See *Network Basic Input/Output System.*

NetBIOS Extended User Interface (NetBEUI) A simple network layer transport developed to support NetBIOS installations. NetBEUI is not routable and is not appropriate for larger networks. NetBEUI is the fastest transport protocol available for Windows NT.

NetBIOS Gateway A service provided by RAS that allows NetBIOS requests to be forwarded independent of transport protocol. For example, NetBIOS requests from a remote computer connected via NetBEUI can be sent over the network via NWLink. See *NetBIOS Extended User Interface, NetBIOS over TCP/IP, Network Basic Input/Output System.*

NetBIOS over TCP/IP (NetBT) A network service that implements the NetBIOS IPC over the TCP/IP protocol stack. See *Interprocess Communications, Network Basic Input/Output System, TCP/IP.*

NetBT   See *NetBIOS over TCP/IP*.

Network   A group of computers connected via some digital medium for the purpose of exchanging information. Networks can be based upon many types of media, such as twisted pair telephone-style cable, optical fiber, coaxial cable, radio, or infrared light. Certain computers are usually configured as service providers called *servers*. Computers that perform user tasks and utilize the services of servers are called *clients*. See *Client/ Server, Network Operating System, Server*.

Network Basic Input/Output System (NetBIOS)   A client/server inter-process communication service developed by IBM in the early 1980s. NetBIOS presents a relatively primitive mechanism for communication in client/server applications, but its widespread acceptance and availability across most operating systems makes it a logical choice for simple network applications. Many of the network IPC mechanisms in Windows NT are implemented over Net-BIOS. See *Client/Server, Interprocess Communications*.

Network Interface Card (NIC)   A physical layer adapter device that allows a computer to connect to and communicate over a local area network. See *Ethernet, Token Ring*.

Network News Transfer Protocol (NNTP)   A protocol for the transmission of a database of topical message threads between news servers and newsreader clients.

Network Operating System   A computer operating system specifically designed to optimize a computer's ability to respond to service requests. Servers run network operating systems. Windows NT Server and NetWare are both network operating systems.

Network Security   Security that governs a network. See *Local Security, Network User, Security*.

Network User   A user who logs on to the network using the Security Accounts Manager (SAM) from a remote domain controller. See *Interactive User, Security Accounts Manager*.

New Technology File System (NTFS)   A secure, transaction-oriented file system developed for Windows NT that incorporates the Windows NT security model for assigning permissions and shares. NTFS is optimized for hard drives larger than 500MB and requires too much overhead to be used on hard disk drives smaller than 50MB.

Newsgroups   Internet-wide threads of topical discussion implemented using the NNTP protocol. See *Usenet News, NNTP*.

NNTP   See *Network News Transfer Protocol*.

NTFS   See *New Technology File System*.

Object   A software service provider that encapsulates both the algorithm and the data structures necessary to provide a service. Usually, objects can inherit data and functionality from their parent objects, thus allowing complex services to be constructed from simpler objects. The term *object oriented* implies a tight relationship between algorithms and data structures. See *Module*.

Object Counters   Containers built into each service object in Windows NT that store a count of the number of times an object performs its service or to what degree. You can use Performance Monitor to access object counters and measure how the different objects in Windows NT are operating. See *Object*.

ODBC   See *Open Database Connectivity*.

Open Database Connectivity (ODBC)   A standard for connecting database clients to database servers regardless of the vendors or systems involved.

Operators   Windows NT users that have a limited ability to manage Web site characteristics.

Optimization   Any effort to reduce the workload on a hardware component by eliminating, obviating, or reducing the amount of work required through any means. For instance, file caching is an optimization that reduces the workload of a hard disk drive.

Packet Filter   A limited security tool that can filter IP packets by type.

Page File   See *Swap File*.

Partition   A section of a hard disk that can contain an independent file system volume. Partitions can be used to keep multiple operating systems and file systems on the same hard disk.

Password   A secret code used to validate the identity of a user of a secure system. Passwords are used in tandem with account names to log on to most computer systems.

Peer Web Services   A limited version of IIS that runs on Windows NT Workstation computers.

Performance Monitor   An NT utility that provides graphical statistics for measuring the performance of your computer.

Perl   A scripting language commonly used in CGI scripts to parse user input from Web pages and dynamically create HTML documents. See *Scripting Language*.

Permissions   Assignments of levels of access to a resource made to groups or users. Security constructs used to regulate access to resources by user name or group affiliation. Permissions can be assigned by administrators to allow any level of access, such as read only, read/write, delete, etc., by controlling the ability of users to initiate object services. Security is implemented by checking the user's security identifier against each object's access control list.

Personal Web Server   A limited version of IIS that runs on Windows 95 computers.

Ping   A protocol used to check the connected route between two systems on an IP network. Also the name of the utility used to generate ping traffic. See *Internet Protocol*.

Plug-Ins   Compiled components that extend the functionality of Web browsers, usually by interpreting specific types of data, such as sound or video. See *Web Browser*.

Point-to-Point Protocol (PPP)   A network layer transport that performs over point-to-point network connections, such as serial or modem lines. PPP can negotiate any transport protocol used by both systems involved in the link and can automatically assign IP, DNS, and gateway addresses when used with TCP/IP. See *Internet Protocol, Domain Name Service, Gateway*.

Point-to-Point Tunneling Protocol (PPTP)   Protocol used to connect to corporate networks through the Internet or an ISP. See *Internet, Internet Service Provider.*

Policies   General controls that enhance the security of an operating environment. In Windows NT, policies affect restrictions on password use and rights assignment and determine which events will be recorded in the Security log.

POP, POP3   See *Post Office Protocol.*

Post   A method of providing operands to a CGI script or Active Server page exterior to the URL.

Post Office Protocol   A protocol used for offline mail readers to manage the contents of their inbox on a mail server.

PPP   See *Point-to-Point Protocol.*

PPTP   See *Point-to-Point Tunneling Protocol.*

Preemptive Multitasking   A multitasking implementation in which an interrupt routine in the kernel manages the scheduling of processor time among running threads. The threads themselves do not need to support multitasking in any way because the microprocessor will preempt the thread with an interrupt, save its state, update all thread priorities according to its scheduling algorithm, and pass control to the highest priority thread awaiting execution. Because of the preemptive nature, a thread that crashes will not affect the operation of other executing threads.

Process   A running program containing one or more threads. A process encapsulates the protected memory and environment for its threads.

Program   A list of processor instructions designed to perform a certain function. A running program is called a process. A package of one or more programs and attendant data designed to meet a certain application is called software.

Programming Interfaces   Interprocess communications mechanisms that provide certain high-level services to running processes. Programming interfaces may provide network communication, graphical presentation, or any other type of software service. See *Interprocess Communications.*

Protocol An established communication method that all parties involved understand. Protocols provide a context in which to interpret communicated information. Computer protocols are rules used by communicating devices and software services to format data in a way that all participants understand.

Proxy Server A server dedicated to the function of receiving Internet Web requests for clients, retrieving the requested pages, and forwarding them to clients. Proxy servers may cache retrieved Web pages to improve performance and reduce bandwidth; they also serve the security function of protecting the identity of internal clients.

PSTN See *Public Switched Telephone Network*.

Public Switched Telephone Network (PSTN) A global network of interconnected digital and analog communication links originally designed to support voice communication between any two points in the world, but quickly adapted to handle digital data traffic when the computer revolution occurred. In addition to its traditional voice support role, the PSTN now functions as the physical layer of the Internet by providing dial-up and leased lines for the interconnections.

Query A request to an index or database server for a specific set of information. See *Database, Index Server, Structured Query Language*.

RAID See *Redundant Array of Independent Disks*.

RAM See *Random Access Memory*.

Random Access Memory (RAM) Integrated circuits that store digital bits in massive arrays of logical gates or capacitors. RAM is the primary memory store for modern computers, storing all running software processes and contextual data. See *Microprocessor*.

RAS See *Remote Access Service*.

Redundant Array of Independent Disks (RAID) A collection of hard disk drives, coordinated by a special controller, that appears as one physical disk to a computer but stores its data across all the disks to take advantage of the speed and/or fault tolerance afforded by using more than one disk. RAID disk storage has several levels, including 0 (striping), 1 (mirroring), and 5 (striping with parity). RAID systems are typically used for very large storage volumes or to provide fault-tolerance features, such as hot swapping of failed disks or automatically backing up data onto replacement disks.

Registry   A database of settings required and maintained by Windows NT and its components. The registry contains all of the configuration information used by the computer. It is stored as a hierarchical structure and is made up of keys, hives, and value entries. You can use the Registry Editor (REGEDT32 command) to change these settings.

Remote Access Service (RAS)   A service that allows network connections to be established over PSTN lines with modems. The computer initiating the connection is called the RAS client; the answering computer is called the RAS server. See *Modem, Public Switched Telephone Network*.

Remote Procedure Call (RPC)   A network interprocess communication mechanism that allows an application to be distributed among many computers on the same network. See *Interprocess Communications, Local Procedure Call*.

Report Writer   A tool provided by Microsoft (as a part of Site Server Express 2.0) to create graphs and charts based on IIS log data.

Requests for Comments (RFCs)   The set of standards defining the Internet protocols as determined by the Internet Engineering Task Force and available to the public domain on the Internet. RFCs define the functions and services provided by each of the many Internet protocols. Compliance with the RFCs guarantees cross-vendor compatibility. See *Internet*.

Resource   Any useful service, such as a shared network directory or a printer. See *Share*.

RFC   See *Request For Comments*.

RIP   See *Routing Information Protocol*.

Routing Information Protocol (RIP)   A protocol within the TCP/IP protocol suite that allows routers to exchange routing information with other routers. See *Transmission Control Protocol/Internet Protocol*.

RPC   See *Remote Procedure Call*.

SAM   See *Security Accounts Manager.*

Script   A list of commands to be executed by an interpreter. Web browsers can be interpreters for scripts embedded in HTML documents. See *Interpreter, Scripting Language, Web Browser.*

Scripting Language   A specific syntax and structure for commands in scripts. See *Interpreter, Script.*

Search Engine   Web sites dedicated to responding to requests for specific information, searching massive locally stored databases of Web pages, and responding with the URLs of pages that fit the search phrase. See *Uniform Resource Locator, World Wide Web, Index Server.*

Secure Socket Layer (SSL)   An encrypted transmission protocol that uses TCP/IP to implement a secure public key encrypted data channel between a client and a server. See *Encryption, Transmission Control Protocol/Internet Protocol.*

Security   Measures taken to secure a system against accidental or intentional loss, usually in the form of accountability procedures and use restriction.

Security Accounts Manager (SAM)   The module of the Windows NT executive that authenticates a user name and password against a database of accounts, generating an access token that includes the user's permissions. See *Security, Security Identifiers.*

Security Identifiers (SIDs)   Unique codes that identify a specific user or group to the Windows NT security system. Security identifiers contain a complete set of permissions for that user or group.

Server   A computer dedicated to servicing requests for resources from other computers on a network. Servers typically run network operating systems, such as Windows NT Server or NetWare.

Server-Side Include (SSI)   A generic term for Web services that use embedded HTML tags to dynamically create HTML documents based on the contents of many different HTML documents.

Service   A process dedicated to implementing a specific function for other processes. Most Windows NT components are services used by user-level applications.

Service Pack   Many NT products have service packs that offer bug fixes or feature enhancements.

Servlet   A server-side application written in Java. See *Java*.

Share   A resource (e.g., directory, printer) shared by a server or a peer on a network.

SID   See *Security Identifiers*.

Simple Mail Transfer Protocol (SMTP)   An Internet protocol for transferring mail between Internet hosts. SMTP is often used to upload mail directly from the client to an intermediate host, but only computers constantly connected to the Internet can use SMTP to receive mail. See *Internet*.

Simple Network Management Protocol (SNMP)   An Internet protocol that monitors network hardware, such as routers, switches, servers, and clients from a single manager on the network. See *Internet Protocol*.

Site   A related collection of documents at the same Internet address, usually oriented toward some specific information or purpose. For example, IIS uses sites for WWW and FTP. See *Hypertext Markup Language, Internet*.

Site Server Express   Microsoft's set of (limited) tools to explore and report on Web sites.

SMTP   See *Simple Mail Transfer Protocol.*

Snap-Ins   Management components used to extend the functionality of the Microsoft Management Console.

Sniffer   A software or hardware troubleshooting device used for the low-level analysis of network protocols.

SNMP   See *Simple Network Management Protocol.*

Software   A suite of programs sold as a unit and dedicated to a specific application. See *Applications, Process, Program.*

SQL   See *Structured Query Language*.

SQL Server   Microsoft's relational database server based on SQL syntax. See *Database, Structured Query Language*.

SSL   See *Secure Socket Layer*.

Stripe Set   A single volume created across multiple hard disk drives and accessed in parallel for the purpose of optimizing disk access time. NTFS can create stripe sets. See *File System, New Technology File System*.

Structured Query Language   An open syntax for the transmission of queries between clients and servers. Database servers interpret SQL to return the data described by the query.

Subnet   A single broadcast network defined by the fact that any two computers in the subnet can communicate without any special routing.

Subnet Mask   A number mathematically applied to Internet protocol addresses to determine which IP addresses are a part of the same subnetwork as the computer applying the subnet mask.

Surf   To browse the Web aimlessly, looking for interesting information. See *World Wide Web*.

Swap File   The virtual memory file on a hard disk containing the memory pages that have been moved out to disk to increase available RAM. See *Virtual Memory*.

TCP   See *Transmission Control Protocol*.

TCP/IP   See *Transmission Control Protocol/Internet Protocol*.

Telnet   A terminal application that allows a user to log into a multiuser UNIX computer from any computer connected to the Internet. See *Internet*.

Thread   A list of instructions running in a computer to perform a certain task. Each thread runs in the context of a process, which embodies the protected memory space and the environment of the threads. Multithreaded processes can perform more than one task at the same time.

Throughput   The measure of information flow through a system in a specific time frame, usually one second. For instance, 56 Kbps can be the throughput of a modem on a 28.8 Kbps transmission medium due to compression.

Token Ring   The second most-popular data link layer standard for local area networking. Token ring implements the token-passing method of arbitrating multiple-computer access to the same network. Token ring operates at either 4 or 16 Mbps. FDDI is similar to token ring and operates at 100 Mbps. See *Fiber Distributed Data Interface.*

Transmission Control Protocol (TCP)   A transport layer protocol that implements guaranteed packet delivery using the Internet Protocol (IP). See *Internet Protocol, Transmission Control Protocol/Internet Protocol.*

Transmission Control Protocol/Internet Protocol (TCP/IP)   A suite of Internet protocols upon which the global Internet is based. TCP/IP is a general term that can refer either to the TCP and IP protocols used together or to the complete set of Internet protocols. TCP/IP is the default protocol for Windows NT.

Transport Protocol   A service that delivers discrete packets of information between any two computers in a network. Higher level connection-oriented services are built upon transport protocols. See *Internet, Internet Protocol, NetBIOS Extended User Interface, Transmission Control Protocol, Transmission Control Protocol/Internet Protocol.*

Trust Relationship   Administrative link that joins two or more domains. A trust relationship enables users to access resources in another domain if they have rights, even if they do not have a user account in the resource domain.

UDP   See *User Datagram Protocol.*

UNC   See *Universal Naming Convention.*

Uniform Resource Locator (URL)   An Internet-standard naming convention for identifying resources available via various TCP/IP application protocols. For example, `http://www.microsoft.com` is the URL for Microsoft's World Wide Web server site, while `ftp://gateway.dec.com` is a popular FTP site. A URL allows easy hypertext references to a particular resource from within a document or mail message. See *Hypertext Transfer Protocol, World Wide Web.*

Universal Naming Convention (UNC)   A multivendor, multiplatform convention for identifying shared resources on a network.

UNIX   A multitasking, kernel-based operating system developed at AT&T in the early 1970s and provided (originally) free to universities as a research operating system. Because of its availability and ability to scale down to microprocessor-based computers, UNIX became the standard operating system of the Internet and its attendant network protocols and is the closest approximation to a universal operating system that exists. Most computers can run some variant of the UNIX operating system.

Usenet News   A distributed news database implemented on NNTP, divided into topical discussion threads called newsgroups, which are distributed among news servers. Clients using newsreaders can subscribe to specific newsgroups and have them automatically downloaded when they open their newsreader.

User Datagram Protocol (UDP)   A non-guaranteed network packet protocol implemented on IP that is far faster than TCP because of its lack of flow-control overhead. UDP can be implemented as a reliable transport when some higher level protocol (such as NetBIOS) exists to make sure that the required data will eventually be retransmitted in local area environments. At the transport layer of the OSI model, UDP is a connectionless service and TCP is a connection-oriented service. See *Transmission Control Protocol*.

User Manager for Domains   A Windows NT application that administers user accounts, groups, and security policies at the domain level.

User Name   A user's account name in a logon-authenticated system. See *Security*.

User Right Policies   Used to determine what rights users and groups have when trying to accomplish network tasks. User Rights Policies are set through User Manager for Domains. See *User Manager for Domains*.

VBScript   A variant of Visual Basic used as a scripting language in Internet Explorer and Active Server Pages. See *Scripting Language*.

Virtual Directory   A directory accessible to IIS that has a registered alias so that it appears to be a subdirectory of a service root directory.

Virtual Machine   A fictitious machine architecture that can be interpreted on a number of actual machines. Programs compiled to the virtual machine specification can run on any computer that can interpret that virtual machine specification. See *Java Virtual Machine*.

Virtual Memory   A kernel service that stores memory pages not currently in use on a mass storage device to free up RAM memory for other uses. Virtual memory hides the memory-swapping process from applications and higher-level services.

Virtual Reality Modeling Language   A syntax that describes the position of three-dimensional objects in a space, which can be transmitted from a server to a client and rendered on the client.

Virtual Server   A set of directories that simulate the functionality of a wwwroot directory in that they appear to be a Web server unto themselves. You can run multiple virtual servers on a single IIS computer.

Virtual Web Site (IIS)   A manageable service providing access to remote resources via the HTTP protocol.

W3C   World Wide Web Consortium.

WAN   See *Wide Area Network*.

Web Browser   An application that makes HTTP requests and formats the resultant HTML documents for users. They are the preeminent Internet client; most Web browsers understand all standard Internet protocols and scripting languages. See *Hypertext Markup Language, Hypertext Transfer Protocol, Internet*.

Web Page   Any HTML document on an HTTP server. See *Hypertext Markup Language, Hypertext Transfer Protocol, Internet*.

Web Site   A set of related HTML pages and the resources they refer to.

WebMap   A stored database describing the contents of a Web site and the links between Web pages.

Webmaster   The administrator of a Web site.

Well-Known Port   The commonly accepted or defined TCP socket for a specific service.

Wide Area Information Service (WAIS)   An Internet-based distributed database connection protocol that allows the simultaneous query of multiple separate databases.

Wide Area Network (WAN)   A geographically dispersed system of networks, connected by routers and communication links. The Internet is the largest WAN. See *Internet, Local Area Network*.

WinCGI   The Windows adaptation of the CGI specification for UNIX computers.

Windows Internet Name Service (WINS)   A network service for Microsoft networks that provides Windows computers with IP addresses for specified NetBIOS names, facilitating browsing and intercommunication over TCP/IP networks.

Windows NT   The current 32-bit version of Microsoft Windows for powerful CPUs. The system includes peer networking services, server networking services, Internet client and server services, and a broad range of utilities.

Windows Sockets   An interprocess communications protocol that delivers connection-oriented data streams used by Internet software and software ported from UNIX environments. See *Interprocess Communications*.

WINS   See *Windows Internet Name Service*.

Workgroup   In Microsoft networks, a collection of related computers, such as a department, that don't require the uniform security and coordination of a domain. Workgroups are characterized by decentralized management, as opposed to the centralized management that domains use. See *Domain*.

Workstation   A powerful personal computer, usually running a preemptive, multitasking operating system like UNIX or Windows NT.

World Wide Web (WWW)   A collection of Internet servers providing hypertext formatted documents for Internet clients running Web browsers. The World Wide Web provided the first easy-to-use graphical interface for the Internet and is largely responsible for the Internet's explosive growth.

WWW   See *World Wide Web*.

X.25   Standard that defines packet-switching networks.

Index

Note to the Reader: First level entries are in **bold**. Page numbers in **bold** indicate the principal discussion of a topic or the definition of a term. Page numbers in *italic* indicate illustrations.

SYBEX BOOKS ON THE WEB

Netscape: Welcome to Sybex, Inc. - Quality Computer Books

Back Forward Reload Home Search Guide Images Print Security Stop

Location: http://www.sybex.com

SYBEX INC. QUALITY COMPUTER BOOKS

Catalog   Order/Sales   Support   Contact   About   International   Home

Catalog
Order/Sales
Support
Contact
About
International

WHAT'S HAPPENING!

Promotions
Read about contests, discounted books & special packages here! We have special promotions for both general and academic readers.

Special Publications
Find out what we're publishing on the latest, most important topics.

Features
Bonus material you can't find elsewhere.

WHAT'S NEW!

Our newest publications!

COMING SOON!

New series, new topics!

WHAT'S HOT!

Look here for the latest and hottest books out from Sybex! We'll be featuring special titles in various categories on a regular basis, so be sure to visit us again to see what's hot!

Games

Our Games site is a hotbed of the latest and greatest computer and video game books. We'll have cheats, hints and walkthroughs as well as links to the hottest Gamer sites.

Network Press

Our aim with Network Press is to cover the key technologies products in networking today. Network Press publishes a full range of books to further your career through skills and certification!

A+: Certification Kit

Catalog | Order/Sales | Support | Contact | About | International | Home | Back to Top

Copyright © 1998 Sybex Inc.

A t the dynamic and informative Sybex Web site, you can:

- view our complete online catalog
- preview a book you're interested in
- access special book content
- order books online at special discount prices
- learn about Sybex

www.sybex.com

SYBEX Inc. • 1151 Marina Village Parkway, Alameda, CA 94501 • 510-523-8233

SYBEX

NETWORK PRESS® PRESENTS
MCSE TEST SUCCESS

THE PERFECT COMPANION BOOKS TO THE MCSE STUDY GUIDES

MCSE Test Success:
NETWORKING ESSENTIALS

EXAM 70-058

TODD LAMMLE

GET READY FOR THE EXAM—
OBJECTIVE BY OBJECTIVE

MASTER ALL THE MATERIAL
YOU NEED TO KNOW

PRACTICE ON 500 REVIEW
QUESTIONS AND SAMPLE
TEST QUESTIONS

Microsoft Certified
Professional
Approved Study Guide

ISBN: 0-7821-2146-2
352pp; 7¹/₂" x 9"; Softcover
$24.99

MCSE Test Success:
NT SERVER 4

EXAM 70-067

LISA DONALD

GET READY FOR THE EXAM—
OBJECTIVE BY OBJECTIVE

MASTER ALL THE MATERIAL
YOU NEED TO KNOW

PRACTICE ON 500 REVIEW
QUESTIONS AND SAMPLE
TEST QUESTIONS

Microsoft Certified
Professional
Approved Study Guide

ISBN: 0-7821-2148-9
352pp; 7¹/₂" x 9"; Softcover
$24.99

MCSE Test Success:
NT WORKSTATION 4

EXAM 70-073

TODD LAMMLE
LISA DONALD

GET READY FOR THE EXAM—
OBJECTIVE BY OBJECTIVE

MASTER ALL THE MATERIAL
YOU NEED TO KNOW

PRACTICE ON 500
REVIEW QUESTIONS AND
SAMPLE TEST QUESTIONS

Microsoft Certified
Professional
Approved Study Guide

ISBN: 0-7821-2149-7
400pp; 7¹/₂" x 9"; Softcover
$24.99

MCSE Test Success:
NT SERVER 4 IN THE ENTERPRISE

EXAM 70-068

LISA DONALD

GET READY FOR THE EXAM—
OBJECTIVE BY OBJECTIVE

MASTER ALL THE MATERIAL
YOU NEED TO KNOW

PRACTICE ON MORE THAN 500
REVIEW QUESTIONS AND SAMPLE
TEST QUESTIONS

Microsoft Certified
Professional
Approved Study Guide

ISBN: 0-7821-2147-0
442pp; 7¹/₂" x 9"; Softcover
$24.99

Here's what you need to know to pass the MCSE tests.

- **Review concise summaries of key information**

- **Boost your knowledge with 400 review questions**

- **Get ready for the test with 200 tough practice test questions**

Other MCSE Test Success titles:

- **Core Requirements Box Set**
  (4 books, 1 CD)
  [ISBN: 0-7821-2296-5] April 1998

- **Windows® 95**
  [ISBN: 0-7821-2252-3] May 1998

- **Exchange Server 5.5**
  [ISBN: 0-7821-2250-7] May 1998

- **TCP/IP for NT® 4**
  [ISBN: 0-7821-2251-5] May 1998

Microsoft Certified
Professional
Approved Study Guide

NETWORK PRESS®
SYBEX

MCSE EXAM NOTES®

MCSE Exam Notes: NT SERVER 4

EXAM 70-067

FULL COVERAGE OF EACH EXAM OBJECTIVE

KNOW WHAT YOU NEED TO KNOW—AND NAIL THE EXAM

INCLUDES EXAM-TAKING STRATEGIES

Microsoft Certified
Professional
Approved Study Guide

ISBN: 0-7821-2289-2
368 pp; 5⁷/8" x 8¹/4"; Softcover
$19.99

MCSE Exam Notes: NT SERVER 4 IN THE ENTERPRISE

EXAM 70-068

FULL COVERAGE OF EACH EXAM OBJECTIVE

KNOW WHAT YOU NEED TO KNOW—AND NAIL THE EXAM

INCLUDES EXAM-TAKING STRATEGIES

Microsoft Certified
Professional
Approved Study Guide

ISBN: 0-7821-2292-2
416 pp; 5⁷/8" x 8¹/4"; Softcover
$19.99

THE FASTEST AND MOST EFFECTIVE WAY TO MAKE SURE YOU'RE READY FOR THE MCSE EXAMS:

- Unique, innovative approach helps you gain and retain the knowledge you need, objective by objective.

- Essential information is arranged for quick learning and review.

- Exam tips and advice are offered by expert trainers.

OTHER TITLES INCLUDE:

MCSE Exam Notes™: NT® Workstation 4
MCSE Exam Notes™: Networking Essentials
MCSE Exam Notes™: Windows® 95
MCSE Exam Notes™: TCP/IP for NT® Server 4
MCSE Exam Notes™: Exchange Server 5.5
MCSE Exam Notes™: Internet Information Server 4
MCSE Exam Notes™: SQL Server 6.5 Administration
MCSE Exam Notes™: Proxy Server 2
MCSE Exam Notes™: Systems Management Server

CORE BOX SET ALSO AVAILABLE:

MCSE Exam Notes™: Core Requirements box set
- 4 books:
    MCSE Exam Notes™: Networking Essentials
    MCSE Exam Notes™: NT® Workstation 4
    MCSE Exam Notes™: NT® Server 4
    MCSE Exam Notes™: NT® Server 4 in the Enterprise
- Bonus CD
- Only $64.99—Save $15.00

NETWORK PRESS®
SYBEX

www.sybex.com

MCSE CORE REQUIREMENT STUDY GUIDES FROM NETWORK PRESS

Sybex's Network Press presents updated and expanded second editions of the definitive study guides for MCSE candidates.

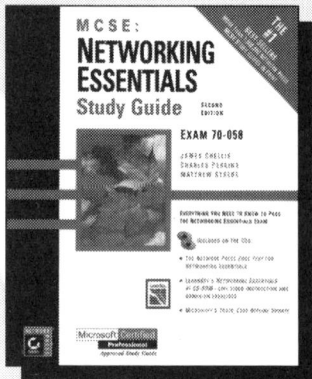

ISBN: 0-7821-2220-5
704pp; 7 1/2" x 9"; Hardcover
$49.99

ISBN: 0-7821-2223-X
784pp; 7 1/2" x 9"; Hardcover
$49.99

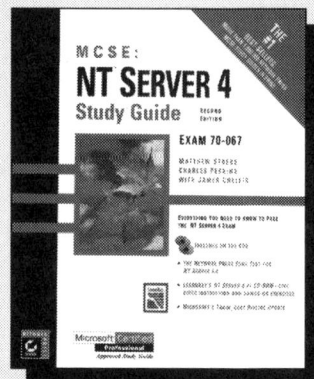

ISBN: 0-7821-2222-1
832pp; 7 1/2" x 9"; Hardcover
$49.99

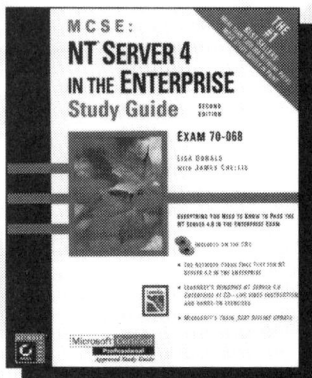

A $50.00 SAVINGS!

ISBN: 0-7821-2221-3
704pp; 7 1/2" x 9"; Hardcover
$49.99

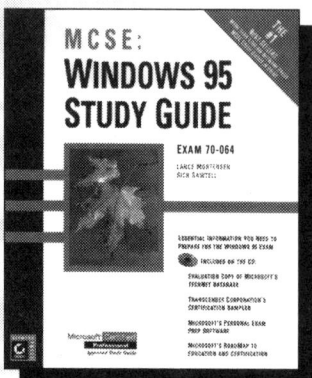

ISBN: 0-7821-2256-6
800pp; 7 1/2" x 9"; Hardcover
$49.99

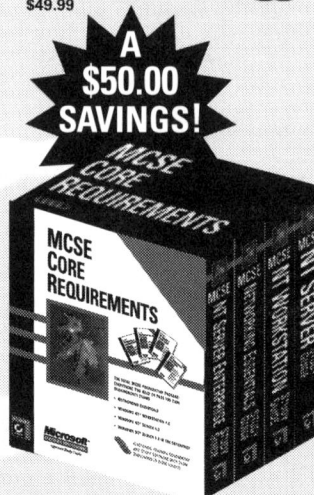

MCSE Core Requirements
Box Set
ISBN: 0-7821-2245-0
4 hardcover books;
3,024pp total; $149.96

Microsoft Certified
Professional
Approved Study Guide

NETWORK PRESS®
SYBEX

STUDY GUIDES FOR THE MICROSOFT CERTIFIED SYSTEMS ENGINEER EXAMS

MCSE ELECTIVE STUDY GUIDES
FROM NETWORK PRESS®

Sybex's Network Press expands the definitive study guide series for MCSE candidates.

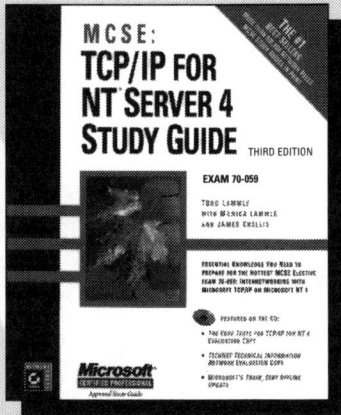

MCSE:
TCP/IP FOR NT SERVER 4 STUDY GUIDE THIRD EDITION

EXAM 70-059

ISBN: 0-7821-2224-8
688pp; 7¹/₂" x 9"; Hardcover
$49.99

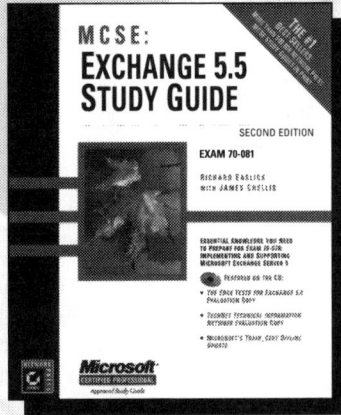

MCSE:
EXCHANGE 5.5 STUDY GUIDE
SECOND EDITION

EXAM 70-081

ISBN: 0-7821-2261-2
848pp; 7¹/₂" x 9"; Hardcover
$49.99

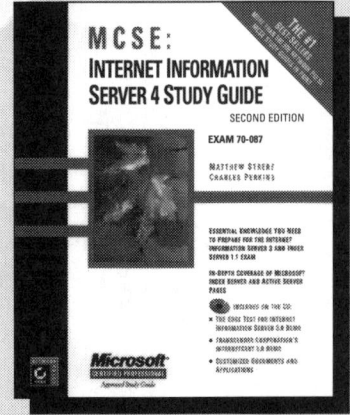

MCSE:
INTERNET INFORMATION SERVER 4 STUDY GUIDE
SECOND EDITION

EXAM 70-087

ISBN: 0-7821-2248-5
704pp; 7¹/₂" x 9"; Hardcover
$49.99

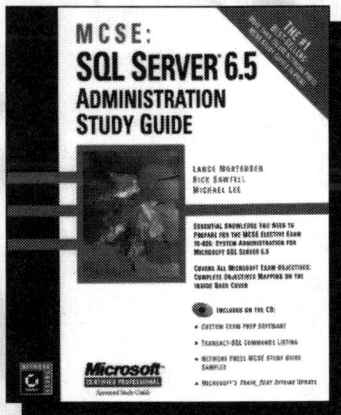

MCSE:
SQL SERVER 6.5 ADMINISTRATION STUDY GUIDE

ISBN: 0-7821-2172-1
672pp; 7¹/₂" x 9"; Hardcover
$49.99

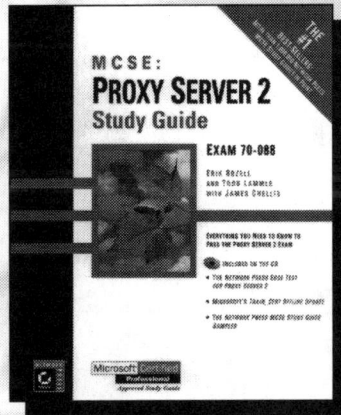

MCSE:
PROXY SERVER 2 Study Guide

EXAM 70-088

ISBN: 0-7821-2194-2
576pp; 7¹/₂" x 9"; Hardcover
$49.99

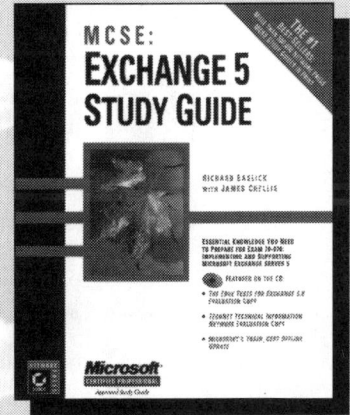

MCSE:
EXCHANGE 5 STUDY GUIDE

ISBN: 0-7821-1967-0
656pp; 7¹/₂" x 9"; Hardcover
$49.99

Microsoft® Certified
Professional
Approved Study Guide

NETWORK PRESS® SYBEX®

STUDY GUIDES FOR THE MICROSOFT CERTIFIED SYSTEMS ENGINEER EXAMS

NT IN THE REAL WORLD

THE INFORMATION YOU NEED TO BUILD, SECURE, AND OPTIMIZE NT NETWORKS

MASTERING
WINDOWS NT SERVER 4
FIFTH EDITION

MARK MINASI

ISBN: 0-7821-2163-2
1,664 pp; 7 1/2" x 9"; Hardcover
$59.99

MASTERING
TCP/IP FOR NT SERVER

MARK MINASI
TODD LAMMLE
with MONICA LAMMLE

ISBN: 0-7821-2123-3
544 pp; 7 1/2" x 9"; Softcover
$44.99

NT NETWORK SECURITY

MATTHEW STREBE
CHARLES PERKINS
MICHAEL G. MONCUR

ISBN: 0-7821-2006-7
929 pp; 7 1/2" x 9"; Hardcover
$59.99

NT ENTERPRISE NETWORK DESIGN

MERGAN SFERR
GARY MONTI
VAHAN SACHMANN

ISBN: 0-7821-2156-X
624 pp; 7 1/2" x 9"; Hardcover
$54.99

NETWORK PRESS
SYBEX